Praise for *Amish Grace*

"*Amish Grace: How Forgiveness Transcended Tragedy* is one of those rare books that inspires deep personal reflection while recounting a moment in history, telling a sociological story, and exploring theological issues. In the fall of 2006, following the murders of Amish school children by a deranged gunman, how did the Amish manage to forgive the murderer and extend grace to his family so quickly and authentically? Making it clear that the answer involves no quick fix but an integrated, disciplined pattern of life—a pattern altogether upstream to the flow of American culture—the authors invite us to ask not just how to forgive but how we should live. In our era of mass violence and the derangement from which it comes, no question could be more timely."

—Parker J. Palmer, author of *A Hidden Wholeness,*
Let Your Life Speak, and *The Courage to Teach*

"*Amish Grace* tells a story of forgiveness informed by deep faith, rooted in a rich history, and practiced in real life. In an American society that often resorts to revenge, it is a powerful example of the better way taught by Jesus."

—Jim Wallis, author of *God's Politics*;
president, Sojourners/Call to Renewal

"An inside look at a series of events that showed the world what Christ-like forgiveness is all about . . . A story of the love of God lived out in the face of tragedy."

—Tony Campolo, Eastern University

"*Amish Grace* dissects the deep-rooted pattern of Amish forgiveness and grace that, after the Nickel Mines tragedy, caused the world to gasp."
—Philip Yancey, author of *What's So Amazing About Grace?*

"Covers the subject in a superb way. It gave me a private tutorial in Amish culture and religion . . . on their unique view of life, death, and forgiveness."

—Fred Luskin, author of *Forgive for Good*;
r, Stanford Forgiveness Projects

"A remarkable book about the good but imperfect Amish, who individually and collectively consistently try to live Jesus' example of love—for one another and for the enemy."

—Dr. Carol Rittner, R.S.M., Distinguished Professor of Holocaust & Genocide Studies, The Richard Stockton College of New Jersey

"A casebook on forgiveness valuable for ALL Christians. . . . drills beneath the theory to their practice and even deeper to the instructions of Jesus."

—Dr. Julia Upton, R.S.M., Provost, St. John's University

"This is a very uplifting and enlightening book. It opens the door and allows us to peek at the hearts of Christian Amish believers who forgave horrid murders from the heart. And that forgiveness became a light on a hill that points to Jesus."

—Everett L. Worthington Jr., professor of psychology, Virginia Commonwealth University

Amish Grace

Amish Grace

How Forgiveness Transcended Tragedy

Donald B. Kraybill
Steven M. Nolt
David L. Weaver-Zercher

JOSSEY-BASS
A Wiley Imprint
www.josseybass.com

Published by Jossey-Bass
A Wiley Imprint
989 Market Street, San Francisco, CA 94103 www.josseybass.com

Jossey-Bass books and products are available through most bookstores. To contact Jossey-Bass directly call our Customer Care Department within the U.S. at 800-956-7739, outside the U.S. at 317-572-3986, or fax 317-572-4002.

Jossey-Bass also publishes its books in a variety of electronic formats. Some content that appears in print may not be available in electronic books.

All Scripture quotations are from the Holy Bible, King James Version.

Library of Congress Cataloging-in-Publication Data
Kraybill, Donald B.
    Amish grace : how forgiveness transcended tragedy / Donald B. Kraybill, Steven M. Nolt, David L. Weaver-Zercher. – 1st ed.
        p. cm.
    Includes bibliographical references and index.
    ISBN 978-0-7879-9761-8 (cloth)
    ISBN 978-0-4703-4404-0 (paperback)
    1. Forgiveness of sin.   2.   Amish–Doctrines.   3.   West Nickel Mines Amish School.   I. Nolt, Steven M., II. Weaver-Zercher, David, III. Title.
    BT795.K73 2007
    364.152'30974815–dc22

                                                                                        2007019071

Printed in the United States of America
FIRST EDITION
HB Printing   10 9 8 7 6 5
PB Printing   10 9 8 7 6 5 4 3 2 1

CONTENTS

❦ Contents ❦

All author royalties from Amish Grace *will be donated*
to the Mennonite Central Committee to benefit
their ministries to children suffering
because of poverty, war, and natural disaster.

For more information on the worldwide relief and service ministries of MCC,
visit www.mcc.org.

PREFACE

Amish. School. Shooting. Never did we imagine that these three words would appear together. But the unimaginable turned real on October 2, 2006, when Charles Carl Roberts IV carried his guns and his rage into an Amish schoolhouse near Nickel Mines, Pennsylvania. Five school-girls died that day, and five others were seriously wounded. Turning a tranquil schoolhouse into a house of horror, Roberts shattered a reas-suring American myth—that the Old Order Amish remain isolated from the problems of the larger world.

The Amish rely less on that myth than do those who watch them from afar. In fact, their history reminds them that even the most deter-mined efforts to remain separate from the world and its iniquities are not foolproof. The Nickel Mines Amish certainly didn't anticipate the horror of October 2. They were, however, uncommonly prepared to respond to it with graciousness, forbearance, and love. Indeed, the biggest surprise at Nickel Mines was not the intrusion of evil but the Amish response. The biggest surprise was Amish grace.

This book explains the Amish reaction to the Nickel Mines shooting, especially their forgiveness of the killer and their expressions of grace to his family. Given our longtime study of Amish life, we weren't entirely sur-prised by the Amish response. At the same time, their actions raised a host of questions in our minds: What exactly did the Amish do in the aftermath of the tragedy? What did it mean to them to extend forgiveness? And what was the cultural soil that nourished this sort of response in a world where vengeance, not forgiveness, is so often the order of the day?

As we explore these questions, we introduce some aspects of Amish culture to show the connection between Amish life and Amish grace.

This tie is important for two reasons. First, it clarifies that their extension of grace was neither calculated nor random. Rather, it emerged from who they were long before that awful October day. Second, embedding the Amish reaction in the context of their history and practice enables us to suggest more easily what lessons may apply to those of us outside Amish circles.

In the Appendix we provide details about some of the distinctive features of this community, but a few words of introduction here will help set the stage for our story. The Amish descend from the *Anabaptists,* a radical Christian movement that arose in Europe in 1525, shortly after Martin Luther launched the Protestant Reformation. Opponents of the young radicals called them *Anabaptists,* a derogatory nickname meaning "rebaptizers," because they baptized one another as adults even though they had been baptized as infants in the state church. These radical reformers sought to create Christian communities marked by love for each other and love for their enemies, an ethic they based on the life and teaching of Jesus. Nearly two centuries later, in the 1690s, the *Amish* emerged as a distinct Anabaptist group in Switzerland and in the Alsatian region of present-day France.

The Amish of Lancaster County, Pennsylvania, are one of many Amish subgroups in North America. Most Amish groups are also known as *Old Orders* because they place a premium on maintaining old religious and social customs. *Mennonites,* who are religious cousins to the Amish, also trace their roots to the sixteenth-century Anabaptists. Many, but not all, of the Mennonite groups in the twenty-first century are more assimilated into mainstream culture and use more technology than the Amish.

Even though the occasion for this book is one we would like to erase from Lancaster County history, we believe it opens a window onto Amish faith. Buggies, beards, and bonnets are the distinctive markers of Amish life for most Americans. Although such images provide insights into Amish culture and the values they hold dear, Amish people are likely to say that they are simply trying to be obedient to Jesus Christ, who commanded his followers to do many peculiar things, such as love, bless, and forgive their enemies. This is not a picture of Amish life that can easily be reproduced on a postcard from Amish Country; in fact, it can be painted only in the grit and grime of daily life. Although it would be small comfort to the families who lost daughters that day, the picture of Amish life is much clearer now than it was before October 2006.

This book is about Amish grace, but it is also about forgiveness, pardon, and reconciliation. *Grace,* as we use it in this book, is a broad concept that characterizes loving and compassionate responses to others. A gracious response may take many forms: comforting a person who is grieving, providing assistance to someone in need, sacrificing for another's benefit, and so on. Amish people are somewhat uncomfortable talking about "Amish grace," because to them, grace is a gift that God alone can give. We use *grace* in a broader way throughout the book, as a synonym for graciousness and gracious behavior toward others.

Forgiveness is a particular form of grace that always involves an offense, an offender, and a victim (in this case, a victimized community). When forgiveness happens, a victim forgoes the right to revenge and commits to overcoming bitter feelings toward the wrongdoer. Some people who have studied forgiveness extend this definition a step further, contending that positive feelings toward the offender—feelings such as love and compassion—are also essential to forgiveness. For their part, the Amish believe that gracious actions extended to the offender are an important aspect of authentic forgiveness. It is not our goal in this book to define forgiveness once and for all. Ours is a more modest goal: to tell the story of Amish forgiveness at Nickel Mines. Although we give priority to the Amish understanding of forgiveness, we sometimes link it to scholarly conversations on the topic.

In telling the Amish story, it is important to distinguish forgiveness from both pardon and reconciliation. Whereas in forgiveness the victim forgoes the right to vengeance, *pardon* releases an offender from punishment altogether. In many cases, pardon can be granted not by the victim but only by a person or institution with disciplinary authority over the offender (such as the judicial system). *Reconciliation* is the restoration of a relationship, or the creation of a new one, between the victim and the offender. Reconciliation is not necessary for forgiveness to take place, and of course it does not always happen, because it requires the establishment of trust between two willing parties. In many situations, however, reconciliation between victim and offender constitutes the ultimate goal, and forgiveness is a crucial step in that process.

We talked with more than three dozen Amish people in the course of writing this book, and we quote many of them liberally in the following pages. Because Amish culture emphasizes humility, the Amish people we interviewed did not want their names to appear in print. We have respected their wishes and simply cite many of our sources as "an Amish grandmother" or "an Amish carpenter." Similarly, we do not identify by name Amish people who wrote letters or essays in Amish magazines and correspondence newspapers.

For the eight individuals we quote extensively, we use typical Amish first names as pseudonyms (Amos, Eli, Gid, Katie, Mary, Mose, Sadie, and Sylvia). Each pseudonym refers to an actual person, not a composite of characters. This is a book about grace, and in that spirit we also use a pseudonym for the killer's widow.

In a few circumstances, we use the real names of Amish people because their names were published so widely in the news media. We use the first names of the girls who attended the West Nickel Mines School, as well as their teacher's first name. We also include the full names of Amish people in forgiveness stories unrelated to the schoolhouse shooting because these names have already appeared in the news media or in other publications when the stories were originally reported.

Finally, we must clarify our use of the phrase *the English*. Amish people often use this term for non-Amish people. The Amish speak a German dialect, Pennsylvania German (also known colloquially as Pennsylvania Dutch), as their first language. They also speak, read, and write English, which they typically learn when they begin school. Amish adults routinely speak English in their interactions with non-Amish neighbors, whom they refer to simply as "the English," even if the outsiders have no formal ties to Great Britain. In the pages that follow, we use the terms *non-Amish, English,* and *outsiders* interchangeably.

We've organized the text into three parts. Part One, which comprises the first five chapters, tells the story of the school shooting and the responses that flowed in its wake. Part Two explores broader understandings and practices of forgiveness in Amish life. Part Three reflects on the meaning of forgiveness, not only for the Amish but for the rest of us as well.

Amish Grace

Part One

CHAPTER ONE

The Nickel Mines Amish

We believe in letting our light shine, but not shining
it in the eyes of other people.

—AMISH FATHER

T he earliest streaks of light were barely breaking the eastern
sky as we turned east in Strasburg, Pennsylvania.* Reading
our MapQuest printout with a flashlight, we drove two
miles and then turned south onto Wolf Rock Road. Ahead of us,
two blinking red lights punctured the darkness, signaling the unhurried pace of a horse-drawn buggy. We slowed the car and followed
the rhythmic *clip-clop, clip-clop* of the horse's hooves toward the
top of a ridge.

We were searching for a place that one hopes never to be looking
for. A shooting had occurred the day before at a one-room Amish school
in a small community called Nickel Mines. As scholars of Amish life, we

---

*The authors use the first-person plural (*we*) as their collective voice. Although each
author received many media queries in the days following the shooting, the on-site
observations at Nickel Mines on Tuesday, October 3, 2006, are those of Donald
B. Kraybill.

had spent that day responding to a flood of phone calls from reporters eager for information. Now we were headed to the scene of the tragedy, to answer more questions from the journalists gathered there.

We continued climbing "the ridge," as the Amish call it, a low east-west range that slices the Lancaster Amish settlement in half. The older section of the settlement, on the north side, was formed about 1760, when Amish moved near what would later become the village of Intercourse. In 1940, Amish pioneers pushed south of the ridge toward Georgetown in search of cheaper land. With the Old Order population doubling every twenty years, Georgetown soon became the hub of a thriving community. Today some eight hundred Amish families live within a four-mile radius of the small town. The "southern end," as this section of the settlement is called, is hillier and also on the "slower, more conservative side," according to the Amish who live in the older area to the north.

The flashing lights on the back of the buggy we were trailing reminded us that the Amish do not shun all technology. Although they spurn television, the Internet, car ownership, and other things they fear could harm their community, the Amish selectively use some innovations and adapt others in ways that help rather than hinder their way of life. Their struggle to tame technology—through the ingenuity of Amish "engineers"—has resulted in a fascinating blend of old and new: LED lights on buggies, steel wheels on modern tractors, cash registers run by batteries, shop saws powered by compressed air, and telephones kept in shanties outside of homes so they don't disrupt family life. Some Amish businesses use the newly developed Classic Word Processor. Advertised as "nothing fancy, just a word horse for your business," this electronic device has an eight-inch screen, a Windows operating system, and standard spreadsheet and word processing software. Unlike most computers, however, this "Old Order computer" has no connections for phone, Internet, or video games.

Even though we had spoken with reporters about the West Nickel Mines School for hours the day before, we were not sure of its location. We knew it was a dozen miles southeast of Lancaster City, tucked away from Route 30, the busy tourist strip overflowing with restaurants and outlet stores. We also knew that the old nickel mines had folded in 1890 when the business fell prey to cheaper imported metals. Now the area was simply a rural region, mostly farms, small businesses, and bungalows scattered along curving country roads.

As we topped the ridge and approached Mine Road, a stop sign appeared in the gray dawn. Police cars blocked Mine Road to the right. An officer with a large flashlight came to our window and asked where we were headed. After seeing our identification, he waved us to the right and told us to park behind the TV trucks that lined Mine Road for as far as we could see.

Mine Road is a narrow, backcountry road with a few scattered houses on the left side and farmland overlooking a small valley on the right. The West Nickel Mines Amish School lay near the bottom of the valley. Dozens of media trucks were parked along the berm of the road, their satellite dishes pointing skyward. A white board fence enclosed the schoolyard, the school building, two outhouses, and a ball field. Horses grazed in the pasture adjacent to the school, the site of another ball field. The one-room, nineteenth-century-style school with its rooftop bell made a lovely backdrop for the morning news. A peaceful and idyllic view, it could have been the vestibule of Paradise. In fact, a small village by that name lies just five miles over the ridge to the north.

We parked and walked down the road through a throng of television crews and journalists. Some of the reporters, disheveled and yawning, had apparently spent the night in their trucks. Several New York journalists, probably wishing for a Starbucks, had just returned from a convenience store five miles away with cups of a generic brew. Ahead of us a small crossroads overflowed with even more media trucks. Dozens of journalists carrying notepads, microphones, and cameras milled around the area. "Where is Nickel Mines?" we asked one reporter as we approached. "This is it!" was his simple reply.

This was it? Only a few houses and a crossroads? An auction building squats on one corner of the intersection. There are no stores, gas stations, or coffee shops. The closest store, bank, and firehouse are located in Georgetown, about a mile and a half to the south. Overnight the parking lot of the auction house had turned into a media bazaar with satellite dishes, bright lights, the hum of diesel generators, and inquisitive reporters everywhere. This humble crossroads, barely a hamlet, had captured the world's attention for a long day that would stretch into a week.

We stood at a soda machine beside the auction building, trying to get our bearings. Only seventeen hours earlier Charles Carl Roberts IV had bought a soda at this very spot, just four hundred yards from the West Nickel Mines School. He had waited while the twenty-six children played softball during their morning recess. An Amish member of the school board had seen him here but thought nothing of it because Roberts often hung out around the auction house. "Charlie could have done the shooting at the Georgetown School closer to his home," said an Amish man, "but he probably thought it was too close to some houses."

The Lancaster Amish settlement has more than 180 local congregations called church districts, each led by a team of ordained men—a bishop, a deacon, and two or three ministers. The men, selected from within their district, serve as religious leaders in addition to their regular employment. They serve for life, without compensation or formal theological training.

Streams and roads mark the borders of each district, which serves as the social and religious home for twenty-five to forty families.

Each Amish family worships with the other families who live within the boundaries of their district. When a district's membership grows too large for families to accommodate worship services at their homes, the district is divided. Because the families live so close and engage in many activities together outside church services, they know each other very well.

The Nickel Mines crossroads divides three districts: West Nickel Mines, East Nickel Mines, and Northeast Georgetown. Children from all three districts attended the West Nickel Mines School. "It was fortunate that the children came from three different districts," said an Amish man in retrospect, "so the grief and funeral preparations didn't fall on the members of just one district."

This is dense Amish country, where Amish farms and businesses nestle alongside those of their English neighbors. Bart Township, the municipal home of the Nickel Mines area, boasts a population of three thousand Amish and English who live in some eight hundred houses within sixteen square miles. As in many other Amish communities in North America, the Amish here have many friends among their English neighbors, and a lot of neighborly activity occurs across the cultural fences. About 75 percent of the firefighters in the Bart Township Fire Company are Amish, and some hold leadership positions. They do not drive the trucks, but they help to fight fires and organize fund-raisers for the company.

The willingness of Amish men to *ride* in the fire trucks they refuse to *drive* mirrors the Amish relationship to motor vehicles in general. In the early twentieth century, Amish leaders forbade car ownership for fear the car would unravel their communities, making it easier for members to drive off to cities and blend in with the larger world. Horse-and-buggy transportation helps to tether members to their local church district and ties them closely to their neighbors. Amish people do hire English "taxi drivers" who use their own vehicles to transport their Amish patrons for business, special events, and long-distance

7

travel. Moreover, some Amish business owners have English employees who provide a truck or car for daily business-related travel. On the day of the shooting, parents of the injured children rode to hospitals in police cruisers and the vehicles of non-Amish drivers. Because flying is off-limits, they declined offers to go by helicopter to the hospitals, although many of the injured were transported that way.

As the sun erased the overnight darkness, the school came into clearer focus. It was a typical one-room Amish school sporting a cast-iron bell in a small cupola on the roof. Built in 1976, the yellow stucco building sat in a former pasture about fifty yards from White Oak Road and about a quarter mile from the nearest Amish homes. There are more than fourteen hundred similar Amish-operated schools across the country. Most, but not all, Amish youth in North America attend private Amish schools like this one. After completing eighth grade, the "scholars," as the Amish call their pupils, begin vocational apprentice-ships at their homes, farms, or home-based shops, or with a nearby neighbor or relative.

The West Nickel Mines School is one of thirty Amish schools within a four-mile radius of Georgetown. These one-room schools, like the Amish church districts they serve, are named for nearby towns and locally known sites—Cedar Hill, Wolf Rock, Georgetown, Valley Road, Bartville, Mt. Pleasant View, Peach Lane, Green Tree, and so on. More than 190 Amish schools are sprinkled across the Lancaster County Amish settlement, which spills eastward into Chester County. A school board composed of three to five men supervises one or two schools—hiring the teachers, caring for maintenance, and managing the finances.

Private Amish schools like this one in Nickel Mines are relatively new. In fact, Amish children attended rural public schools until the advent of large, consolidated schools in the mid-twentieth century. Consolidation meant that Amish pupils could no longer walk to school;

8

it also meant that their parents had less control over the schools their children attended. Increasingly the teachers in the big schools came from faraway places and had little knowledge of Amish life. To their dismay, Amish parents found their high-school-age children exposed to topics and classes they disapproved of, such as evolution and physical education.

The Amish objected to this revolutionary change in public schools. In their view, a good eighth-grade education in the basics of reading, writing, spelling, and arithmetic was all that was needed for success in Amish life. In fact, in Lancaster County dozens of Amish parents were jailed in the early 1950s because they refused to send their children to consolidated schools beyond the eighth grade. Eventually the U.S. Supreme Court, in a 1972 case known as *Wisconsin* v. *Yoder,* allowed Amish children to end their formal education when they turned fourteen. Both the threat of consolidated schools and the court decision spurred the growth of Amish private schools.

Compared to homes, barns, and shops, schools contain the least amount of technology in Amish society. Typically this technology includes only a battery-run wall clock, a propane gas light, and a kerosene, coal, or wood stove. There are no calculators, microscopes, computers, electrical outlets, security cameras, or televisions. One Amish teacher, often with the help of an aide, teaches all eight grades in the same classroom. The curriculum, taught in English, focuses on the basics: spelling, reading, penmanship, grammar, arithmetic, and some geography. A quiet but orderly hum hovers over the room as children whisper and help one another while the teacher works with one or two grades at a time. A student's raised hand, asking for permission to get a library book or use the outhouse, usually receives a subtle nod from the teacher. At the end of the day, the scholars turn into janitors—sweeping the floor, replacing books on the library shelves, and tidying up the bats and balls in the foyer.

9

Many people are surprised to learn that religion is not taught as a separate subject in Amish schools. Instead, it is imparted through Bible reading, prayer, hymns and songs, and the exemplary behavior of the teacher. The Amish believe that formal religious instruction belongs in the family and church, not in the school. Of course, values permeate the school "all day long in our curriculum and in the playgrounds," according to one Amish school manual. This occurs, the manual explains, "by not cheating in arithmetic, by teaching cleanliness and thrift in health . . . by learning to make an honest living . . . and by teaching honesty, respect, sincerity, humbleness, and the golden rule on the playground."

As we peered across the road at the West Nickel Mines School, journalists gathered around us in search of information. Their questions were sensible and to the point: What do the Amish think about . . . ? How do the Amish react to . . . ? What do the Amish teach in their schools?

As straightforward as their questions were, the reporters often began with the wrong assumption: that all Amish people in North America are shaped by the same cultural cookie cutter. In fact, there are many different subgroups of Amish, each with their own unique practices. For example, some, such as the Lancaster Amish, drive gray-topped carriages, but others drive carriages with black, yellow, or white tops. Occupations, dress patterns, wedding and funeral practices, and accepted technology vary across the many Amish subgroups. In a few subgroups, business owners are permitted to own cell phones; most Amish homes have indoor toilets but some do not; certain groups permit the use of in-line roller skates but others do not; and so on. With sixteen hundred church districts across the country, with religious authority anchored in local districts, and without an Amish "pope," there are many different ways of being Amish in North America.

We tried to respond to the reporters with specifics about the Amish in the Nickel Mines area, but even here there are different personalities and practices. The diversity found in other ethnic and religious groups is also rife among the Amish. How could we squeeze all of this cultural complexity into short sound bites for the evening news?

Part of the reason we were in such demand the day of the shooting was the Amish aversion to publicity. No lawyers or family spokespersons represented the grieving Amish parents or provided statements to the media. With a few exceptions, the Amish did not want to talk with the media or appear on camera. This reticence came not from the sudden shock of the shooting but from a deep aversion to publicity that is grounded in their religious beliefs and cultural traditions.

Taking their cues from the Bible, the Amish have long declined the media spotlight, preferring to live quietly and privately. They take seriously Jesus' words, "Take heed that ye do not your alms before men, to be seen of them . . . do not sound a trumpet before thee, as the hypocrites do . . . let not thy left hand know what thy right hand doeth. . . . And when thou prayest, thou shalt not be as the hypocrites are: for they love to pray . . . in the corners of the streets, that they may be *seen of men*" (emphasis added). These verses from Chapter Six of Matthew's Gospel appear right before the Lord's Prayer, the model prayer that Jesus taught his disciples. The instruction is clear: do not practice your religion in public to show off your piety. Practice your faith privately, and your Father in heaven will reward you.

The Amish also refrain from publicity because, as a collective society, they believe that the community should come first, not the individual. Having one's name in a newspaper story manifests pride by calling attention to one's opinions; therefore, some Amish people will talk to the press but only if they can remain anonymous. Faith must at times be practiced in public but should not, in the Amish view, be showcased.

"We believe in letting our light shine," said one Amish father, "but not shining it in the eyes of other people."

Posing for photographs is also discouraged. The Amish cite the second of the Ten Commandments, "Thou shalt not make unto thee any graven image, or any likeness of any thing" (Exodus 20:4), as a reason for not posing for photographs. To pose for a picture is considered an act of pride that places the individual on a pedestal. Such self-promotion not only calls excessive attention to the individual, but it also borders on self-worship.

So the reporters covering the West Nickel Mines School shooting faced a quandary. How could they cover a people who didn't want to be covered, let alone at a time of deep grief and shock? The shooting was relatively easy to cover: police reports and public records were readily available within a day of the tragedy. Reporting about the Amish community was a different matter altogether.

As we retraced our steps on Mine Road to prepare for an interview, we yielded to an Amish farmer approaching with a bench wagon pulled by two mules. Sitting on an elevated seat at the front of the enclosed wagon, he looked like a stagecoach driver. As we waited for the mule-drawn wagon to pass a string of mobile TV studios beaming their news around the world, it felt for a moment as if we were in a time warp.

The large gray wagon held benches, songbooks, and eating utensils. Because the Amish have no church buildings, enclosed wagons transport supplies from home to home as families take turns hosting the biweekly church service. The three-hour Sunday morning service, called *Gmay* (a dialect shortcut for the word *church*), is followed by a fellowship meal and may be attended by as many as two hundred people. The church service is held in large first-floor rooms or the basement of a home, in the upper level of a barn, or in a shop.

The wagons also bring benches to the homes of grieving families after a death. Hundreds of friends and family members come to the home for viewing and visitation after a body returns from an English mortuary. The visitation period typically stretches over several days and evenings before the funeral. Sixteen hours after the school shooting, the bench wagons were converging on the homes of families who would soon bury their children. The benches carried by the wagons would be used for seating in the barns where the funerals were slated for Thursday and Friday.

The bench wagon illustrated a point we repeated over and over again to reporters who asked, "Are the Amish prepared to deal with a tragedy like this?" Our answer was a paradox, perhaps a little unexpected. Of course, the Amish were not prepared, we said—except, of course, they were.

In one sense, no community is ever prepared for such a calamity. There have been few murders in Amish history, and never before had there been a school massacre. Certainly adults and children had died in tragic accidents, but there were no parallels to the Nickel Mines shooting. Amish schools, with no history of violence, are not designed with such incidents in mind. There are no metal detectors at the doors, no daily body searches for concealed weapons, no police officers patrolling the hallways, no policies for emergencies, and no drills to prepare for hostage situations. The children who attend a one-room Amish school come from ten or so nearby families. Doors are unlocked and sometimes stand open when school is in session. Amish schools offer children a deep sense of security: their peers are neighbors and their teachers are frequent visitors to their homes. Some of the younger children would likely not recognize a pistol if they saw one. Almost without exception, young Amish children have not seen violent movies, video games, or television; they can hardly imagine violence, apart from a fistfight. So were the Amish prepared for the outburst of violence that hit them that Monday in October? Of course not.

At the same time, the Amish are better prepared than most Americans to deal with a tragedy like this. The Amish are a close-knit community woven together by strong ties of family, faith, and culture. Members in distress can tap this rich reservoir of communal care during horrific events. The typical Amish person has seventy-five or more first cousins, many living nearby. Members of a thirty-family church district typically live within a mile or so of each other's homes. When tragedy strikes—fire, flood, illness, or death—dozens of people surround the distressed family with care. They take over their chores, bring them food, set up benches for visitation, and offer quiet words of comfort. The Amish call this thick web of support *mutual aid*. They literally follow the New Testament commandment to "bear ye one another's burdens and so fulfil the law of Christ" (Galatians 6:2). So while no one is ever ready to deal with a tragedy like this, historic practices had prepared the Amish well.

As the bench wagon came closer, we were surprised that the mules were not spooked by the TV crews and their noisy generators. What did frighten them, however, was a yellow plastic strip, two inches high and six inches wide, stretching across the road. The plastic cover protected electric cords running from an English residence to some of the media trucks. The mules stopped and refused to cross the yellow strip. After trying to persuade them from his seat on the wagon, the driver finally got off, walked in front of them, and tugged on their bridles. They still refused. After several more minutes of their owner's persuasion and gentle tugs, the animals gingerly stepped across the yellow line. Despite the sudden appearance of electric cords and satellite dishes, the viewings in the grieving community at Nickel Mines would proceed on schedule.

Word of trouble in a school had begun spreading at 10:30 A.M. on Monday, October 2, 2006. A distraught, sobbing teacher ran to a nearby Amish farmhouse with an alarming report: a man with a gun was in the school. The farmer called 911 from his telephone shanty to say that children had been taken hostage in a school. The news traveled quickly via word of mouth. "The Amish grapevine is faster than the Internet," said one Amish man, who has never sent an e-mail. Some neighbors began gathering at the farmhouse; others went to the school to see if they could help. By 11:26 A.M. local television stations were reporting a multiple shooting in an Amish school. Word of the horror soon appeared on Fox News and CNN.

Amish people ran to their phone shanties to pass the word. "Something bad happened at the West Nickel Mines School. Children were shot. A neighbor man went crazy. Helicopters are taking them to hospitals." Voice-mail messages were left on Amish phones in Ohio, Indiana, Wisconsin, and many of the other 370 Amish communities in twenty-seven states and the Canadian province of Ontario. An Amish contractor in Indiana received a call about the shooting on his cell phone from his financial advisor in Chicago. A Pakistani customer in New York called his Amish harness supplier in Lancaster to report the shooting. The news—of a shooting, of dying children, of very bad things south of Paradise—spread fast in Amish communities in North America despite the absence of phones inside their homes.

The horror of school shootings at places like Columbine had reached Lancaster County. For many Americans living in fear of guns, violence, and terror it had been comforting to imagine a safe place somewhere—a place where children could giggle and learn their ABCs without worrying about guns, knives, and bullies. If something like this could happen in a small Amish school nestled in a peaceful rural community, it could happen anywhere. In many respects, the last safe place in America's collective imagination had suddenly disappeared.

CHAPTER TWO

The Shooting

This was our 9/11.

— Amish leader

The cloudless skies on Monday, October 2, 2006, reminded some Nickel Mines residents of the blue skies of September 11, 2001. The shock and trauma of the tragedy brought comparisons too. "I will never forget where I was, what I was doing, and who told me first about the shooting," said one Amish father.

Fall is a festive time for the Amish of Lancaster County because dozens of weddings take place on Tuesdays and Thursdays during that season. By early October, children are counting the days until their siblings or cousins will marry. Amish weddings are happy occasions stretching from early morning until late evening, with three to four hundred friends gathering at the bride's home. It's not uncommon for an Amish person to receive invitations to a half dozen weddings in a single fall season. Those invited to multiple weddings on the same day circulate from one celebration to another.

17

The fall harvest in Nickel Mines was almost finished. Tobacco was already turning tan in the drying sheds and the last cutting of alfalfa would soon be baled into hay for winter feeding. Chopped green corn, blown into sixty-foot-high silos, was fermenting into sweet-smelling silage for cattle feed. Horse-pulled corn pickers, powered by gasoline engines, would soon be husking yellow ears of corn and dropping them onto wagons that would haul them to storage bins near Amish barns.

Hunting season was just around the corner. In late November, many Amish men would climb into vans driven by English people and head to hunting cabins in northern Pennsylvania. Each of them hoped to bag a white-tailed deer at their favorite mountain site. Some diehard hunters would go to Maryland or West Virginia in search of a white-tailed trophy. Twelve-year-old sons eagerly awaited the rite of passage when they would join their fathers in the woods for the first time.

The Nickel Mines Amish who operate stands at farmers markets in Delaware, Maryland, and New Jersey were beginning to stock up on meats, cheeses, and other deli items for the holiday season. The brisk air and clear October sky usually heralded a season of celebration and plenty among the Amish of Nickel Mines. This autumn, however, would be different.

At about 3:00 on Monday morning, thirty-two-year-old Charles Carl Roberts IV parked his eighteen-wheel milk truck in the parking lot of the Nickel Mines Auction. He jumped into his small pickup and drove a mile and a half down the road to his home in Georgetown to catch some sleep before sunrise. His work day had begun at 6:00 the night before when he had begun making the rounds with his tank truck to local Amish and English farms. After pumping the milk from the stainless steel tank at each farm into his truck, he hauled his fifty-thousand-pound load to a regional processing plant before heading back to the auction house and then home to bed.

The trucking job suited Roberts's introverted personality because he could work alone most of the day. He spoke only if someone addressed him first, and his answers were typically short. He had worked as a carpenter before learning the trucking trade from his father-in-law. On occasion little things would agitate him. One farmer reportedly kept his children out of the milk house while Roberts pumped the milk because Roberts swore a lot and seemed frustrated. Other stories also bespoke a troubled soul beneath the shy surface. Coworkers at the processing plant noticed, however, that he seemed friendlier and more relaxed the last week of September, as though something had settled in his mind.

By 7:30 on Monday morning, twenty-six children aged six to thirteen were trudging toward the West Nickel Mines School from ten different homes. Some walked along the road while others took their favorite shortcuts across fields, carrying their red and blue plastic lunch pails and colorful small coolers. They chattered and teased each other along the way. The ones arriving early played briefly in the schoolyard until the school bell called them inside.

Emma, their twenty-year-old teacher, with two years of experience, knew all her students and their parents quite well. She lived less than two miles from the school and her pupils lived within walking distance. Informal visits between parents and teacher, at school and in homes, happen frequently in Amish life. Four special guests had arrived that day—Emma's mother, her sister, and two of her sisters-in-law. One of the young women was nearly eight months pregnant; another had

19

two small children in tow. Hosting familiar visitors without advance notice is a common practice in small, family-oriented Amish schools.

The walls of Amish schools are typically covered with colorful student artwork, samples of homework, homemade posters, and lesson themes prepared by the teacher. The West Nickel Mines School was no exception. Students' drawings and short sayings of Amish wisdom decorated the classroom. A sign on the blackboard read, "Visitors Bubble Up Our Days." Underneath the sign, a teddy bear was blowing bubbles, and in each bubble was written the name of a school visitor. An acronym posted in many Amish schools is *JOY*—*Jesus* first, *Others* next, *Yourself* last.

Emma called the children to order and welcomed her special guests. She began the day by reading a Bible passage in German, because later she would be teaching German to some of the grades. In Amish schools, the lessons, the Bible readings, and the Lord's Prayer are typically spoken in English, but on this day the students used German for the Bible reading and prayer. Emma read from Acts 4, in which the biblical writer Luke describes the early church in Jerusalem: They "were of one heart and of one soul: neither said any of them that ought of the things which he possessed was his own; but they had all things common. And with great power gave the apostles witness of the resurrection of the Lord Jesus: and great grace was upon them all" (Acts 4:32–33).

Following the reading, the children stood and repeated the Lord's Prayer in German. It came easily to them because they had memorized it in both German and English before they turned five.

After saying the Lord's Prayer but before beginning their lessons, the children sang three songs, two in German and one in English. One of the German songs, "Bedenke Mensch das Ende" ("Consider, Man, the End"), warns of the final judgment, when "each one will have his turn and receive his reward according to what he has done." The words are

20

sometimes read at Amish funerals. The children sang them to the tune of the Christian gospel song "Bind Us Together with Love."

> Consider, man! the end,
> Consider your death,
> Death often comes quickly;
> He who today is vigorous and ruddy,
> May tomorrow, or sooner,
> Have passed away. . . .

The children then sang the seventeenth-century hymn "In der stillen Einsamkeit" ("In Quiet Solitude") to the tune of "Jesus Loves Me."

> In quiet solitude,
> You will find your praise prepared,
> Great God hear me,
> For my heart seeks you.
> You are unchanging,
> Never still and yet at rest.
> You rule the seasons of the year,
> And bring them in at the proper time.

Finally, before turning to their lessons, the scholars sang "Multiply," a song by gospel singer Dottie Rambo that describes how a barefoot boy gave his bread and fish to Jesus to multiply them for others.

Emma then commenced teaching. Like many Amish teachers, she combined two grades for their lessons. She began recitations with the first and second graders at the blackboard, then worked with the third and fourth graders, and so on. As she taught each cluster, the other students completed their homework, reviewed their lessons, or did independent work. The older boys, eager to play softball in the lovely weather, were soon counting the minutes to recess.

Down the road in Georgetown, after catching a few hours of sleep, Roberts ate breakfast with his wife, Amy, and their three children. Shortly after breakfast, Amy left with their youngest, an eighteen-month-old, for a Moms in Touch prayer group meeting at a local Presbyterian church. Mothers gathered weekly in this group to pray for their children, their teachers, school safety, and other issues of concern in local schools. On this particular morning, a young Amish woman was caring for the preschool children in the church nursery.

Back at his modular home along the main street of Georgetown, Roberts walked his six- and eight-year-old children to the school bus stop and kissed them goodbye at 8:45 A.M. He was scheduled for a routine drug test that morning for his trucking license, but he had other plans. In the house he laid out a suicide note for each family member. Then he carried supplies from his shed to the enclosed back of a pickup truck he had borrowed from his wife's grandfather, who lived next door. Roberts had been buying supplies over the past week and storing them in the shed beside his home. He still needed some more plastic zip ties—plastic strips that can be pulled tight to hold together a bundle of loose wires—so he drove two miles east to the Amish-owned Valley Hardware store.

With the plastic ties in hand, he now had all the supplies on the list scribbled in the notebook he kept in his tank truck: a 9-mm handgun, a 12-gauge shotgun, a 30-06 rifle, a stun gun, and six hundred rounds of ammunition. In addition, stowed away in the pickup truck were a tube of lubricating jelly, a hammer, nails, wrenches, binoculars, earplugs, batteries, a flashlight, a candle, tape, two-by-four and two-by-six wood planks, and an extra set of clothing—all the things he would need to barricade himself inside the schoolroom for an extended standoff.

He was on schedule. In fact, he arrived in Nickel Mines a little early; the children were still playing softball during their morning recess. With a few minutes to spare he bought a soda at the vending machine beside the auction house and watched the ball game by the school four hundred yards away. A school trustee, riding in the truck of his English driver, waved to the children as he passed the ball field. A few moments later he saw Roberts by the vending machine but thought nothing of it.

At about 10:15 A.M., after Emma called the children back to their lessons, Roberts drove down White Oak Road to the schoolhouse. He backed his truck into the schoolyard through the open gate of the white board fence, all the way to the small porch at the main entrance. An English neighbor who had just picked up some tools at an Amish rental agency had to wait on the road as Roberts backed his truck into the schoolyard.

Hearing the commotion, Emma went to the front door, which was open on the warm day. Turning their heads to see the visitor on the porch, some of the children recognized him as the trucker who picked up milk from their farms. He held a rusty metal object in his hand. Had anyone seen something like this along the road? he asked. Could they help him look? He never looked Emma in the eye but she told him, "Sure, we'll try."

Roberts went back to his truck and soon returned with a semi-automatic pistol. Entering the schoolhouse, he waved the gun and ordered everyone to lie facedown on the floor at the front of the room, near the blackboard. Seeing the gun and knowing that other adults were in the room, Emma and her mother fled out the side door and ran nearly a quarter of a mile across the fields for help. They arrived at a nearby Amish farm, where the distraught Emma begged for help.

23

At 10:35 A.M., a 911 operator received a call from the farm's phone shanty: "There's a guy in the school with a gun."

Back in the schoolhouse, Roberts was agitated. He was surprised to find other adults in the schoolhouse and astonished that the teacher had run for help. He sent one of the boys to bring her back.

Roberts tied the feet and legs of some of the girls with zip ties and also bound some of the girls to each other. Several times he promised not to hurt them if they obeyed. The children, raised to trust and obey adults, believed him—at least at first.

To conceal his activities, Roberts pulled down the school's blinds, but one of them snapped back to the top of the window and fell to the floor. In order to reattach it, he climbed atop a desk. Meanwhile, nine-year-old Emma, whose legs were free, heard a woman's voice say, "Run," and run she did. No one else heard the voice, and some Amish believe it was the voice of an angel. Next Roberts shoved a ten-year-old boy, who was lying on the floor, out the side door. The pregnant visitor was comforting Naomi Rose, a sobbing seven-year-old, but the gunman soon ordered the adult women to leave. Next he told the boys—eleven of whom had sisters in the schoolhouse—to get out. Stunned and terrified, the boys gathered near the boys' outhouse to pray. Roberts quickly carried in the rest of his supplies from the truck.

Now he was alone with his prey. As he nailed the doors shut to barricade the girls in the dark room, Roberts heard one of them praying. "Would you pray for me?" he asked. One of the girls responded, "Why don't you pray for us?" He purportedly replied, "I don't believe in praying." He had come to molest them, not to pray for them. "If one of you will let me do what I want to, I won't hurt the rest of you," he said. One of the younger girls, not understanding his request but hoping to save the others from harm, offered to help. The older girls quickly said in Pennsylvania German, *"Duh's net! Duh's net!"* (Don't do it! Don't do it!)

At one moment in the unfolding tragedy, Roberts mumbled something about giving up and even walked toward the door, according to one of the survivors. For some reason, however, he returned to his plan, telling the girls that he was sorry he had to "do this." According to the survivors, he said, "I'm angry at God and I need to punish some Christian girls to get even with Him."

At 10:44 A.M., just nine minutes after the 911 call from the phone shanty, three state troopers arrived at the school. They found the doors locked and the blinds pulled. Seven more officers arrived shortly thereafter and quickly surrounded the schoolhouse. A police negotiator, using the bullhorn on his cruiser, tried to contact Roberts, asking him numerous times to put down his gun.

During the standoff, Roberts called his wife on his cell phone to say he was not coming home and that he had left notes for everyone. He was angry at God, he said, for the death of their firstborn daughter, Elise, who had lived for only twenty minutes after her birth nine years earlier. In the note to his wife Roberts had written, "I'm not worthy of you, you are the perfect wife, you deserve so much better. . . . I'm filled with so much hate towards myself, hate towards God, and an unimaginable emptiness. It seems like every time we do something fun I think about how Elise wasn't here to share it with us and I go right back to anger."

Roberts grew even more agitated when he realized that the police had arrived and his plan to molest the girls had failed. At 10:55 A.M. he called 911: "I just took ten girls hostage and I want everybody off the property or else. . . . Right now, or they're dead in two seconds . . . two seconds, that's it!"

Roberts then turned to the girls: "I'm going to make you pay for my daughter." Marian, one of two thirteen-year-olds in the room, quickly assumed leadership of the younger girls, doing everything she could to help protect them. Realizing he planned to kill them, she said,

25

"Shoot me first," hoping to save the others and fulfilling her duty to watch over the little ones in her care.

At about 11:05 A.M. the police heard three shotgun blasts followed by rapid-fire pistol shots. A shotgun blast, fired through the window by the main door, narrowly missed several officers. Troopers rushed the building, smashing windows with batons and shields. The killer turned the pistol on himself and fell to the floor as troopers broke through the windows. In execution style, he had gunned down the lineup of girls on the floor. Five would die. The other five, critically injured, had survived by rolling around and burying their heads in their arms.

Police dispatchers radioed a "mass casualty," and before long the site was flooded with a hundred state and local police, twenty ambulance crews, and trucks from five fire companies. The Lancaster County coroner who arrived on the scene called it "blood, glass, trash, chaos." It was impossible to fit ten stretchers inside the schoolhouse, so troopers covered the children and carried them outside, where they tried to control the bleeding until ambulance crews could transport them away. Naomi Rose died in a trooper's arms outside the school.

The view could hardly have been more surreal: the serene pasture surrounding the schoolhouse looked like a combat zone. Five medevac helicopters arrived as four police helicopters and an airplane patrolled the skies. At one point, as the media converged on the site, eleven helicopters and several airplanes flew overhead until the police declared a no-fly zone above the school.

A medevac helicopter lifted the first child skyward at 11:21 A.M., just eleven minutes after troopers reported the mass casualty alert. It headed northwest toward Penn State Hershey Medical Center in Hershey, Pennsylvania. Amish farmers in northern Lancaster County, who had already heard of the shooting, saw the helicopter carrying one of their own as it flew over their farms. Other helicopters flew to hospitals in Lancaster, Philadelphia, and Reading. One child was flown to Christiana Hospital in Newark, Delaware.

Parents, surrounded by family and neighbors, stood at a distance, watching the horrific scene without knowing the conditions of their daughters. Eventually about one hundred family members and friends gathered at a nearby Amish farm—the same one the teacher and her mother had run to for help—to console one another and wait for news. For several hours it remained unclear who was dead and who was alive. The children carried no identification, and with similar dress and many head injuries it wasn't clear who had gone to which hospital. Photos taken at the hospitals were e-mailed back to a mobile command center so the parents could learn about the status and location of their children.

Later in the day, word of the deadly toll began to spread. In addition to Naomi Rose, two others had died at the schoolhouse: thirteen-year-old Marian, who had offered to be shot first, and twelve-year-old Anna Mae. Indicative of the confusion that reigned that day, Anna Mae's father had been driven to Christiana Hospital in Delaware expecting to see her, only to find a child from another Amish family. It wasn't until 8:30 that evening that Anna Mae's mother learned that she had died in the schoolhouse and concluded, "Now we know where she is [in heaven]."

One family lost two daughters. Eight-year-old Mary Liz, who had been taken to Christiana Hospital, died in her mother's arms shortly after midnight. Her parents were then driven seventy miles northwest to Hershey Medical Center. There, at 4:30 A.M., Lena, Mary Liz's seven-year-old sister, also died in her mother's arms.

Within sixteen hours of the shooting, five of the girls were "safe in the arms of Jesus," as Amish parents repeated many times. Five others, critically injured, struggled for their lives. An Amish woman in Iowa spoke for hundreds of Amish people: "My mind went to the following song many times: 'Safe in the arms of Jesus / Safe on his gentle breast / There by His love o'er shaded / Sweetly my soul shall rest.'"

The five girls had joined the sixteenth-century martyrs of the Amish faith. The old martyr stories are recorded in a thousand-page book, *The Bloody Theater or Martyrs Mirror of the Defenseless Christians,* known simply as *Martyrs Mirror.* Amish ministers often cite this massive tome in their sermons. Beheaded, burned at the stake, and tortured for their faith, the martyrs died because they were considered heretics during the Protestant Reformation. Nearly five hundred years later, the five girls at the Nickel Mines School died quicker deaths, although not directly for their faith. Still, in the minds of many Amish people, they were martyrs. "They were willing to die, and that makes them martyrs," said one Amish mother. "The oldest one said, 'Shoot me first.'"

Perhaps it was the stories of the martyrs in her people's history that imbued the oldest girl with such courage on that terrifying day. The stories and songs of the faith that she had learned will certainly be passed down to generations after hers. And for the Amish survivors of Nickel Mines, the song she and her classmates had sung that morning will carry a sad and profound resonance for years to come:

> Consider, man! the end,
> Consider your death,
> Death often comes quickly;
> He who today is vigorous and ruddy,
> May tomorrow or sooner,
> Have passed away.

CHAPTER THREE

The Aftermath

We were all Amish this week.

—NICKEL MINES AMISH MAN

The news of the Nickel Mines massacre spread quickly across the nation and around the world. Not only was the cold-blooded violence awful in its scope, but it had struck a people and a place that many imagined was immune from such terror.

As satellite dishes beamed the story around the world, even people who knew little or nothing of the Amish found themselves overcome with sadness. At several Amish farmers markets in the Baltimore-Washington area, outsiders brought flowers and knelt to pray in front of Amish deli stands. At several stands, non-Amish people set up collection boxes for cash donations. "People didn't know what to say to us," recalled an Amish man who runs a farmers market in Philadelphia's Rittenhouse Square. "There were cloudy eyes and tears. 'What can we do?' they asked."

In fact, people did many things. Grief counselors from the Lancaster County Emergency Management Agency arrived at the Bart

Township firehouse early Monday afternoon, only hours after the shooting. They remained busy throughout the week, helping Amish and English alike to process the terror and pain. Other mental health professionals provided counseling for several weeks thereafter, serving anyone in need, including panic-stricken Amish children. "They did a great job," said an Amish fire official. "They told us that things will never be the same again, that we must find 'a new normal.'" He kept repeating the phrase as we talked: "a new normal, a new normal." The expression was clearly helping him get his bearings in the aftermath of the tragedy.

The Bart firehouse soon became the command center for police, firefighters, emergency medical technicians, and hundreds of volunteers who converged on the village of Georgetown. Sixty-nine fire companies from other areas provided support throughout the week. Fire company personnel, in cooperation with the police, managed the deluge of media vehicles and coordinated the four Amish funeral processions, which plodded through Georgetown a few days after the shooting. Fire company volunteers and neighbors served thousands of meals at the firehouse, feeding some five hundred people a day for most of the week. Local stores contributed food and drinks for the hungry volunteers.

The Bart Post Office received thousands of cards, letters, checks, and gifts from around the world. Some letters arrived with only a simple address: "Amish Families of Nickel Mines, USA." For four weeks, volunteers came to the firehouse five days a week and sorted the mail into large plastic tubs. Each tub had a label: the name of a particular Amish family, "the Roberts family," or "the Amish." One Amish family received about twenty-five hundred letters. By mid-November, as the mail began to dwindle, the sorters came in only three days a week. An entire office at the firehouse overflowed with teddy bears—hundreds more than the surviving children could use. The extra teddy bears and other toys eventually found their way to children in other Amish schools.

The care demonstrated by their English neighbors made a deep impression on the Amish. "I can't put into words what the people are doing for our community," wrote a Georgetown correspondent in *Die Botschaft*.* "The police tried to keep the newsmen away. Fire companies and ambulance people were here from far around. Almost all the roads were closed around here almost all last week to keep the tourists and the newsmen away." He continued, "Words can't express what the English are doing for our people. We're getting cards and letters from all over the world. A lot of people gathered at the firehouse.... Some were neighbors and others were total strangers."

Indeed, outsiders who wondered if the tragedy would drive a wedge between the Amish and the English needed only to look inside the firehouse: Amish and state police officers worked side by side; Amish and non-Amish women prepared and served meals together. As a result, the cultural barriers between the Amish and the English diminished somewhat in the wake of the shooting. Everyone, both Amish and English, agreed that the incident drew them closer together. "We were all Amish this week," said one Amish man.

The Amish also received support from more distant places. On impulse, several out-of-state grief counselors boarded a plane for Pennsylvania, hoping to help the grieving families. Philadelphia residents offered housing to Amish families so they could stay near their hospitalized children. A manufacturer of playground equipment pledged to donate all the outside equipment for a new Amish school. Some outsiders, demonstrating a remarkable degree of sensitivity, inquired whether their gifts would be culturally appropriate. Students and teachers at an elementary school in Florida who were preparing a box of school supplies for the surviving children asked

Die Botschaft (The News) is one of several Amish correspondence newspapers. These publications consist of letters written in English by "scribes" (correspondents) who describe recent events in their local areas.

whether they could include a globe, crayons, and coloring books, or whether such items might be offensive. Their gifts, in fact, fit the culture perfectly.

Some of the goodwill came in response to previous acts of grace. After Hurricane Katrina devastated the Gulf Coast in 2005, fifty Amish carpenters went to Picayune, Mississippi, to repair the roofs of hurricane-damaged homes. When the residents of Picayune heard about the school shooting, they wanted to return the favor. Despite their ongoing struggle to recover from Katrina, the people of Picayune presented the Amish community with a check for $11,000. Some expressions of care had even deeper roots. In 1972, after the destructive floods of Hurricane Agnes, Amish people helped to clean up the mud and mess in devastated areas of central Pennsylvania. Thirty-four years later, people in several of those communities called and asked what they could do to return the kindness.

Hundreds of phone calls flooded the Bart Township Fire Company, from people asking how to help and where to send money. The Georgetown branch of the Coatesville Savings Bank quickly set up two funds: the Nickel Mines Children's Fund and the Roberts Family Fund. Other banks and charitable organizations also established funds. In one example of the many community fund-raisers that were organized after the tragedy, three thousand motorcyclists came to Lancaster County on a ride named "Because We Care" and raised $34,000 for the families of the victims.

With the avalanche of gifts growing hourly, it soon became clear that coordination was needed. Two days after the shooting, sixteen Amish and English leaders met at the Bart firehouse to develop a response. Within a few hours they had formed the Nickel Mines Accountability Committee and appointed nine men—seven Amish and two English—to serve on it. The leaders elected two Amish men to serve as chair and vice chair and asked Herman Bontrager, a local Mennonite leader, to be the committee's spokesperson.

"We are not asking for aid, but we will receive it," the Accountability Committee explained at the outset. The long-standing Amish tradition of mutual aid that encourages members to care for one another in time of need also discourages them from relying too heavily on aid from non-Amish people and outside agencies. For this reason, they reject commercial insurance and, with a few exceptions, do not participate in Social Security. In this case, however, the Nickel Mines shooting trumped tradition. "The whole nation is grieving," said one Amish leader. "By letting them give, it helps them too." The committee therefore agreed to accept outside donations so that others wouldn't be deprived "of the blessing of giving."

In a public statement released a few days later, the Nickel Mines Accountability Committee thanked the local community for its many expressions of love. "Each act of kindness, the prayers and every gift," wrote the committee, "comfort us and assure us that our spirits will heal, even though the painful loss will always be with us." After thanking the standard list of helpers—police, emergency workers, medical providers, and church and community groups—the committee extended its gratitude to one more group, which may have surprised some people: the news media. The media "helped the world grapple with values that are dear to us—forgiveness, nonviolence, mutual care, simplicity," the committee wrote, and demonstrated many "acts of kindness" even while doing their reporting work. Finally, the committee reported that financial contributions would be used for medical and counseling services, transportation needs, rehabilitation, disability care, "and other expenses resulting from the event." Within several months of the tragedy, the committee had received $4 million from contributors around the world.

The generosity of neighbors and compassionate strangers around the world stirred a deep sense of gratitude among the Amish. The front-page headline of a weekly Amish newspaper proclaimed "THANK YOU." The accompanying editorial began with special thanks to the state police commissioner, Jeffrey Miller, for his work during the crisis. The column also extended warm thanks to a host of professionals and volunteers "for their quick action in their protection of our privacy during the days of sorrowing and grief . . . and the many unselfish hours they volunteered to keep law and order in the community." The editorial ended by thanking "the whole community, both English and Amish, for everything that was done to help carry this burden . . . [and] all people of all nations around the world, for all the donations that have been sent to us and for all the prayers that have been offered on our behalf."

The parents of one of the deceased girls, in a letter to a Lancaster newspaper, echoed the gratitude: "We will never forget the feelings of protection and comfort it gave us to have the state police protecting us from the hungry media on our way to the burial services of our daughter. . . . There are many other things to be thankful for, and even in our sorrow, we are counting our blessings. And we thank the whole nation for prayer support."

Some Amish people acknowledged that they might have underestimated the potential goodness of outsiders. In a letter to the editor of the *Philadelphia Inquirer,* an Amish father admitted, "Our perceptions of 'worldly' and 'outsiders' have been challenged and changed. It has been reaffirmed to us that there is much good in the rest of the world." He continued his letter by noting, "It is reassuring that in spite of our different identities we can still reach out to each other as human brothers and sisters with the same hopes, fears, desires, and feelings in difficult times."

To be sure, Amish writers continued to emphasize the primary importance of their own church community. "We are thankful to have such a sharing community and church, where there is Christian fellowship under an Almighty and loving, caring Savior and God," wrote the editor of one Amish newspaper. Indeed, the Amish families most directly affected by the shooting relied on their fellow church members as their chief source of support and, compared to what many grief-stricken people experience, they received extraordinary care. Unlike the English, who donated playground equipment, teddy bears, and money, the Amish caregivers offered more modest gifts: meals, quiet words of condolence, and often just the gift of presence. On October 3 and 4, hundreds of family members and friends streamed into the homes of the bereaved parents. Drawing on the bonds of kinship, these visitors responded to the parents' unimaginable grief with heartfelt gestures of support.

Despite the tragic circumstances, the viewings conformed to typical Amish practice. After a death in the Amish community, an English mortician takes the body to a funeral home, embalms it, and then promptly returns it to the home, where family members dress the body in preparation for burial. Young girls are usually dressed in white and wear a white head covering as they lie in a simple wooden coffin. In keeping with the Amish tradition of being candid about death, the girls' coffins were open, a reminder to those filing by of the schoolhouse horror only a few days past.

At word of a death, members of the local church district assume the chores for the grieving family, freeing them to meet with the hundreds of friends and relatives who visit in the days before the funeral. Mary, a young mother, explained, "Often at a viewing many people just shake hands but don't say anything. I often say, 'We will think about you a lot.' I don't say, 'I'm praying for you,' because that would sound too proud." A minister agreed: "When you visit parents during these viewings, it's just your presence. Just be there a few moments and then leave. Just a few moments of silence."

In the Lancaster Amish settlement, viewings are open to anyone, but funerals are typically for invited guests only. A friend or relative, on behalf of the bereaved family, issues invitations to the funeral by word of mouth. To accommodate the large number of people in attendance—often three hundred or more—the funeral service is usually conducted in a barn or large shop. A small, private service is held first in the home, followed by the large, formal funeral.

The funerals for the five girls took place three and four days after the shooting. Three of the funerals—for Naomi Rose, Marian, and the two sisters, Mary Liz and Lena—were held on Thursday, October 5. The funeral for Anna Mae was held on Friday, October 6. Like other Amish worship services, funeral services are usually conducted in Pennsylvania German. However, as a courtesy to English friends, visitors from Chicago, and police officers in attendance, one of the services included both German and English.

Along with sermons emphasizing the importance of yielding to God's will, Amish funerals often include the reading, but not the singing, of a hymn. The song read at the funeral of seven-year-old Naomi Rose was "Ich war ein kleines Kindlein" ("I Was a Little Child"). The text underscores the uncertain nature of one's earthly life and the blessed assurance to come:

> I was a little child
> Born into this world;
> But my hour of death
> God has sent quickly.
> I have nothing to say
> About the world and its doings;
> I have in my days
> needed nothing of that.
> My most beloved father

Who begat me into the world,
And my dearest mother
Who has nursed me herself,
They follow me to the grave
With inward sighs;
Yet I was God's gift
Which He now takes to Himself.
He takes me with grace
To an inheritance in His kingdom.
Death cannot harm me
I am like the angels;
My body shall live again
In rest and eternal joy,
And soar with my soul
In greater glory.

Following each of the four funeral services, a procession of some three dozen carriages wound its way through the village of Georgetown on its way to the Bart Amish Cemetery. Each procession was led by two state troopers on horseback and a horse-drawn hearse that carried the simple wooden coffin. As the processions passed the Bart firehouse, firefighters stood along the road and doffed their helmets. One of the killer's relatives, who watched a procession pass his home, later recalled, "Neighbors, people, and families were embracing each other. There was just a lot of grace and sympathy."

When each procession finally reached the cemetery, pallbearers carried the coffin to the open grave. After a brief service that included the reading of a hymn and a prayer, the body was lowered into the ground. The two sisters, Mary Liz and Lena, who were "very close" and "loved to play together," according to their grandfather, were buried in separate coffins in the same grave.

The Amish were deeply touched that the state police provided mounted officers to lead and follow each procession. After arriving at the cemetery, the four officers barricaded the entrance, keeping a watchful eye out for intruders who might violate the privacy of the solemn moment. "It was a very humbling experience to see those mounted troopers. I just cried," said an Amish businessman.

On Saturday, the family and friends of Charles Carl Roberts IV gathered for his burial. Following a private service at a local funeral home, Roberts's body was taken to the cemetery of the Georgetown United Methodist Church, a short three hundred yards from his home. There he was laid to rest beside the pink, heart-shaped gravestone of his infant daughter, Elise, whose death nine years earlier had tormented him for so long.

With the girls and their killer now buried, questions about the reason for Roberts's rampage resurfaced. "We all keep asking why," said Roberts's grandfather-in-law, who had lived next door to him. "Everyone had a good word for Charlie, but he just lost his mind." The brutal violence did not fit with what he knew about Roberts's care for his children. Moreover, as far as he knew, the gunman "had no bad feelings against the Amish." The only thing he could tie to Roberts's behavior was his intense reserve. "He was very quiet. He would stand here in the driveway and throw the ball to the dog, but not say anything, not even to me. To get a conversation going, you had to start it."

A possible explanation for his outburst came from the killer himself. When Roberts called his wife from the schoolhouse, he said he was plagued by memories of having molested two family members twenty years earlier. But this explanation, like every other, seemed insufficient to explain the rampage. In addition, the family members he referred to had no recollections of abuse.

One week to the day after the shooting, school classes for the surviving Amish children resumed in a garage on a nearby Amish property. To prepare for the move to the new location, parents, friends, and the surviving boys returned to the old schoolhouse in rented vans to retrieve their remaining books and supplies. Emergency workers had already cleaned up the blood and broken glass that had littered the floor. When the boys entered the building they went to the front, knelt down where the girls had been bound together, and poked their fingers through the bullet holes in the floor. Then they went to their desks to gather up their supplies. The parents searched the desks of their daughters to retrieve artwork, pencils, and any memorabilia they could find. The blackboard was taken down and, with its chalk lessons still intact, loaded into a waiting van.

Before they left the school, one of the parents asked an Amish bishop to say a prayer. "He wished us all God's richest blessings and talked about how the Lord works in everything. Tears were flowing again, but these were tears of peace," recalled an Amish witness. The bishop thanked the boys for showing the courage to return to the school and go through their desks; he then prayed the Lord's Prayer. "It was such a sacred moment, such a sacred place," said one Amish person. "I could just feel God's power. There was lots of crying, and it was very, very sad, but on the other hand there was peace, peace. God's presence was so real I could almost touch it."

As they prepared to leave, the boys gathered around the rope of the school bell. They were eager to pull it at exactly 10:45 A.M., when churches across Lancaster County would ring their bells to mark the passing of the first week since the tragedy. A state policeman who was guarding the schoolhouse gave a nod at the exact time. With so many hands pulling so hard, the bell rang just once and then got stuck. Some of the boys scampered onto the roof and continued to ring it from up there.

Returning to the school was a healing experience, but it could not alter the fact that things had changed. Before leaving their old schoolyard, the boys began planning the location of the ball diamond they would create at the temporary school down the road. The West Nickel Mines School had two ball fields, so all of the children could play at the same time. Now it dawned on the boys that they would need only one, because ten of their classmates were missing.

One person who wasn't missing, however, was their teacher. When the students reassembled in their makeshift classroom, Emma was there to meet them and resume her teaching duties. It would be best for her and for her scholars, she reasoned, if she were there to help them find their "new normal."

Within days of the shooting, word had spread among the media that the Amish might raze the old school building. "Why would they do that?" asked one reporter. "Is it part of a religious ritual of purification?" The easy answer was no: the Amish do not have purification rituals. They simply did not want their children to be reminded of the terror of that hour, day after day, season after season, as they sat in a room where five of their peers had died and another five were wounded. The Amish were also concerned about the possibility that thousands of tourists would converge on White Oak Road to see the now historic site. "We want to move on," said an Amish farmer. "The community doesn't want all the publicity and all the tourists that would come to Nickel Mines if the school remained standing." In short, common sense dictated demolition.

At 4:45 A.M. on October 12, ten days after the shooting, the teeth of a huge backhoe bit into the schoolhouse. In fifteen minutes it was

40

rubble. Working in the early dawn under large spotlights, the demolition crew hoped to avoid the media glare. Nevertheless, a few photographers and a handful of Amish turned out to witness the destruction of this peculiar site of death.

Several weeks after the shooting, state police officers and Amish families gathered in the Bart firehouse on a Friday evening. The gathering was marked by the appearance of three of the surviving girls, who had recently returned home from the hospital. The girls recognized the troopers who had rescued them and rushed over to talk to them. "It was very emotional. It was something that's hard to put into words—how the state police put their hearts out on the floor and the Amish did the same," said the father of one of the survivors. "It was good for both sides. It was comforting for the girls."

The Amish had only words of praise for the police. "The police were magnificent," said one Amish shop worker, who added, "I'll wave at them the next time I see them." It appeared that many Amish people in Lancaster County had made the same decision. Typically reticent in their interactions with outsiders, some Amish people began lifting their hands in greeting as they passed officers on the road. As members of "another kingdom," the Amish had gained a new respect for the agents of the state, who had guarded their community and given them space to grieve after their own September 11.

Reporters continued to wonder if the shooting would bring changes in Amish schools, especially in the area of safety. The Amish wondered the same thing. On October 10, eight days after the shooting, Amish leaders held a meeting at an Amish home to discuss the safety questions that many people, both Amish and English, had been asking for a week. Should electronic alarms be installed? What about cell phones programmed to call 911?

The leaders decided that electronic forms of protection would probably not prevent future shootings and, according to one elder, could even weaken "our trust in God, losing His blessing on our schools." Mechanical enhancements gained greater favor than electronic ones: installation of locks on schoolhouse doors, panic bars so people could exit but not enter, and sturdy fences with strong locks. Some proposed the use of evacuation drills and others suggested locating schools closer to Amish homes. But these suggestions were simply that: suggestions. In the end, each of the hundreds of small Amish school boards across the country would decide what safety changes, if any, they would implement. Each school board would draw the delicate line between trusting in God or in human devices.

By mid-November, a site had been selected for the new school, which would be built in early 2007. New grass sprouting on the old schoolyard was blending in with the adjoining pasture. The surviving girls were recovering; in fact, three were already back at school. Another, needing constant care, had returned home, and the fifth, still at Children's Hospital in Philadelphia, hoped to be home by Christmas. Indeed, she amused many in the Amish community when word got out that she had begged a nurse to wrap her in a big gift box as a present for her parents.

And there was a new Naomi Rose. The twenty-two-year-old pregnant visitor, who had comforted the distraught Naomi Rose before being ordered to leave the schoolhouse, gave her newborn daughter that name eight days later.

The Amish in Nickel Mines were moving on. Though the survivors carried deep scars, both physical and emotional, they were committed to moving on as a community, to caring for each other, and to practicing their faith. With God's help, they were starting to live "a new normal."

CHAPTER FOUR

The Surprise

You mean some people actually thought we got together to plan forgiveness?

—AMISH GRANDMOTHER

T he schoolhouse shooting in quiet Amish country shocked the world. Then, with a swiftness that also startled the world, the Nickel Mines Amish forgave the killer and offered grace to his family.

Even as outsiders were responding with compassion for the Amish community in the wake of the shooting, the Amish themselves were doing another kind of work. Softly, subtly, and quietly, they were beginning the difficult task of forgiveness.

The Amish quickly realized that Roberts's widow and children were also victims of the shooting—victims who had lost not only a husband and father, but also their privacy. Unlike the Amish victims, the Roberts family had to bear the shame of having a loved one inflict such pain on innocent children and families. Within a few hours of the shooting, some Amish people were already reaching out to the killer's family.

Amos, an Amish minister in one of the nearby church districts, described it to us like this: "Well, there were three of us standing around at the firehouse on Monday evening. We just thought we should go and say something to Amy, Roberts's widow. So first we went to her house, and no one was there. Then we walked over to her grandfather's house and no one was there. So we walked over to her father's house and she, her children, and her parents were there alone. So we just talked with them for about ten minutes to express our sorrow and told them that we didn't hold anything against them."

That same evening, several miles away, an Amish man went to see the killer's father, a retired police officer who provided taxi service for local Amish residents. Dwight Lefever, a spokesperson for the Roberts family, later told the media that an Amish neighbor had come to comfort the family. "He stood there for an hour, and he held that man [Mr. Roberts] in his arms and said, 'We forgive you.'" In the next days, Roberts's parents received many visits and calls from other Amish people who also expressed forgiveness and gracious concern.

The day after the shooting, Amy's grandfather visited one of the bereaved Amish families, one for whom the gunman had hauled milk. "I knew the father and grandfather of the children who were killed. We met in the kitchen and shook hands and put our arms around each other," recalled Roberts's relative. "They said there are no grudges. There's forgiveness in all of this. It was hard to listen to, and hard to believe." Describing what happened in the following days he said, "There have been many Amish stopping at Amy's house and expressing their forgiveness and condolences and bringing her gifts. I can see them from my window when they come to her house."

Other Amish people in the Nickel Mines community expressed their commitment to forgiveness in different ways. At about 5:30 on Wednesday morning, two days after the shooting, the sleepless grandfather of the two slain sisters was walking by the schoolhouse, reflecting on his loss. A little more than twenty-four hours earlier, he had made grueling trips to two different hospitals only to see the young girls die in their mother's arms. Suddenly TV cameras caught him in the glare of floodlights, and a reporter stepped toward him.

"Do you have any anger toward the gunman's family?" she asked.
"No."
"Have you already forgiven them?"
"In my heart, yes."
"How is that possible?"
"Through God's help."

Later that morning, an Amish woman from Georgetown, appearing in silhouette on CBS's *Early Show,* also spoke about forgiving the killer. "We have to forgive," she said. "We have to forgive him in order for God to forgive us."

Another story, widely reported in the national media, involved the grandfather of another of the victims. Looking at his granddaughter's mutilated body lying in a coffin in her home, he told the younger children surrounding him, "We shouldn't think evil of the man who did this." This spirit of grace was echoed by an Amish craftsman in Georgetown who had relatives in the schoolhouse. He told the Associated Press, "I hope they [Roberts's widow and children] stay around here. They'll have lots of friends and a lot of support."

Amish grace soon moved beyond spontaneous words and personal gestures. The parents of several of the slain children invited members of the Roberts family to attend their daughters' funerals. More surprisingly, when the Roberts family gathered on Saturday to bury the gunman in the cemetery of Georgetown United Methodist Church, more than half of the seventy-five mourners were Amish. Amos, an Amish neighbor who was present at the gravesite, thought it was simply the right thing to do. "A number of us just talked and thought we should go," he said. "Many of us knew the family very well. So we met at the firehouse, just informally, and then we walked across the back way, behind a long garage. We waited there until we saw them bring the body to the cemetery. . . . Many of our people went up to Amy and greeted her and the children." In fact, some of the parents who had buried their own children just a day or two before offered condolences and hugs to Amy at the gravesite.

The funeral director recalled the moving moment: "I was lucky enough to be at the cemetery when the Amish families of the children who had been killed came to greet Amy Roberts and offer their forgiveness. And that is something I'll never forget, not ever. I knew that I was witnessing a miracle."

A Roberts family member, also an eyewitness to the "miracle," described it this way: "About thirty-five or forty Amish came to the burial. They shook our hands and cried. They embraced Amy and the children. There were no grudges, no hard feelings, only forgiveness. It's just hard to believe that they were able to do that."

The presence of Amish mourners at Roberts's burial may have been the most dramatic expression of their grace, but it was not the final one. Several weeks after the shooting, a meeting took place at the Bart firehouse between members of the Roberts family—Amy, her sister, her parents, and Charles's parents—and the Amish families who lost children. It was a profound time of grief and healing, according to some present. "We went around the circle and introduced ourselves," an Amish leader said. "Amy just cried and cried and cried. We talked and cried and talked and cried. She was near me, and I put my hand on her shoulder, and then I stood up and I talked and cried. It was very moving and very intense." In the words of another Amish participant, "There were a lot of tears shed that day. There was a higher power in the room."

Forgiveness also flowed in the form of dollars. When the Nickel Mines Accountability Committee formed two days after the shooting, committee members discussed their desire to help the Roberts family. In searching for a committee name, they decided to forgo the word *Amish* and instead use *Nickel Mines,* said one committee member, "because this is a community tragedy beyond us Amish. We want to reach out to the Roberts family as well." In the ensuing discussion, another committee member asked, "Who will take care of them now since they will have no income? It's not right if we get $1,000 and they get only $5." After contacting the Roberts family, the committee designated some its funds for the killer's widow.

In addition to assisting the Roberts family through the Accountability Committee, Amish people contributed to the family personally by making donations to the Roberts Family Fund established by the Coatesville Savings Bank. Dozens of Amish people donated money to the fund, said one knowledgeable source. One English man recalled making a contribution at the bank, turning to leave, and finding two Amish people behind him in line waiting to donate.

These concrete acts of grace were not lost on the widow's family. "It's hard to accept what has happened," said one of Amy's relatives, "but the kindness of the Amish has helped us tremendously. . . . It helps us to know that they forgave us." Another relative agreed, echoing what many commentators had already noted: "If this had happened to some of our own [non-Amish] people, there would have been one lawsuit after another. . . . But this experience brought everybody closer together." In a public statement released ten days after the shooting, the Roberts family specifically thanked the local Amish community: "Your compassion has reached beyond our family, beyond our community, and is changing our world, and for this we sincerely thank you." A confidant of the killer's parents said, "All of the expressions of forgiveness provided a great freedom that enabled them to move on with healing despite all the sadness and sorrow. It gave them hope for the future and released them from the heavy burden."

A friend of the killer's widow said, "The forgiveness and generosity of the Amish had a powerful impact on Amy. She was overwhelmed and very moved by it. Many Amish neighbors came to visit her in the weeks following the shooting. They came to the burial, they brought flowers to her home, and they brought meals."

These simple acts of Amish grace soon eclipsed the story of schoolhouse slaughter. On Wednesday, two days after the shooting, the media calls we received suddenly turned from questions about Amish schools to questions about Amish forgiveness. How could they forgive so quickly? Did their leaders demand that they do it? Or was it all a gimmick, designed only to garner good publicity for their community?

As the media gathered answers to these questions, Amish forgiveness became the focal point in hundreds of news stories around the world. From the *Washington Post* to *USA Today,* from *NBC Nightly News* to *Larry King Live,* from the *Christian Science Monitor* to the Christian Broadcasting Network, from the *Khaleej Times* to Australian television, journalists found themselves reporting a story they had not set out to cover.

The initial news stories were soon followed by legions of commentaries and editorials reflecting on the virtues of forgiveness, dismissing it as emotionally unhealthy, or asking what might have happened if the United States had responded with forgiveness to the terrorist attacks of September 11. Ordinary people entered the conversation as well; thousands of reader letters reflected on this surprising extension of grace and wondered whether it was a model for others to emulate. (We explore some of these reactions in the next chapter.)

What these letters and media stories often lacked, however, were accounts of the concrete acts of Amish grace that we have just noted. Given the reluctance of Amish people to talk with the media, this dearth of information is hardly surprising. In this instance, however, the silence cannot be reduced to the fact that Amish people do not boast to the media about what they do. In this case, they did not talk about their forgiving acts because, to them, granting forgiveness was a natural, spontaneous, and quite ordinary thing. Refusing to forgive "is not an option," said Bishop Eli, a welder. "It's just a normal part of our living."

How did the Amish decide so quickly to extend forgiveness? That question brought laughter from some Amish people we interviewed. "You mean some people actually thought we got together to plan forgiveness?" chuckled Katie, a seventy-five-year-old grandmother, as she worked in her kitchen. "Forgiveness was a decided issue," explained Bishop Eli. "It's just what we do as nonresistant people. It was spontaneous. It was automatic. It was not a new kind of thing." Every Amish person we spoke with agreed: forgiveness for Roberts and grace for his family had begun as spontaneous expressions of faith, not as mandates from the church.

That the outside world was surprised at Amish forgiveness in turn surprised the Amish. "Why is everybody all surprised?" asked one Amish man. "It's just standard Christian forgiveness; it's what everybody should be doing." Sadie, a bookkeeper and mother of three, was similarly taken aback by the national attention Amish forgiveness had generated. "Before the media made such a big deal of forgiveness, I never realized that it was so much a part of our life. I just never realized before how central it is to us."

Suddenly the Amish had a new problem, one as challenging for them as forgiving the killer and his family: living up to the high expectations of the outside world. "The news reporters have set a high standard for us because of all this talk about forgiveness," an Amish craftsman who lives near the school told us. "It's a new burden that's hard to carry," lamented another community member. Many Amish turned the overwhelming attention that they were receiving into an opportunity for self-reflection. A perplexed young father asked, "Why is the world so hungry for forgiveness now? It humbles us. It gives us a big responsibility. We don't want to be exalted. Now we're under the public eye, being scrutinized to see if we really do forgive. We wonder: can we Amish people really be what the public expects of us now?"

Over and over again, the Amish with whom we spoke expressed anxiety about being placed on a pedestal by the media and the watching world. For people who seek humility and avoid publicity, garnering praise from the larger world caused deep discomfort. "Everybody knows who we are now," said a grandmother who lives near the village of Bird-in-Hand. That puts the Amish community on "thin ice," she continued. Not only are people thinking about the Amish, but "everybody puts us up so high. . . . We are not exactly like the reporters say we are. We are being put up on a pedestal as 'too-good' people."

Amish concern about being placed on a pedestal stemmed in part from their awareness that, long before the school shooting, some non-Amish neighbors had thought the Amish received too much favorable treatment in the press. Irritated at times by slow-moving buggies on high-speed roadways, some locals "think that the Amish don't do anything right," Gid, a minister and farmer, said. "It makes them annoyed when we look so good in the media because they think we can't really be that good." In fact, in the weeks following the school shooting, some English neighbors grumbled about ungracious encounters with Amish employers, including Amish employers who had fired English employees.

More than worrying about outsiders' appraisals of them, however, the Lancaster County Amish worried about God's expectations, which to them seemed clear: their lives should demonstrate humility and avoid vanity. The last sentence of the Lord's Prayer, which the Amish revere, reads, "For *thine* is the kingdom, and the power, and the glory" (Matthew 6:13; emphasis added). Suddenly the "glory" had focused on them. Jesus' words about practicing one's faith in private troubled them greatly; they didn't want to be lumped with the hypocrites who Jesus condemned for their public displays of piety. Yet in the media maelstrom that was engulfing their community, practicing their faith in private was hardly an option.

Motivated in part by this discomfort, some Amish people made special efforts to speak publicly about the foundation of their faith. The father of one of the children who was killed emphasized that "God is the one who should get the blessing in this when it's all over and done. It should be God, not us." The parents of another girl who died in the schoolhouse wrote a letter to a Lancaster newspaper saying, "It is only through our faith in Jesus Christ that forgiveness is possible. He is the one who deserves the praise and glory, not us Amish."

Speaking publicly about faith is not a common practice in most Amish communities. Generally, the Amish do not support or engage in organized evangelistic work; in fact, the Amish are criticized by some evangelical Christians for their lack of missionary zeal. Preferring actions over words, the Amish provide material aid to refugees and disaster-stricken people rather than try to convert others to their views. In their minds, verbal evangelism involves the subtle use of coercive persuasion that focuses on individual conversion rather than community faithfulness.

For this reason, the Amish are drawn to the metaphor from Jesus' Sermon on the Mount: a light on the hill that shines in the darkness and provides a witness to God's grace by faithful practice. An Amish shop worker referred to this image as he considered how stories of Amish forgiveness had spanned the globe: "This forgiveness story makes me think of Matthew 5 and a light set on the hill. 'Ye are the light of the world. A city that is set on an hill cannot be hid'" (Matthew 5:14).

"Sometimes some of our people think we should do more evangelistic work or begin a prison ministry," said one Amish farmer, reflecting on all the press coverage of forgiveness. "But this forgiveness story made more of a witness for us all over the world than anything else we can ever do." Gid agreed: "Maybe this was God's way to let us do some missionary work. Maybe He used the media to help spread the word." Not every Amish person drew this missionary-minded conclusion, but some clearly did. "The message [of forgiveness] really was a light to the world," said Amos, the minister. "We're supposed to be a light to the world, but we're not supposed to say, 'See what I'm doing.' . . . It's important that we put the honor where the honor belongs [to God]."

A father who lost a daughter at the schoolhouse stressed again and again that forgiveness is more than words. Sitting at his kitchen table, he told us, "Our forgiveness is not in our words, it's in our actions; it's not what we said, but what we did. That was our forgiveness." At the bottom of his faxed correspondence, another Amish man included a phrase that he had borrowed from a church sign: "Preach the gospel, and if necessary, use words." The Amish were preaching, but rarely with words.

When forgiveness arrived at the killer's home within hours of his crime, it did not appear out of nowhere. Rather, forgiveness is woven into the very fabric of Amish life, its sturdy threads having been spun from faith in God, scriptural mandates, and a history of persecution. The grace extended by the Amish surprised the world almost as much as the killing itself. Indeed, in many respects, the story of Amish forgiveness became *the* story—the story that trumped the narrative of senseless death—in the days that followed the shooting. Amish grace, and the way it affected the world, did not rob the tragedy of its horror, nor did it eradicate the grief of those left behind. Still, it may have been an answer to Amish prayers that somehow, somewhere, some good would come out of this terrible event.

CHAPTER FIVE

The Reactions

What if the Amish were in charge of the war on terror?

—DIANA BUTLER BASS, RELIGION COLUMNIST

I t's not often that forgiveness becomes the topic of a national conversation. Wayward religious leaders repenting of their sins have sometimes triggered talk about the virtues of forgiveness. President Clinton's confessions following his dalliances with Monica Lewinsky stirred similar discussions. Rarely, however, has this spiritually oriented topic gained much traction at the nation's dinner tables and water coolers.

The Amish response at Nickel Mines kick-started a national conversation—with the help, of course, of the news media. Within two days of the Monday shooting, Amish forgiveness had become the primary theme in the media's coverage of the incident, outpacing both the details of the rampage and the killer's curious motives. On Thursday and Friday, the girls' funerals assumed center stage, but even then the media's theme of healing suggested that the Amish had forgiven the person whose actions had made the funerals necessary. At about the same time, a swell of op-ed pieces pondering Amish forgiveness began to appear, a rising tide that crested a week after the shooting. In all of this, the Amish had suddenly vacated their standard role in the American imagination as technophobic, buggy-driving, plain-dressing folks. To the endless wonder of observers, and to their own surprise, the Amish had become the world's most forgiving people.

Understanding why a story gains attention in the media is never easy. What makes an event newsworthy? Needless to say, the media first came to Lancaster County because of the killing itself, a vicious crime magnified by its context: a one-room schoolhouse in a quiet hamlet. The shock that such horror could visit Amish Country offered a compelling storyline, and the gracious acts that followed it only added to the drama. Perhaps too the media hoped to offer something redemptive in the midst of tragedy, something that would reassure their audiences of the enduring goodness of America's heartland. Many journalists, astonished by what they had heard and seen, also sensed that the story would appeal to readers and viewers. Whatever the reasons, the story of the shooting at Nickel Mines quickly stimulated a national conversation, both about the Amish and about forgiveness.

Lauding Amish Forgiveness

The most prominent response to emerge from the story was amazement. Time and again commentators expressed astonishment that the Amish were able to forgive, and to forgive so quickly. Occasionally the bewilderment turned to skepticism, as when reporters asked if the Amish were simply seeking good publicity. Generally, however, observers believed that the Amish had genuinely forgiven Roberts and his family—acts they found utterly amazing. One columnist, writing in

Helena, Montana, summed up the sentiment of many observers: "I am profoundly moved by what is happening in Nickel Mines."

In addition to being surprised, the vast majority of pundits also lauded Amish forgiveness, calling it worthy of admiration. "What wonderful people they are," wrote a woman living nearby in Lititz, Pennsylvania. "If all people would follow their examples of faith and forgiveness, what a much better world this would be." A writer in Philadelphia concurred; not only should Americans "feel indebted" to the Amish for what they did, but they should also endeavor to "learn from their example." In the *Sacramento Bee,* a columnist cautioned that she didn't want to "idealize" the Amish community, which "has its problems, too." Still, she wanted her readers to consider "for just a moment how remarkable their calm display of human kindness is." "We should all be that odd, strange, and offbeat," wrote yet another observer.

Such views of Amish forgiveness led many commentators to ask what it was about the Amish that enabled them to forgive. For many, the answer was relatively simple: the Amish embodied an uncorrupted Christian faith. "The Amish have shown the rest of the world what true Christianity is really like," wrote a columnist for a Fort Wayne, Indiana, newspaper. Other observers cited a simple authenticity among the Amish. Still others tied the Amish response to an altruism to which all people could aspire. "This is not about being Amish," wrote one commentator. "This is about living our lives with a calm courage that understands that survival lies in reaching out, not striking back."

Finally, many observers found that the Amish response at Nickel Mines gave them an opportunity to reflect on their own lives and American society. These reflections often revealed a sense of unease about modern culture, which most found wanting compared to Amish life. Numerous observers lamented rising secularism in the country, including one commentator who, in a debatable comparison, equated "the faith of the Amish" with "the Christian faith of our forefathers." After the shooting a Binghamton, New York, newspaper ran an op-ed piece titled "A Society So Modern It's Sickening," which noted four words that have lost currency in contemporary American life: *innocence, decency, reverence,* and *manners.* The commentary mentioned the Amish only at the end, when the writer identified *forgive* as a fifth word she hoped would now make a comeback. "Modern society's sophisticates sneer at the Amish for their 'backward' ways," she concluded, but their extension of forgiveness at Nickel Mines demonstrates "that they may be far more advanced than the rest of us."

Contrary to this writer's assertion, few people sneered at the Amish in the aftermath of the shooting. In fact, these four themes— amazement at the act of forgiveness, admiration of the Amish who did it, a largely favorable view of Amish life, and a lament about mainstream American life—characterized the vast majority of op-ed pieces and commentaries following the tragedy.

Together these themes built on a much longer tradition of public tribute to Amish life. The Amish have long captivated outsiders with their tight-knit communities and resistance to modern technologies, prompting some to wonder if the Amish have something good the English are missing. In the aftermath of the Nickel Mines shooting, this tune of amazement played in a slightly different key. Not only did the Amish *have* something good that others lacked, but in many people's eyes the Amish *were* good— or at least better than the vast majority of their American neighbors. Three months later, when the editors at Beliefnet.com named the "Most Inspiring People of 2006," their selection confirmed the overwhelming choice of their readers: the Amish of Nickel Mines, Pennsylvania.

Questioning Amish Forgiveness

Despite the widespread admiration of Amish forgiveness, a small but insistent chorus emerged on the other side. An early and stinging critique of Amish forgiveness appeared in the *Boston Globe* the Sunday after the shooting. In a frequently reprinted op-ed piece titled "Undeserved Forgiveness," Jeff Jacoby admitted that it was "deeply affecting" to watch the Amish strive to follow Jesus' admonition to return good for evil. Still, he insisted, "hatred is not always wrong, and forgiveness is not always deserved." Jacoby asked his readers, "How many of us would really want to live in a society in which no one gets angry when children are slaughtered?" The problem was not with forgiveness per se, he said; in fact, "to voluntarily forgive those who have hurt you is beautiful and praiseworthy." No, the problem in this case, wrote Jacoby, was that the persons who granted forgiveness forgave a person who hurt *others*. "I cannot see how the world is made a better place by assuring someone who would do terrible things to others that he will be readily forgiven afterward." Appealing to the Bible, the same authority that the Amish often cite, Jacoby reminded his readers that Ecclesiastes teaches that "there is a time to love and a time to hate." He concluded by quoting from Psalm 97: "Let those who love the Lord hate evil."

Jacoby was not alone in his criticism of Amish forgiveness. "Why Do the Amish Ignore Reality?" was the headline for Cristina Odone's opinion piece in Britain's *Observer*. Odone called the Amish community's response to their daughters' killer "disturbing." "They have responded to the massacre of their innocents by repeating that the Lord giveth and the Lord taketh away," she complained. In many respects, Odone's concern was less about forgiveness than it was about what she called the "fatalism" inherent in Amish life. In her view, the Amish acceptance of whatever comes their way, combined with their commitment to pacifism, means that they "inhabit a hopeless universe where senseless massacres are accepted. Not even the charming old-fashioned horse and buggy can make up for that."

These critiques, though relatively few in number, provided a sharp counterpoint to the acclaim heaped on the Amish in the days after the shooting. Moreover, they picked up on themes that some critics of Amish life had cited long before writers at the *Boston Globe* and the *Observer* had ever heard of Nickel Mines. In a poem published in 1996, Denise Duhamel recounted the death of an Amish boy at the hands of a drunk driver and his family's response to that tragedy. "My Amish neighbors / forgive," wrote Duhamel, who then offered her perspective. "I prefer seeing it all," she wrote. "I prefer a good fight / a wailing of grief," quite unlike the gift-shop Amish dolls that "want it silent." Duhamel's implication was that Amish people deal with their grief like soulless dolls—by simply stifling emotional pain. In the days following the Nickel Mines shooting, a *USA Today* blogger made a similar complaint: "This extreme event needs time for emotions to settle, not suppress and suppress. After all, this was not someone who broke a window and was sorry!"

The lack of appropriate emotion, a fatalistic approach to evil, a willingness to forgive the unrepentant, the extension of forgiveness on behalf of others, and its swiftness—all of these critiques of the Amish response echo concerns that some scholars raise about forgiveness more generally. Much has been made in recent years about the virtue of forgiveness, both as a means to heal the victim and, in some cases, as a path to mend the relationship between victim and offender. We explore some of these issues later in this book. At this point we simply note that, in response to those who advocate the virtues of forgiveness, dissenting voices offer caution about extending forgiveness, at least in certain circumstances.

For instance, legal scholar Jeffrie G. Murphy has written that, while he is not an "enemy of forgiveness," he is troubled by those who are too enthusiastic in their "boosterism" of it. In Murphy's view, forgiveness is often a legitimate response to being wronged, although it is only valid "if directed toward the properly deserving (e.g., the repentant) and if it can be bestowed in such a way that victim self-respect and respect for the moral order can be maintained." Sharon Lamb, who collaborated with Murphy on a book titled *Before Forgiving,* applies Murphy's concerns to domestic abuse against women. In most situations of abuse, Lamb contends, "the idea of offering forgiveness toward unrepentant perpetrators . . . is dangerous and plays into deep stereotypes of women's 'essential' nature."

By counseling caution, Lamb and Murphy continue a long-standing debate about forgiveness that emerged in the wake of the Holocaust. In his book *The Sunflower: On the Possibilities and Limits of Forgiveness,* first published in 1969, Simon Wiesenthal describes a request for forgiveness he received from a dying SS officer when Wiesenthal was a prisoner in a Nazi concentration camp. The officer, haunted by his involvement in atrocities against Jews, approached Wiesenthal in a final attempt to be forgiven for his crimes. "I have longed to talk about [my evil deeds] to a Jew and beg forgiveness from him," the officer said. "Without your answer I cannot die in peace." Wiesenthal recounts this event in gripping detail and reports that, in the end, he responded to the man's request with silence. Was silence the right response? Wiesenthal wonders. He then turns to his readers and asks them, What would you have done? What *should* you have done?

In Wiesenthal's concentration camp story, the wrongdoer was repentant, or at least seemed to be, thus overriding one of Murphy's cautions about forgiveness.* Nevertheless, the incident raises two other questions that the critics of Amish forgiveness asked in the wake of the Nickel Mines shooting. First, is it appropriate to forgive someone for evil acts he or she committed against *other* people? Second, are some acts so heinous that they should not be forgiven?

*As we point out in Chapter Ten, some forgiveness scholars think that forgiveness should be unconditional, not dependent on the remorse or repentance of the wrongdoer. In their view, forgiveness is entirely the victim's choice. This view of forgiveness means making a clear distinction between forgiveness and reconciliation, the latter of which requires good-faith efforts by both the victim and the offender.

In the second half of *The Sunflower,* a panel of respondents offers a wide range of answers to those questions. "If asked to forgive, by anyone for anything, I would forgive because God would forgive," writes Roman Catholic priest and educator Theodore Hesburgh. So would I, says the Dalai Lama, although "I would not forget about the atrocities committed." Radio talk show host Dennis Prager, who describes himself as a "religious Jew," responds differently: "People can never forgive murder, since the one person who can forgive is gone, forever." Holocaust survivor Sidney Shachnow offers an even harsher judgment: "I personally think [the SS officer] should go to hell and rot there."

The spectrum of responses reveals two pertinent things about Amish grace in the wake of the Nickel Mines tragedy. First, forgiveness is a valued, but disputed, virtue. Some people find forgiveness noble in the abstract but much more complicated when real-life factors—Who is being forgiven? Of what? By whom? In what circumstances?—are added to the mix. Second, forgiveness is defined differently by different people. Indeed, part of the challenge of talking about forgiveness stems from different definitions of what forgiveness entails. Is it *successfully* letting go of anger, or is it simply *trying* to let go of anger? Does it demand positive *acts* on the part of the victim as well as positive *feelings*? Does it mean that the wrongdoer is now pardoned and is therefore no longer accountable for his or her crime? We return to some of these questions in Part Three of this book when we look more closely at the nature of forgiveness as it was expressed at Nickel Mines.

Another question emerged in the aftermath of the shooting, a critique that is unique to the Amish story. Some onlookers, pointing to the practice of shunning within Amish communities, asked whether the Amish were inconsistent, even hypocritical, in their application of forgiveness. How can the Amish be cited as shining examples of forgiveness, some people wondered, when they seem unwilling to forgive their own people? One online newspaper, reporting the experience of an ex-Amish woman a few weeks after the shooting, put it this way: "Her story paints a very different picture of the Amish than the scenes in Nickel Mines." In a certain sense, the newspaper's observation was correct: Amish responses to their wayward members differ from their responses to English offenders. But is that hypocritical? We return to that question in Chapters Nine and Eleven, when we look at forgiveness and shunning within Amish communities.

Using Amish Forgiveness

Despite a few warning lights, responses to the grace extended at Nickel Mines were overwhelmingly positive, so much so that pundits lined up behind the Amish to score points for their own causes. Soon both the shooting and the Amish response became raw material for making arguments about issues of national, even international, significance.

As they have after other school shootings in the United States, arguments about gun control and America's culture of violence emerged quickly. "Why does a tormented, suicidal adult, such as the one who shot ten Amish school girls . . . have ready access to a semi-automatic pistol, a shotgun, 600 rounds of ammunition and a high-voltage stun gun?" asked an editorial from Scripps News. Of course, anti-gun-control advocates saw the school shooting quite differently. "This shooting . . . and every school shooting in the past ten years all had one thing in common," remarked Alan M. Gottlieb, chairman of the Citizens Committee for the Right to Keep and Bear Arms. "They all happened in so-called 'gun-free school zones,' where students and adult staff are essentially helpless," that is, unable to use guns to defend themselves.

Arguments for and against gun control drew more on the shooting than on the forgiveness that flowed in its wake. But the idea of forgiveness packed great ideological wallop as well, particularly for people who saw acts of retribution they could not support. The biggest target in this regard was the Bush administration and its war on terror. The Amish response to Charles Roberts was a "blueprint" for how President Bush should have responded after September 11, wrote Doug Soderstrom on the Axis of Logic Web site. If only President Bush had been the "follower of the Lord Jesus Christ" he claimed to be, "the world may have been spared the unfathomable travesty of a 'nation of believers' driven insane by an uncontrollable urge to kill in the name of an all-loving God."

Diana Butler Bass, writing on the Faithful America blog, expressed similar sentiments: "What if the Amish were in charge of the war on terror? What if, on the evening of Sept. 12, 2001, we had gone to Osama bin Laden's house (metaphorically, of course, since we didn't know where he lived!) and offered him forgiveness? What if we had invited the families of the hijackers to the funerals of the victims of 9/11?" Acknowledging that it was too late for that, Butler Bass concluded with what she called a modest proposal: Americans should ask the Amish to assume leadership of the Department of Homeland Security. "After all," she said, "actively practicing forgiveness" is far better than living in perpetual fear.

Other commentators were not quite willing to hand over national security to the Amish, but they still thought the Nickel Mines Amish deserved better grades than Washington politicians in their handling of a crisis. "You respect people who are true to their words," wrote George Diaz of the *Orlando Sentinel*. While the Amish "are committed to their beliefs," the Republican congressional leadership "is committed to saving its posterior." From there Diaz proceeded to flay House Speaker Dennis Hastert and others for their handling of scandals in the Republican-led House of Representatives. Writing just weeks before the 2006 midterm elections, Diaz quoted an Amish man who, in an interview with CNN, said, "In forgiveness there is healing." Diaz respected the man's simple assertion but added that it "would be nice if somebody [in Washington] accepted accountability" for all the inside-the-beltway shenanigans. "Then, and only then, can forgiveness and healing truly begin."

The Religious Right likewise became a target of these Amish-inspired reflections—and so did the Religious Left. "The so-called Christian Right should look closely at the Amish lifestyle for lessons in what is wrong with their approach to faith and politics," wrote Stephen Crockett of Democratic Talk Radio. Unlike James Dobson and his ilk, the Amish "do not seek to impose their values on others by law or force," and "hate has no power or legitimacy among them." David Virtue, writing for "The Voice for Global Orthodox Anglicanism," found a different lesson in the aftermath of Nickel Mines. Recalling the bravery of the Amish school-girls and the courage of those who offered forgiveness, he observed that their response grew out of "raw naked faith," not out of the "pathetic liberal gospel" advanced by the U.S. Episcopal Church's hierarchy. He then invoked the name of liberal clergyman John Shelby Spong, asking his readers if they would "stand up and die" for the theological beliefs held by Spong in the way the Amish girls had stood up for their faith.

It may be stretching things to say that the Amish schoolgirls died *defending* their faith, although they and their surviving community members clearly *demonstrated* their faith in their responses to Roberts and his family. Thus it's not surprising that the most consistent and wide-reaching discussion after the shooting focused not on politics per se but on the nature of the Christian life. To be sure, many political issues—gun control, school violence, the war on terror, capital punish-ment, penal reform, and violence against women, among others—were debated along the way, but the most prominent questions were these: What does it mean to live a truly Christian life? Have the Amish set a standard for other Christians to aspire to?

At least for some observers, the answer to the second ques-tion was yes. Sister Joan Chittister, writing for the *National Catholic*

Reporter, suggested that "it was the Christianity we all profess but which [the Amish] practiced that left us stunned." The Nickel Mines Amish, Chittister concluded, astounded the twenty-first-century world the way the earliest Christians astounded the Roman world: simply by being "Christian."

Theologically speaking, this may be the case. For centuries Christian theologians have cited the centrality of forgiveness to the Christian faith, not only as something Jesus modeled but also as something he commanded his followers to do. Nonetheless, it's important to recognize that the Amish are, and always have been, quite unlike most people who call themselves Christians. From a sociological standpoint, they are not simply Christians; they are *Amish* Christians. As Amish Christians, they share a basic set of beliefs with other Christians, but they come to their faith with a unique history, culture, and theology. To really understand the grace offered at Nickel Mines, we must explore the history, the spirituality, and the culture of the people who extended it.

Part Two

Contra Costa County Library
Concord
7/27/2020 10:15:25 AM

- Patron Receipt -
- Charges -

21901020792705

em: 31901043648825
tle: Amish grace : how forgiveness transcenc
all Number: 364.1523 KRAYBILL
Due Date: 8/17/2020

ontra Costa County Libraries are open for
ont door pick up of holds. Masks and
ocial distancing are required. For faster
rvice, book an appointment at:
ttps://ccclib.org/front-door-service/.
ok drops are open.
l Contra Costa County Libraries will be
osed on September 7th. Pinole Library
emains temporarily unavailable. Join
ummer Reading, June 6- August 6
o to: https://ccclib.org/summer/

CHAPTER SIX

The Habit of Forgiveness

I forgive them, and I'd like to forget it. We all make mistakes.

—AMISH ROBBERY VICTIM

W as the grace at Nickel Mines a one-time event, a spontaneous aberration that happened because of the unique circumstances of the crime? The killer, Charles Roberts IV, was a deeply disturbed man. Although Roberts's action had been premeditated, Amish compassion in the wake of his crime might have been shaped by the fact that they, along with others, understood that Roberts was a mentally sick person who evoked pity alongside horror and anger. Moreover, Roberts was now dead. There was no need to testify in court, press charges, visit him in prison, or control desires for revenge.

But what if the killer not only had survived but also had been defiant or lacked remorse? Would the Amish have forgiven such a person? What if the perpetrator had ended up in court? Would the Amish have brushed aside all concerns for justice and punishment? And what if the media had not converged on Nickel Mines after the tragedy? Did the Amish offer forgiveness for the sake of public relations?

All of these questions point to a larger one: How typical was the forgiveness that surprised the public in October 2006? We were familiar with some stories that would begin to answer these questions, but we searched for more. We talked with Amish people, read Amish-authored books and memoirs, and dug into archives and newspaper records. What we found were dozens of accounts that provide a wider context for considering Amish forgiveness, stories that help us assess whether the response at Nickel Mines was typical.

Anabaptist Habits

Our actions are rarely random. We all embrace patterns of behavior and habits of mind that shape what we do in a given situation. When we consider the behavior of groups, we call such patterns *culture*. One way to understand culture is to compare it to a musical repertoire. A repertoire is a set of musical pieces that a performer knows especially well from frequent practice. It reflects an artist's background and training, and serves a performer in a situation in which there is no time to learn something new. When a musician is asked on short notice to "play something," or a choral group finds that its manager has suddenly scheduled a concert for next week, these artists fall back on their repertoire—the material they can perform almost instinctively. It's not that musicians can't learn new music; they often do. Even then, however, a repertoire forms the core around which new material is added.

Culture is the term we use for a group's repertoire of beliefs and behaviors. It involves assumptions and conduct that are so deeply rooted and so often practiced that most people are not even aware of them. Culture reflects people's history and teaching, and is especially visible in times of stress that demand immediate response, when there is no time or emotional energy to think through all the possible actions.

Like musical repertoires, cultures change over time, but they change in ways that extend present patterns.

Although the Amish are far from static, their culture draws on values and practices set in motion hundreds of years ago, amid events in Europe's tumultuous sixteenth century. Out of that era of religious turbulence, which saw Reformation figures such as Martin Luther and John Calvin charge the powerful medieval church with corruption, a small but feisty group of reformers called for more than just reform of the church. These radicals insisted on a new concept of the church as a voluntary gathering of those committed to obeying Jesus' teachings. They symbolized their commitment with adult baptism. But because all of them had been baptized into the church as infants, these new baptisms constituted, in the eyes of church and state officials, *second* baptisms. So the radicals received the disparaging nickname *Anabaptists,* which means "rebaptizers," and found themselves condemned as heretics.

Both Catholics and mainstream reformers wanted a state-supported church, which the Anabaptists challenged. For their part, the Anabaptists insisted that they were simply trying to live as Jesus had commanded, relying on an uncomplicated and often literal reading of the Bible. They renounced self-defense, the swearing of oaths, and military participation. As they held one another accountable to lead Christian lives, they sometimes resorted to expelling members from their fellowship (excommunication) as a sort of shock therapy to jolt the unrepentant into mending their ways. But the Anabaptists would not use violence, nor would they ask government officials to coerce or otherwise maintain religious belief. In fact, they believed that the faithful church should not rely on state support or sanction at all. For them, any links to the state were a sure sign that the church had compromised its primary commitment to God.

Such ideas immediately earned Anabaptists the ire of both Catholic and Protestant church leaders, who saw their authority undercut, and civic officials, who relied on religious fear to keep citizens in line. Condemned on all sides, Anabaptists soon found themselves imprisoned and even executed for their beliefs. Although the Anabaptist movement was never large, it accounted for 40 to 50 percent of all Western European Christians who were martyred for their faith during the sixteenth century. Of course, martyrs are a minority in any movement, and most Anabaptists never faced the prospect of capital punishment. Nevertheless, brutal death has been a part of the Anabaptists' story from the time they began creating their cultural repertoire.

By the 1540s the notoriety of one Dutch Anabaptist leader, Menno Simons, was such that the name *Mennonite* came to label many Anabaptist descendants. Then, in 1693, a disagreement among Anabaptists produced the Amish. A fervent Anabaptist convert, Jakob Ammann, feared that Anabaptists in Switzerland and eastern France had become too eager for social acceptance. The emergence of religious toleration, which some Anabaptists greeted as a breath of fresh air, struck Ammann as a dangerous temptation to seek worldly approval. Under Ammann's leadership, Amish churches formed, with a determination to distinguish themselves from the surrounding society, which they considered to be corrupt.

Within a generation, both Mennonites and Amish began immigrating to North America, where many settled in the same communities and recognized one another as fellow Anabaptists, even while cultivating distinct traditions. With some exceptions, Mennonites engaged the wider society more readily than did their Amish counterparts. By the twenty-first century, many Mennonites were seeking to harmonize Anabaptism with higher education, professional pursuits, and urban and suburban living, while Amish people embodied their Anabaptist convictions in rural areas and in traditional customs that they called an "Old Order" way of life.

Anabaptist habits that undergird Old Order Amish culture include their responses to violence, crime, and undeserved suffering.

These are not the only situations in which Amish people practice forgiveness, but they are circumstances of stress, pain, and grief in which the Amish repertoire of values creates particular patterns of practice. These values incorporate a willingness to place tragedy in God's hands without demanding divine explanation for injustice. They also include a desire to imitate Jesus, who loved those who harmed him and who refused to defend himself. Wider society's police and judicial powers merit respect, and even appreciation, the Amish say, but as institutions of "the world" they are fundamentally alien to the Amish, who do not use them to seek revenge.

We examine these and other Anabaptist habits in more depth in Chapters Seven, Eight, and Nine, where we explore the roots, spirituality, and practice of Amish forgiveness. For now, we turn to a sampling of stories that illustrate Amish habits in the face of crime—stories that are part of the larger repertoire of faith that stood behind the Amish response to the violence of Nickel Mines. These stories, filled with both pain and grace, tell us that the Amish reaction to the shooting, remarkable as it was, was neither exceptional nor rare.

Forgiveness as First Response

Forgiveness seemed to come quickly for an Amish mother in northern Lancaster County when her five-year-old son was hit by a car in 1992. The boy was riding his scooter, crossing the road that separated their house and barn, and his injuries were so severe he didn't survive to see the next day. Still, as the investigating officer placed the driver of the car in the police cruiser to take him for an alcohol test, the mother of the injured child approached the squad car to speak with the officer. With her young daughter tugging at her dress, the mother said, "Please take care of the boy." Assuming she meant her critically injured son, the officer replied, "The ambulance people and doctor will do the best they can. The rest is up to God." The mother pointed to the suspect in the back of the police car. "I mean the driver. We forgive him."

In this case, an expression of forgiveness came swiftly, at the accident scene, before the driver's breath alcohol test and before the victim's death. Still, three years later, the mother again asserted her forgiveness of the driver in the pages of a short book she wrote titled *Good Night, My Son*. Forgiveness did not take away the pain that still tore at the parents' hearts, nor was their acceptance of their son's death without struggle. Yet upon reflection several years later, the mother did not retract the forgiveness she had offered at the scene of the accident.

Another story that highlights the speed with which an Amish family extended forgiveness in the aftermath of tragedy came to us from the recipient of that gift of grace. In late October 1991, Aaron and Sarah Stoltzfus had enjoyed a happy day together. Married in an all-day wedding at her home the previous Tuesday, the couple had set out on their honeymoon. Unlike English couples, who might fly to a Caribbean island, the Stoltzfuses, following traditional Amish honeymoon custom, arranged to visit extended family for several weeks. During that time they received gifts, enjoyed a break from their work routines, and became better acquainted with their new in-laws. Now, five days after their wedding, they were returning home on Sunday afternoon after their first honeymoon visit.

That same day, seventeen-year-old Joel Kime came home from church, grabbed some lunch, and headed to a soccer game with his brother and two friends. Driving his family's old AMC Concord station wagon, and eager to show off its power, he had already hit seventy miles an hour when he topped the crest of a hill on a narrow country road, only to find a buggy one hundred yards ahead. Unconcerned, he decided to "blow past those guys, because I thought it was so incredibly cool!" His daring turned into terror as the horse began to turn left into the passing lane. At his high speed, Kime had failed to see the buggy's turn signal. Newlywed Sarah died in the hospital that evening.

According to Kime, Amish forgiveness transformed this tragedy in many ways. On Monday evening, the day after the accident, Kime's parents took him to the Stoltzfus home. He had never been to an Amish home before and was frightened. To his surprise, Aaron's grandmother hugged him and expressed her forgiveness. So did Aaron's father. It happened again when Sarah's parents, Melvin and Barbara, put their arms around him and said, "We forgive you; we know it was God's time for her to die." In Kime's words, it was "unbelievable. It was totally, absolutely amazing. . . . They proceeded to invite my family to come over for dinner. . . . I cannot express the relief that floated over me."

In a back room of the farmhouse Kime met Aaron, the shattered husband, staring at his deceased bride in the wooden coffin. "Like his parents, he came to me with open arms," Kime recalled. "I said, 'How can I ever repay you?' He simply forgave me. We hugged as the freedom of forgiveness swept over and through me."

Some time later, Kime and his family had dinner with Sarah's parents in their home, along with Aaron and some of his family. "Never once did they attempt to make us feel bad. . . . I still have a pile of at least fifty cards that I received from various Amish people across the county. They were constantly encouraging and pointing me to God."

At his trial, expressions of Amish grace surfaced again. "Numerous Amish people wrote letters to the judge begging for my pardon, asking that I be acquitted on all counts." Legally it was impossible for the judge to acquit Kime, but because he was a minor, he was able to bypass prison.

The relationship between the Kime and Stoltzfus families continues. They get together about once a year in each other's homes. In Kime's words, "I came to realize that [my] relationship with Aaron and the rest of the Stoltzfus family had grown into a legitimate, normal relationship. They had forgiven me and never went back on that decision. Five years after the accident I invited them to my wedding, and they came for the ceremony and reception, bearing gifts." Later, when Kime and his wife spent time overseas as missionaries, the Stoltzfus family supported them financially. "Forgiveness, they taught me, is not a one-time event," Kime concluded.

Forgiveness in the Media Spotlight

Other tragedies, and the Amish responses that followed them, have been much more public. The murder of Paul Coblentz, a twenty-five-year-old Amish farmer, on August 19, 1957, drew intense national media attention to the Amish settlement in Mount Hope, Ohio. Around 10:30 P.M. two young non-Amish men looking for cash randomly targeted the rural home of Paul and Dora Coblentz. Robbing the young couple of $9 and beginning to assault Dora—who was seeking to shield their seventeen-month-old daughter—one of the intruders, Cleo Peters, shot Paul twice at close range. The robbers then fled, first in a stolen truck and later in a stolen car. A cross-country manhunt eventually cornered the two in Illinois, where they shot a county constable before surrendering to police. The subsequent murder trial flooded rural Ohio with reporters and photographers. The case even appeared as a feature in a true-crime magazine.

In 1957 Amish-themed tourism was still in its infancy, and few Americans even knew of the Amish, let alone anything about their culture and beliefs, so journalists arriving in rural Holmes County struggled to interpret the story for their readers. They were particularly puzzled by the fact that the Amish "revealed no hatred against the fugitives" and that "no wish for vengeance was expressed by any member of the dead man's family."

Reporters focused much of their attention on Coblentz's father, Mose, who spoke freely with them before and during the trial. Mose seemed to express the grief typical of any parent in that situation "as he wondered aloud how he could go on after everyone left and he would be alone to think of his loss." But he astonished observers by going to visit his son's killer, Cleo Peters, in prison. Afterward, Mose reported that the meeting was emotionally very difficult for him, but in the end he had managed to tell Peters, "I hope God can forgive you."

The state was less generous, and the killer's speedy trial ended with a death sentence. At that point, Amish people from Ohio and elsewhere began to write letters to Ohio's governor asking for clemency for Peters. An Ontario Amish man admonished readers of the Amish correspondence newspaper *The Budget,* "Will we as Amish be blameless in the matter if we do not present a written request to the authorities, asking that his life be spared?" As letters piled up on the governor's desk, he commuted Peters's sentence seven hours before the scheduled electrocution.

The Amish did believe that the crime should carry consequences. They had not interfered with the state's rendering of justice— the widow, Dora Coblentz, had even testified at the trial—but they were reluctant to have an execution carried out in their name. Mose Coblentz and other Amish close to the family reported that they pitied Peters, whose time in the Air Force, it was said, had led him to drinking and delinquency. When Peters's parents came to Ohio for the trial, several Amish families invited the couple for dinner, approaching them as fellow victims of their son's actions.

In another case, two decades later, that garnered heavy media attention, including a feature article in *Rolling Stone,* the assailants were well-known to their Amish victims. Four non-Amish teenagers from Berne, Indiana, spent a warm, late summer night in 1979 harassing area Amish—a frequent activity for them. Riding in the back of a pickup

75

truck, they threw stones and pieces of tile at the windows of Amish homes and into passing buggies. This night their projectiles hit a buggy occupied by Levi and Rebecca Schwartz and their seven children. One chunk of tile bounced off Rebecca's arm, causing her to hold seven-month-old Adeline, who was wrapped in her lap, closer.

The attack was particularly unnerving because it happened after dark, so the Schwartzes hurried home. Arriving at their modest farm without further incident, Rebecca gave baby Adeline to an older daughter while she helped the younger children out of the buggy and into the house. Taking off their coats by lamplight, the family discovered that Adeline was dead. The piece of tile thrown into the buggy had struck the infant in the back of the head and, as examiners later concluded, killed her instantly and silently.

Within an hour, police had arrested the four assailants, aged eighteen and nineteen. "The boys were caught soon after," wrote Adeline's maternal grandmother in the next week's issue of *The Budget.* "Some were our neighbors." None of the teens had been in trouble with the law before, and it was hard to know how to make sense of their actions on that night. The grandmother, in an account filled with emotion over the death of Adeline, could only call the young men's actions "foolish."

Reported across the nation, the incident generated hundreds of letters expressing sympathy for the Schwartzes and calling for harsh punishments for the accused. The Schwartz family responded differently, deliberately forgoing vengeance even in the way they talked with others about the assailants. Levi Schwartz told a journalist, "If I saw the boys who did this, I would talk good to them. I would never talk angry to them or want them to talk angry to me. Sometimes I do get to feeling angry, but I don't want to have that feeling against anyone. It is a bad way to live." The next summer at their trials, the young men received heavy fines but only suspended jail sentences and probation, in part because the Amish asked the judge for mercy. "We believe," began a letter endorsed by the Schwartzes and presented by their bishop, "that the four boys have suffered, and suffered heavily, since the crime, and they have more than paid for what they did. Sending the defendants to prison would serve no good purpose, and we plead for leniency for them."

Consequences, but Not Revenge

Amish people understand that evil deeds carry consequences—which are often meted out by the state—but they are keen not to allow that worldly process to entice them to seek revenge. Public statements of forgiveness, then, also serve to distinguish the response of Amish victims from a vindictive judicial process, especially when the Amish participate in that process as witnesses and cooperate with the police. That was the case, it seems, when twenty-four-year-old Michael J. Vieth of Monroe County, Wisconsin, went on a rampage against area Amish. Although doctors later described Vieth as "seriously disturbed," he blamed his actions on a long-held grudge stemming from a time when a buggy had forced his car off the road. Since then, he had looked for a way "to get even with them."

In November 1995, after drinking some noontime beers at a local bar, Vieth decided to drive by an Amish school and unload his anger. Pointing his rifle through the open window of his car, he shot at a buggy that had just left the school. As the bullets hit the horse, it reared up and shielded the Amish youth in the buggy from injury. Vieth fled the scene but returned later, after school had been dismissed. Brandishing a gun, Vieth abducted a fifteen-year-old young woman who had completed her Amish eighth-grade education and was now serving as an aide in the school. He drove her to a secluded location and raped her.

The young woman cooperated with the police by providing a description of the assailant. After searching for three days, police

77

received a tip about Vieth and soon found evidence of the crime at his home, where he lived with his mother.

It was the first armed abduction in the history of Monroe County—and it was unusual for other reasons as well. The families of sexual assault victims are "usually seething mad with the perpetrator," said the district attorney, "but that wasn't the case here." Instead, the district attorney found expressions of forgiveness. An Amish bishop told him, "We forgive the young man. . . . I hope he can change his life around." "What good would it do to know why he did it?" asked another Amish man. "Can you usually figure out why God sent this or that? Not really." "It's not our place to judge. God is the great one," said yet another.

After convincing the judge to give Vieth a sixty-year sentence, the district attorney admitted he was impressed with the Amish readiness to forgive, but he also considered it wishful thinking—or at least unconnected to his role as an instrument of public justice. "It's just not the case," he said, "that God will take care of everybody when you have a tragic situation, when there is evil, and [you] just hope to cleanse it with prayer." As the rape victim's father pondered the tragedy, he said, "It's tested our faith, but hasn't shaken it." Still, he admitted to difficulty in dealing with his emotions as he thought about what happened to his daughter: "That's something we have to work on."

About the same time, not far away, another Amish reaction startled lawyers and judges. In the spring of 1996, Mahlon Lambright, an Amish carpenter from near Mondovi, Wisconsin, turned down $212,418 offered by an insurance company representing an English man whose truck had struck the Lambright buggy and killed his wife, Mary. Moreover, the media later reported, Lambright had asked a judge to dismiss a petition for a wrongful death settlement because his family was receiving all the financial help it needed from the Amish church. Another Amish man, who spoke to the press about the case, stressed an additional reason that Lambright refused a financial settlement: "It shows that he's not seeking revenge, or he would have accepted the money. Our Bible says revenge is not for us." In both cases, Amish victims had participated in the judicial process but distanced themselves from the outcomes, substituting forgiveness as their own response.

Forgiveness, Fear, and Sympathy

The stories we uncovered did not suggest that forgiveness in the aftermath of violent crime was simple or easy. Some accounts, in fact, forthrightly mixed the theme of forgiveness with accounts of ongoing fear and the struggle to let go of anger. The 1982 murder of Naomi Huyard, the first Amish person murdered in Lancaster County history, was one such story. On the evening of November 27, fifty-year-old Naomi Huyard was killed in an especially gruesome and sexually violent way by two young men bent on imitating the murders committed by Charles Manson. One of the killers was a neighbor of the victim.

Typical of many Amish households in Lancaster County, the Huyards had rented space in an electric chest freezer at the home of a non-Amish neighbor. Naomi had gone there to retrieve some frozen food when she was attacked by the teenage son of the homeowners and an accomplice. The murder sparked a chilling fear in the female members of the Huyard family who lived in the neighborhood. For months some found it difficult to sleep; others would not walk outside or go away alone. Reflecting back on the tumultuous events, a relative remembered that, in the initial whirlwind of activity and emotional numbness that followed the killing, "we did not have time to really concentrate on trying to forgive [the killers], as some might have thought. . . . Everything still looked confusing to us." Moreover, recalled this relative, "many people were afraid that since this happened

79

to someone Amish, we would be so willing to forgive that we wouldn't be concerned about [the killers] being locked up." Such fears "were mistaken," she wrote, "as we were very concerned about this and certainly wanted [them] locked up and taken care of by the law."

The nature of the murder, and the protracted court trial that slowly leaked details of Huyard's final minutes of life, deepened the agony for family members. A niece, writing two years after the events, freely admitted her struggle to forgive the killers. The Amish family also wrestled with how to relate to their neighbors. Immediately after the murder they met and cried together, and the Amish "told them it is not their fault and we do not blame them." But later, as the parents began to insist on their son's innocence, despite mounting evidence and an eventual court conviction to the contrary, the Huyards became angry and frustrated, and broke off most interaction with the couple.

Naomi's niece admitted that, of the two murderers, it was harder to forgive the one who was a neighbor, because "he knew Naomi." "But," she said, "a Christian must forgive, yes, even the worst murderers. My thoughts were of how Jesus prayed for those who crucified Him: 'Father forgive them for they know not what they do.'" Even so, her written account, published a decade after the murder, contains real ambivalence. On the one hand, she concludes her story with a call to "all Christians to pray for them [convicted murderers]." On the other hand, the sexual violation of her aunt disturbed her so deeply that letting go of her anger toward the killers was obviously no easy matter. She believed that both killers were "sick," but she had no time for their attempts to manipulate sympathy and fabricate alibis.

In other cases, the fact that the offender was a stranger may have helped make forgiveness easier and allowed victims to see wrongdoers sympathetically, as troubled but nevertheless fellow human beings. At least that was one theme in the response to a hit-and-run accident in

Seymour, Missouri, in January 2000. A logging truck, trying to pass an Amish buggy on a backcountry road, crashed into the buggy, killing Leah Graber, the mother of thirteen children. Several days after Graber's death, her family offered forgiveness to the trucker in a face-to-face conversation. They talked about friendship and about safety improvements on the local roads. "We don't believe in pressing charges or going to courts," said an Amish spokesperson. "Instead, let's sit down and be friends and try to prevent this from happening again. That's the only way to solve things." Moreover, he noted, "It's not our way [to press charges], we believe it's just an accident that happened. . . . It may have been a part of God's plan for Leah."

Similar sentiments marked responses to a series of violent robberies in the summer of 1996 near Nappanee, Indiana. There, assailants riding in cars accosted at least twelve Amish bicyclists, knocking them off their bikes and then robbing them. At first the victims did not report the incidents. Joe Miller, who was hit and robbed of $280, said, "I forgive them, and I'd like to forget it. We all make mistakes; if we forgive we will be forgiven."

Realizing that the drive-by robberies were not ending, one of the victims informed the police, who immediately arrested five individuals. All of them pleaded guilty. Earl Slabaugh, one of the Amish bike riders who reported an incident, went to visit the twenty-one-year-old driver of one of the cars. He told her that he had forgiven her and held nothing against her. According to news reports, she broke down and cried, crushed by her own shame and moved by this act of grace. A committee of Amish leaders and victims asked the prosecutor to convey their forgiveness at the sentencing, and numerous Amish people from the community told reporters that they were forgiving the assailants. Knowing in advance that the victims were to announce their forgiveness, the prosecutor preparing a plea bargain included a requirement that the defendants write letters of apology.

Playing the Repertoire in Georgetown

Eight days before the shooting at the West Nickel Mines School, another tragedy had visited the Amish community near Georgetown. On Sunday morning, September 24, twelve-year-old Emanuel King left his home around 5:30, as he did most mornings, to help a neighboring Amish family milk their cows. He rode his scooter out his family's mile-long farm lane and turned right onto Georgetown Road. As he rounded a slight turn, an oncoming pickup truck crossed the center line, struck Emanuel on the far side of the road, hit a fence post, and sped away. Hearing the crash, a non-Amish neighbor came out to investigate and discovered Emanuel's lifeless body, thrown from the site of impact.

The next day, a newspaper correspondent covering the hit-and-run accident went to Emanuel's home and found some family members too distraught to speak. Others agreed to talk, but their words were not what the journalist had expected. "There were tears, yes, and sadness," the reporter noted, "but also something else here"—a gracious spirit toward the woman whom police considered and later confirmed to be the hit-and-run suspect. Emanuel's mother, grief-stricken, nevertheless wanted to convey a message to the woman. "She should come here. We would like to see her," she told the reporter. "We hold nothing against her. We would like to tell her she should not feel bad about this. We just think Emanuel's time was up now. That is how it was supposed to be." One of the boy's aunts, her eyes filled with tears, added, "Tell [the suspect] our thoughts are a lot with her, and our prayers."

When the driver read the newspaper headline, "A Boy's Death, a Family's Forgiveness," she did a surprising thing: she went to the King home to receive the words of forgiveness. An Amish neighbor reported, "When the driver read that we forgive her and that we wish she would come down here for forgiveness, she came right away on Monday evening." The driver returned again for the viewing and for visitation with the family. Over the next several weeks "she came back three more times," explained Emanuel's father, "and later she even brought a new scooter for the children on what would have been Emanuel's thirteenth birthday."

In this time of intense grief the King family relied on a repertoire of grace, forgiveness, and trust in divine providence to make sense of events that otherwise seemed senseless and that, in many other settings, would have triggered calls for retribution. As we will see, none of these habits is simple or uncomplicated. But all were religious habits so deeply rooted in Amish life that they seemed as instinctive to Emanuel's relatives as they were incomprehensible to outsiders. Seven days later, when five more Amish children in this corner of Lancaster County died in a horrific way, the repertoire was played again, this time for the entire world to see.

CHAPTER SEVEN

The Roots of Forgiveness

If we don't forgive, we won't be forgiven.

—AMISH CARPENTER

W e began to uncover the roots of Amish forgiveness by asking members of the community to describe it. A carriage maker met our request with a puzzled look: "It's just standard Christian forgiveness, isn't it?" When asked the same question, a twenty-eight-year-old Amish craftsman replied, "Amish forgiveness is just Christian forgiveness." But after thinking for a moment, he wondered out loud, "Is it *different* from Christian forgiveness?" The thought had apparently never crossed his mind before. It had never crossed ours either.

Many religious traditions consider forgiveness a virtue, but Christianity has awarded it a particularly high place. This esteem is no doubt rooted in Christianity's understanding of God as One who absorbs evil and willingly forgives sinful humans. Not only did Jesus ask God to forgive those who placed him on the cross (Luke 23:34), the Apostle Paul observed that, in the midst of Jesus' suffering, "God was in Christ, reconciling the world unto himself, not imputing their trespasses unto

85

them" (2 Corinthians 5:19). Throughout the New Testament, Christians are urged to follow Christ's example by extending grace to their offenders. Leave vengeance to God, Paul instructs the church in Rome. "Be not overcome of evil, but overcome evil with good" (Romans 12:21).

The importance of forgiveness in the Christian tradition, when combined with the fact that so many Americans identify themselves as Christians, raises an interesting question: Did the keen public interest in the grace of the Amish stem from the fact that their forgiveness differed from other understandings of forgiveness, or did it arise from the Amish community's willingness to practice what others only preach? One non-Amish observer remarked, "All the religions teach forgiveness, but the Amish are the only ones that do it." Was it really just a difference between holding an ideal and practicing it, or were the basic notions of Amish forgiveness unique?

That's the question we set out to answer. We speculated that the present-day Amish might trace their views of forgiveness back to the Protestant Reformation, when hundreds of their ancestors had died for their faith. But when we asked them about the roots of forgiveness, they began with Bible stories, not the sixteenth-century martyrs. More specifically, they focused on the New Testament, in particular the Gospels of Matthew, Mark, and Luke. In these New Testament texts, filled with stories about Jesus and the parables he told, the Amish find strong and inescapable reasons to forgive. We soon discovered that those reasons both parallel and depart from the way Christians from other theological traditions understand forgiveness.

The Amish and Discipleship

Many scholars have described the Anabaptist tradition, from which the Amish descend, as a discipleship tradition. From their beginning in the sixteenth century, Anabaptists have emphasized "following Jesus" as an essential mark of the Christian life. Of course, other Christian traditions value Jesus' life and example, but they find the essence of the Christian faith in something other than discipleship. Roman Catholics, for instance, give priority to the Eucharist, and Pentecostals stress the work of the Holy Spirit. For Anabaptists, the primary expression of faith is following—even imitating—Jesus.

It's not surprising, then, that Amish churches focus their attention on the words and actions of Jesus as recorded in the Gospels. The New Testament clearly takes precedence over the Old Testament in the biblical texts that preachers use in their sermons. For example, although Amish preachers recite Old Testament stories in their sermons, all the biblical texts read in Amish church services come from the New Testament. Moreover, the Gospels take priority over the other New Testament books. Out of the sixty chapters in the Lancaster Amish lectionary,* forty come from the four Gospels, with nineteen from Matthew's Gospel alone. During the first twelve weeks of each calendar year, the Amish lectionary directs every member's attention to Matthew 1–12, which includes Jesus' Sermon on the Mount (Matthew 5–7), a passage that receives much attention in Amish theology.

Do the Amish emphasize discipleship because they focus on the Gospels, or does their interest in the Gospels flow from their commitment to discipleship? This chicken-and-egg question may be impossible to answer. Clearly, however, Anabaptists generally and the Amish in particular see Jesus as worthy not just of worship but also of emulation. One early Anabaptist leader put it this way: "Whoever boasts that he is a Christian, the same must walk as Christ walked." The Amish would admit that traveling this spiritual road is not always easy, but in their view following Jesus is the way that leads to eternal life. A hymn in the *Ausbund,*

---

*A lectionary is a yearlong calendar of biblical texts used in public worship. Many Christian traditions use lectionaries, though the texts may vary from one theological tradition to another.

the Amish songbook that includes dozens of sixteenth-century texts, offers these words of encouragement: "Who now would follow Christ in life / Must scorn the world's insult and strife / And bear the cross each day. / For this alone leads to the throne / Christ is the only way."

Reading Matthew and Practicing Forgiveness

In keeping with their emphasis on following Jesus, the Amish people we interviewed focused much of their attention on his teachings, especially those in the Gospel of Matthew. One bishop explained that Matthew 5–7, Jesus' Sermon on the Mount, is considered among the most important texts in the scriptures. A minister, speaking in his cabinet shop, echoed the bishop: "Forgiveness is all about Matthew 5 and the Sermon on the Mount and loving our enemies." For these leaders, forgiveness is rooted in the teachings of Jesus, which infuse the preaching, reading, and liturgy of their churches.

Even Amish persons who talked more generally about forgiveness as a "biblical" theme eventually spoke of the Sermon on the Mount. When we talked to Amos, a young minister who runs a painting business, he told us, "When you start looking in the New Testament, forgiveness is everywhere. When you open up the New Testament, it's the first thing that's there. That's what the Bible is all about: forgiveness. It says we are to take up our cross and follow Jesus. No matter what happens, we must follow him." As Amos continued, he focused directly on the Gospels: "Just look at Matthew, Mark, Luke, and John. They're all about forgiveness. You don't have to go far in the New Testament and you find it all over the place. Look at the Sermon on the Mount. It's filled with forgiveness."

In fact, Jesus' instructions about forgiveness can be found in many parts of Matthew's Gospel. An Amish carpenter referred to Matthew 18:21–22 as his basis for understanding forgiveness. In this short passage, the Apostle Peter asks Jesus whether forgiving an offense seven times is sufficient, to which Jesus responds that *seventy times seven* would be closer to the mark. In the carpenter's mind, "Seventy times seven means that we could have 490 tragedies [school shootings] and we'd still have to forgive." Many others also cited this verse as a reason for Amish forgiveness.

The rationale for Amish forgiveness does not stem entirely from the Gospel of Matthew, however. Several Amish people mentioned the stoning of Stephen, the first Christian martyr, whose execution is recorded in Acts 7:54–60. As he was dying, Stephen "cried with a loud voice, Lord, lay not this sin to their charge," a testimony that an Amish man summed up neatly: "*That's* forgiveness!" An Amish grandfather pointed to another story, this one in the Gospel of John. "When Jesus caught a prostitute [the Pharisees brought a woman caught in adultery to Jesus], he asked who could throw the first stone at her. No one could do it." Another model of forgiveness that many Amish people cited was Jesus' prayer from the cross: "Father, forgive them; for they know not what they do" (Luke 23:34). Perhaps because of their martyr history, this image of forgiveness in the face of torture and death looms large in the Amish mind.

Several of our Amish contacts also reiterated the advice of Paul: "Forbearing one another, and forgiving one another, if any man have a quarrel against any: even as Christ forgave you, so also do ye" (Colossians 3:13). "When I think of forgiveness," said Mary, a thirty-five-year-old seamstress, "the first verse I think of is 'Be ye kind to one to another, tenderhearted, forgiving one another even as God for Christ's sake hath forgiven you'" (Ephesians 4:32). A few Amish people also referred to Old Testament stories, such as Esau's forgiveness of Jacob (Genesis 33:1–17) and Hosea's grace toward his wife, Gomer, and her infidelities (Hosea 1–3).

Still, the Gospel of Matthew remained central in the reflections of the Amish people we interviewed. Indeed, the story that emerged most prominently in Amish explanations of forgiveness came from Matthew

18:23–35: Jesus' parable of the unforgiving servant. This parable is well-known among the Amish, because their ministers read and preach about it during the Sunday service two weeks prior to each spring and fall communion service. For the Amish, the two weeks between that service and the Lord's Supper on Communion Sunday constitute a period of serious spiritual reflection. This time of soul-searching stresses not so much one's personal relationship with God but one's relationship with other people as the key to a righteous life.

The parable immediately follows Peter's question about how often he should forgive those who sin against him. After answering "seventy times seven," Jesus launches into a story about a king and a servant who owes the king a huge sum of money. When the debt-ridden servant begs the king to forgive his massive debt, the king graciously agrees. Immediately, the forgiven servant collars one of his fellow servants, who owes him a small debt. When that man promises to pay the debt but asks for patience, the recently forgiven servant refuses to pass on the grace he has received and casts his fellow servant into prison. The king, hearing of the vindictive act, reneges on his earlier promise to forgive the indebted servant and now condemns him and delivers him "to the tormentors." Jesus completes his parable with a pointed theological application: "So likewise shall my heavenly Father do also unto you, if ye from your hearts forgive not every one his brother their trespasses" (Matthew 18:35). The story serves to remind every Amish man and woman that only a forgiving heart is prepared to participate in communion.

The Lord's Prayer

As prominent as the parable of the unforgiving servant is in Amish minds, the Lord's Prayer holds an even higher place. Recorded in Matthew 6:9–13, in the middle of Jesus' Sermon on the Mount, it is the primary prayer of the Christian tradition. If the Gospel of Matthew serves as the root system for Amish forgiveness, the Lord's Prayer is the taproot.

> Our Father which art in heaven, Hallowed be thy name. Thy kingdom come. Thy will be done in earth, as it is in heaven. Give us this day our daily bread. And forgive us our debts, as we forgive our debtors. And lead us not into temptation, but deliver us from evil: For thine is the kingdom, and the power, and the glory, for ever. Amen.

We first learned the importance of this prayer one evening while eating pizza and ice cream with Gid, a minister who is also a farmer. Gid invited us and some of his extended family for supper—if we would be satisfied with take-out pizza so that his wife, Sadie, wouldn't have to cook after working all day. We offered to treat and drove Gid to the pizza place, where we were greeted by a waitress who knew him as a regular customer. On the way home we bought soda and ice cream at a convenience store.

Sitting around a metal folding table in the middle of Gid and Sadie's living room, we talked about forgiveness. We expected to hear Bible stories or accounts of the Anabaptist martyrs who forgave their executioners, but Gid started elsewhere. "The Lord's Prayer plays a big part in our forgiveness. If we can't forgive, then we won't be forgiven." We had to think for a moment to make the connection, but we soon remembered the relevant phrase. Many Christians know it by heart: "Forgive us our debts, as we forgive our debtors."

Gid continued by noting the prominence of this prayer in Amish church life. "The Lord's Prayer is said in *every* church service. We don't have a church service, a wedding, a funeral, or an ordination without the Lord's Prayer." Sadie added, "Our morning prayers [with our family] also have the Lord's Prayer, and it's also read by the father in our evening prayers."

"It's the first thing you learn as a child," Gid continued. "Parents teach and drill children to say it. Preschoolers learn the Lord's Prayer. They may

91

memorize it in German when they are four years old. The Lord's Prayer is one of the first things that children learn—after the little prayer about keeping the angels over my bed that's sort of like the English prayer 'Now I lay me down to sleep.' In our family, after they learn that, then they learn the Lord's Prayer. In the morning at school, the scholars stand and recite the Lord's Prayer."

Mary also confirmed the prayer's importance in the lives of Amish children. "The Lord's Prayer was the first thing I learned at the age of five," she told us. "I could quote it in German and our children do too. I got an award from my aunt for learning the Lord's Prayer. My children learned it when they were four or five years old. My husband quotes it when he puts the children to bed, and they could quote it before they went to school."

Another Amish woman spoke of the significance of the Lord's Prayer in the lives of Amish adults as well. "The Lord's Prayer is in our minds all the time," said a seventy-year-old grandmother. "It's not just in the evening when we think of it." She then recounted a conversation with an outsider she met at an Amish wedding who told her that the Lord's Prayer is not often used in English weddings. "That was a real eye-opener to me to hear her say that."

As we continued exploring the roots of Amish forgiveness, we found the Lord's Prayer almost everywhere we looked—in every interview we conducted as well as in sections of Amish books, newspapers, and magazines. But why does the Lord's Prayer carry so much weight for the Amish? True, they use it in every church service, and their children memorize it early in life, but that is also the case in some other Christian traditions. What is it about Amish life and culture that gives this prayer such authority?

We believe the answer lies in the communal nature of Amish life. In the Amish faith, the authority of the community overshadows the freedom of the individual. In fact, a different understanding of the self is the deepest wedge between Amish life and mainstream American culture. "Individualism," said a forty-year-old Amish father, "is the great divide between us and outsiders."

Contemporary American culture tends to accent individual rights, freedoms, preferences, and creativity. From a young age, children are encouraged to distinguish themselves through personal pursuits and creative expression; later in life adults highlight their achievements with see-what-I-have-accomplished résumés. These individually oriented values have produced a society marked by great innovation, awe-inspiring creativity, and a remarkable array of choices. At the same time, some critics complain that these values have contributed to a "culture of narcissism," a culture of self-love. In fact, in his book *The Saturated Self*, psychologist Kenneth J. Gergen argues that many modern people are practically obsessed with their personal desires.

In contrast, the core value of Amish culture is community. On bended knees at baptism, Amish individuals agree to follow Christ, to place themselves under the authority of the church, and to obey the *Ordnung*, the unwritten regulations of the church.* Here the key words are *self-denial, obedience, acceptance,* and *humility*—all of which require yielding to the collective wisdom of the community. This doesn't mean that individuality withers away, but it is constrained. Rather than making their own way alone, Amish people must yield to the authority of the church community and ultimately to God.

These sentiments pervade Amish religious life in ways that many outsiders find puzzling. For instance, verbal expressions of personal faith in public settings are seen as prideful, as if one were showing off one's religious knowledge. Reciting Bible verses publicly signals a "proud heart," and individual interpretations of the Bible and personal testimonies in a church service are seen as exemplifying haughtiness

---

*The *Ordnung*, which provides proscriptions and prescriptions for Amish living, applies to dress, recreation, technology, and many other issues. It changes slowly and is reaffirmed twice a year by a vote of the members of each church district.

rather than genuine faith. For the Amish, genuine spirituality is quiet, reserved, and clothed in humility, expressing itself in actions rather than words. Wisdom is tested by the community, not by an individual's feelings, eloquence, or persuasion.

Within this culture of restraint, prayer is also cloaked in humility. In an attempt to avoid using prayer as a means to impress others—a practice Jesus warns against in the verses right before the Lord's Prayer—Amish individuals do not compose their own spoken prayers, as worshipers in many other religious traditions do. Even Amish ministers do not compose their own prayers for church services. In a typical Amish worship service, which includes two sermons and two prayers, the first prayer is a silent one. When we asked Amish people what they pray during the time of silent prayer, without exception they answered, "The Lord's Prayer." The second prayer is read by a minister from a centuries-old prayer book, *Die ernsthafte Christenpflicht* (Prayer Book for Earnest Christians), and always includes the Lord's Prayer.

As we have noted, the Lord's Prayer is also read during each family's Scripture reading and prayer time, which many Amish families observe both morning and evening. At these times, the father typically reads a prayer from *Die ernsthafte Christenpflicht* as the family kneels. So the Lord's Prayer is heard by many families twice each day, but they may "hear" it in other ways as well. For example, Amish people do not offer audible prayers at mealtime but rather pray silently before and after eating. "What are people praying?" we asked. One man spoke for many when he said, "The Lord's Prayer. It says in there 'give us this day our daily bread,' so it's a mealtime prayer."

For the Amish, then, the Lord's Prayer is *the* prayer. Many Amish people reflect on it several times a day, even more on church days. A young business owner summed it up like this: "We don't think we can improve on Jesus' prayer. Why would we need to? We think it's a pretty good, well-rounded prayer. It has all the key points in it." From an Amish perspective, trying to improve on the Lord's Prayer would reflect a proud heart. This simple, ancient prayer is therefore the key to Amish spirituality.

Forgiving to Be Forgiven

To say that the Lord's Prayer is a "good, well-rounded prayer" covers a lot of territory. But the prayer's words about forgiveness—"forgive us our debts, as we forgive our debtors"—ring loud in Amish ears. One elder explained emphatically, "Forgiveness is the *only* thing that Jesus underscored in the Lord's Prayer. Do you know that Jesus speaks about forgiveness in the two verses right after the Lord's Prayer? So you see, it's really central to the Lord's Prayer. It's really intense."

The fundamentals of Amish forgiveness are embedded in those two verses: "For if ye forgive men their trespasses, your heavenly Father will also forgive you: But if ye forgive not men their trespasses, neither will your Father forgive your trespasses" (Matthew 6:14–15).

The Amish believe if they don't forgive, they won't be forgiven. This forms the core of Amish spirituality and the core of their understanding of salvation: forgiveness from God hinges on a willingness to forgive others. The crucial phrase, repeated frequently by the Amish in conversations, sermons, and essays, is this: *to be forgiven, we must forgive.*

This notion was never clearer than in the aftermath of the Nickel Mines shooting. In response to a flood of inquiries about how the Amish could forgive, local leaders provided an explanation in an unsigned letter: "There has been some confusion about our community's forgiving attitude, [but] if we do not forgive, how can we expect to be forgiven? By not forgiving, it will be more harmful to ourselves than to the one that did the evil deed."

Even before the school shooting, Amish people understood the close tie between forgiving others and receiving God's forgiveness. In the Amish magazine *Family Life,* one writer told the story of a teenager who was hurt by his parents and who used this pain as an excuse for not becoming a Christian. He had "suffered verbal abuse from his father and his mother had expected too much from him. . . . His parents were not perfect, far from it. They had made mistakes, perhaps some major ones." But then the writer added, "We come to the word FORGIVE. Henry could miss heaven altogether, because he has not learned the meaning of true forgiveness."

Commenting on the story, the writer offered some additional words of explanation. "When we pray the Lord's Prayer, we ask the Father to forgive us as we FORGIVE others. Forgiving and being forgiven are inseparable. The person who does not forgive others will not be forgiven. . . . The person who refuses to forgive others has cut himself off from love and mercy. We must forgive, accept, and love, if we want God to FORGIVE us our daily trespasses."

According to another Amish writer, "There is perhaps no other factor that is so far-reaching as forgiveness. In the Lord's Prayer, we avow a profound responsibility upon ourselves—we ask the Lord for forgiveness on the condition that we forgive those who sinned against us. It [the Lord's Prayer] should remind us daily that in a very real sense we are in control of our forgiveness. And hereby we perceive why so many people are miserable—they do not forgive those who have wronged them, and therefore they are not forgiven."

The Amish formula of forgiveness is unfamiliar to many Christians. In fact, Amish assumptions about forgiveness flip the standard Protestant doctrine upside down. The more common understanding asserts that because God has forgiven sinners, they should forgive those who have wronged them. In the Amish view, however, people receive forgiveness from God *only if* they extend forgiveness to others. To those who are surprised that Amish forgiveness differs from other Christians' views, the Amish response is simple: look at the Scriptures and see what they say. As Sadie told us, "It's pretty plain, don't you think?"

Of course, Christians have long debated the meaning of "forgive us our debts, as we forgive our debtors." In fact, many have rejected a literal interpretation of Matthew 6:12 not simply on the grounds that it is daunting, but on the grounds that it puts the cart before the horse. "Forgiveness is never dependent on our initiative," one biblical scholar writes. "It begins with God's grace first given to us while we are yet sinners." Moreover, "God forgives us when we are hard-hearted and unforgiving, precisely so that our souls may become forgiving toward others." In this writer's mind, when a person experiences God's grace, he or she is enabled to forgive others, and the gift of grace is humbly passed along. According to this view, a better reading of Matthew 6:12 is this: "Help us to forgive others as Jesus forgives us."

Other Christians have said that it is not so easy to bypass a literal reading of Matthew 6:12. They cite the two verses following Jesus' prayer that the Amish emphasize: "For if ye forgive men their trespasses, your heavenly Father will also forgive you: But if ye forgive not men their trespasses, neither will your Father forgive your trespasses" (Matthew 6:14–15). In his commentary on this section of Matthew, William Barclay observes that "Jesus says in the plainest possible language that . . . if we refuse to forgive others, God will refuse to forgive us." It is quite clear, Barclay continues, that "if we pray this petition with an unhealed breach, an unsettled quarrel in our lives, we are asking God *not* to forgive us."

Amish people's understanding of the forgiveness petition mirrors Barclay's interpretation. They know, of course, that God's gracious activity in Jesus Christ came long before they were born—and long before Charles Roberts made forgiveness necessary at Nickel Mines. "The main 'forgiveness' was when Jesus gave his life for our sins," wrote one correspondent in the Amish newspaper *Die Botschaft* shortly after the shooting. At the same time, the Amish see God's forgiveness of human beings as both present and future, an offer of grace that can

97

be secured only if one shows grace to others. This cross-stitch between divine and human forgiveness also appears in Jesus' parable of the unforgiving servant, told earlier in this chapter. In the parable, the king's forgiveness, representing divine forgiveness, comes *first,* before the servant's actions. But although the king's graciousness does not *initially* depend on the servant's actions, the *continuation* of his graciousness does. When the servant is not willing to treat others with grace, the king withdraws his forgiveness.

This story clarifies the Amish view that God's continuing forgiveness depends on their willingness to forgive. Even though they are aware of God's gracious activity in the past—in the world, their churches, and their lives—they are clear that they continue to need God's grace. They not only anticipate a judgment day when God will reward the faithful and punish the unfaithful, but they believe their actions will influence how they will be judged. To the Amish, granting forgiveness to one's debtors is an act that God requires of those who seek divine forgiveness.

Before the shooting, Amish people would have heartily agreed that forgiveness was woven into the fabric of their faith. But many didn't realize how tightly intertwined it was until the publicity on forgiveness stirred them to deeper reflection.

CHAPTER EIGHT

The Spirituality of Forgiveness

We daily need forgiveness, because we are frail.

—ANABAPTIST MARTYR, 1572

T wo weeks after the Nickel Mines shooting, we visited an Amish family that lives about five miles from the school. Even at that distance they had heard the sirens and seen the helicopters flying overhead on the day of the shooting. Now, two weeks later, the mother wept openly as she recalled the excruciating losses of October 2. Like so many in the tight-knit Amish community, Mary has friends and relatives near Nickel Mines. "I can't imagine the grief they're feeling," she confided. Clearly, however, she had some sense of it. Mary is the mother of six children, two boys and four girls. The oldest, a thirteen-year-old daughter, moved quietly around the dining room, collecting our dishes as we talked over dessert.

Have your ministers made references to the martyrs? we wondered. Mention of "the martyrs" needed no explanation in this setting. For almost one hundred years, beginning in the 1520s, civil and religious authorities hounded and harassed Anabaptists, condemning hundreds to the medieval equivalent of the electric chair. Eventually some twenty-five hundred were beheaded or burned at the stake. Mary, who had attended one of the schoolgirls' funerals as well as a recent Sunday church service, nodded her head. "Yes, the ministers have talked about the martyrs since the shooting," she said, but quickly added that such references are not unusual. "We hear about the martyrs almost every time we have church."

Although they lived and died almost five hundred years ago, the martyrs hover close to the Old Order present, offering flesh-and-blood blueprints for how to lead lives that are yielded to God. Stories of the martyrs, told and retold in church services, family conversations, and school curricula, teach the Amish a variety of lessons—about God's providence, the world's evils, and the necessity for Christians to remain faithful to God even in the most difficult of circumstances. And while Jesus' teaching, especially in the Lord's Prayer, is the theological taproot for Amish understandings of forgiveness, the movement from prayer to practice draws strength from the witness of the martyrs. In retelling the martyr stories, the Amish surround themselves with historical role models who not only submitted their lives to God but also extended forgiveness to those who were about to kill them. These illustrations, converted into story, song, and sermon, link forgiveness to other theological themes, such as humility, submission, nonresistance, and love of enemy, all of which nourished the community's response to the shooting.

Amish Spirituality

Quaker theologian Sandra Cronk describes Old Order spirituality with the German word *Gelassenheit,* commonly translated "yieldedness" or "submission." The Amish, Cronk says, "see God working in the world with the power of powerlessness." As they seek to emulate this paradoxical pattern,

"Old Order people believe they are living the divine order revealed by Christ." The Amish believe that submission should characterize one's relationship with God, as suggested by the phrase "thy will be done" in the Lord's Prayer (Matthew 6:10). But a spirituality of yielding "is not just a personal experience," according to Cronk. It expands into an ethic of yielding to one another, renouncing self-defense, and giving up the desire for justification or efforts at revenge.

Gelassenheit does not necessarily breed fatalism, however. In their everyday lives Amish people make choices, calculate risk, and plan for the future. And although they often speak of "God's plans" behind events that are tragic or painful, they do not believe that God predestines history or that they are merely puppets in a divinely determined script. The Amish believe that humans possess choices of ultimate significance, choices such as whether or not to make a commitment to Christ. For the Amish, this decision—made as an adult and sealed by baptism—signifies a person's entrance into church membership. Submission to the will of God can also translate into stubborn refusal to follow the government's rules, as when Amish men rejected military induction or when Amish parents refused to send their teenagers to public high schools.

Gelassenheit has many dimensions. One aspect reflects an individual's willingness to surrender self-will to God's will. Ideally, a person filled with *Gelassenheit* does not argue with God. The martyrs burned at the stake for their faith epitomize the deepest form of spiritual yieldedness, of literally giving up their lives to God. Yet in the daily lives of twenty-first-century Amish, *Gelassenheit* means yielding to church authority and being willing to accept the *Ordnung,* or rules of the church, and the collective wisdom it embodies. Moreover, a lifestyle of humility and modesty also gives witness to the gentle spirit of *Gelassenheit.* For the Amish, the Pennsylvania German verb *uffgevva* (to give up) captures one aspect of *Gelassenheit:* the willingness to give

101

up one's self to the authority of the community and its God-ordained leaders. Indeed, *uffgevva* is the word the Amish typically use when speaking about submission. Its multiple meanings include giving up self-will, submitting to an authority (a parent or the church), and yielding to God's will.

Gelassenheit also shapes Amish perspectives on women's roles in their community. Based on their understanding of certain New Testament passages and in a fashion similar to other traditional societies, the Amish hold that men are the spiritual head of the home and that wives should submit to their husbands' authority. Women with young children rarely hold full-time jobs outside the home, although they are increasingly involved with running family businesses in addition to managing households. And although women vote on various church matters, they do not hold ministerial office or wield official authority. Men's and women's spheres of work and influence are clear, and the idea of submission is frequently invoked to describe women's relationship to men. At the same time, *Gelassenheit* is valued across gender boundaries and understood to be a desirable trait among both men and women.

What is most striking to persons accustomed to the assertive individualism of Western culture is *Gelassenheit*'s ability to trump personal desire and produce submissive and self-giving behavior. Amish people practice *Gelassenheit* every day as they dress in prescribed clothing, decline to pose for photographs, and make themselves vulnerable by driving buggies amid fast-moving traffic. *Gelassenheit* shapes personalities that are not aggressive, that hesitate before responding to questions, and that express joy with a gentle smile or quiet chuckle rather than a loud, boisterous laugh. *Gelassenheit* is closely related to nonresistance, the Amish commitment to taking literally Jesus' teaching to "resist not evil, but whosoever shall smite thee on thy right cheek, turn to him the other also" (Matthew 5:39). The spirit of *Gelassenheit* rejects self-defense and revenge.

The spirituality of *Gelassenheit* is "caught" as much as it is taught. Children are brought up in a world soaked in rituals and habits that express submission and endorse self-surrender. That world is also filled with people from the past—a past that touches the present—who witness to the importance of submission, nonresistance, and forgiveness.

Stories and Songs

The Amish are a story-telling people, and perhaps the best-known story in Amish circles is that of Jacob Hochstetler, an eighteenth-century Amish man who lived with his family on the Pennsylvania frontier. In 1757, as the French and Indian War reached their corner of the world, the Hochstetlers awoke one night to find Native Americans attacking their cabin. Two of Hochstetler's sons, Christian and Joseph, reached for their hunting guns, but Jacob would have none of it; he forbade them to use violence. Instead, the family took refuge in the cellar. The mother, one son, and one daughter were killed. Two of the surviving sons later fathered large families, from which a sizeable percentage of today's Amish population can trace its ancestry—no doubt one of the reasons the story is so often repeated.

The tale is also told because it conveys a central cultural concern for nonretaliation and submission. A father who does not try to protect his children might appear negligent to outsiders, but the Amish see Jacob Hochstetler as modeling faithfulness to Jesus' call to nonresistance. Jacob did so, the story suggests, as a loving parent who curbed his sons' impulse to defend their lives through violent means. In this story, reprinted in genealogies, included in Amish school textbooks, and repeated around dinner tables, Jacob Hochstetler is no fool. In contrast to many popular models of manhood, Jacob offers a model of Amish masculinity that illustrates the character of *Gelassenheit*.

Nowhere do examples from the past merge with the spirituality of the present more than in Amish worship. Amish church services are awash in the language and rituals of self-surrender. Sunday morning gatherings, three hours in length, begin with hymn singing from the *Ausbund,* the sixteenth-century hymnal that includes songs written by imprisoned Anabaptists. Amish hymn singing, like other aspects of Amish life, is remarkably unhurried by modern standards. Singing a four-verse hymn may take fifteen to twenty minutes. The tunes, passed on orally because the hymnal includes no musical notation, linger in the air as members extend syllables and hold notes. In the spirit of *Gelassenheit,* not even time is forced.

Ausbund hymns speak of dependence on God and the fleeting nature of human life on earth. The Lord's Prayer is one of the hymns. Others are martyr ballads, recounting stories of biblical figures, early Christians, or Anabaptists who died as Christ did—without a fight—and left justice in God's hands, praying for the salvation of their executioners. One hymn, written by Christopher Baumann, describes his torture at the hands of authorities:

> They stretch me [on the rack] and torment me,
> They tear at my limbs.
> My God! To you I lament,
> You will see into this.

Baumann goes on to confess total dependence on God, but his prayer is not for divine retribution on his torturers:

> My God, I plead from my heart,
> Forgive them their sin,
> Those who inflict upon me this pain.

Another hymn, by the martyr Georg Wagner, presents Jesus' crucifixion and refusal to defend himself as an example for others:

Take notice how
That we also in such manner
Patiently suffer here
To help Him bear the reproach.

Reflecting Forgiveness in a Martyrs Mirror

Amish worship involves kneeling for prayer, listening to the reading of two chapters from the New Testament, and hearing two sermons, one about twenty minutes long and the other about an hour long. Without fail, the bishops or ministers who preach begin by emphasizing their own shortcomings and unworthiness to speak. This embodiment of humility resurfaces again at the end of the sermon. The preacher concludes by apologizing for his weaknesses and calls on other ministers to correct any errors he may have made. The other ministers might do so, but not without first citing their own limitations.

Delivered extemporaneously by men without seminary training, sermons rely heavily on the retelling of stories from the Bible and from Anabaptist history, mixed with observations and lessons drawn from everyday life. It is not uncommon for sermons to refer to stories recorded in *Martyrs Mirror,* a thousand-page book filled with accounts of early Christian martyrs and sixteenth-century Anabaptist men and women who died for their faith. Their example of dying well is offered as a model of patience even for twenty-first-century Amish listeners who are not sitting in dungeons.

Compiled in Dutch in 1660 by a Mennonite minister, *Martyrs Mirror* was later translated into German and English. An Amish publisher sells several hundred copies each year in both German and English. Despite its dense and often difficult prose, *Martyrs Mirror* is widely known in Amish circles and can be found in many homes. Its message reinforces the distinction between the church and the world, and confirms the Amish concern about putting too much trust in worldly authorities.

Martyr traditions are hardly unique to the Amish. Many religious groups and some political movements have honored heroes who died for noble causes. But the memory of martyrs has often been used to fuel revenge. Whether in sixteenth-century Protestant stories of the St. Bartholomew's Day massacre, which incited French religious conflict and justified retaliation against Catholics, or in the rhetoric of the al-Aqsa Martyrs' Brigade at the turn of the twenty-first century, a powerful impulse ensures that undeserved deaths are repaid in kind.

Rather than fueling retaliation, however, the Amish martyr heritage nourishes an ethic of nonretaliation and love of enemy. From the beginning, the Anabaptists believed that "their martyrs were true Christian martyrs, [precisely] because Anabaptists had not shed the blood of other Christians, as had Catholic and Protestant officials," historian Brad Gregory observes. They were true martyrs, in part because "they had persecuted no one."

Through the years the Amish have remembered the martyrs' experiences as examples of self-surrender to be emulated, not as scores to be settled. Indeed, in recently published reflections on Anabaptist martyr hymns, one Amish minister warns fellow Old Orders against any temptation to blame today's Catholics for the persecution that Amish forebears suffered, often at the hands of magistrates loyal to Rome. Not only, he writes, is there "no point made in accusing any church of today for what happened four and five hundred years ago," but the very act of using a martyr memory to find fault with others negates the message of humility and forgiveness that the stories are supposed to teach. "Shouting down the beliefs of other people is surely not what we are here on earth for," he insists. "None of us can be sure that we have all the truth." Instead, "what needs to be deplored and regretted is the abuse of power that almost always goes with [any] group of people having the upper hand."

The self-surrender at the heart of *Gelassenheit* cultivates Amish forgiveness. In a study guide published by an Old Order Amish press to accompany *Martyrs Mirror,* the author draws the connection directly, asserting that "when the persecutors prepared to put them to death, the Anabaptists wanted to die as Jesus did, praying for their persecutors and forgiving them." Both in the sixteenth century as well as today, their example "would have been a powerful encouragement to lay down one's life in a spirit of forgiveness."

Forgiveness is a regular feature of *Martyrs Mirror* stories. Hendrick Alewijns, executed in 1569, connected God's forgiveness of his own sins with his willingness to forgive his persecutors: "May God forgive you all [the] wrong you did against me, as I forgive you, and as I would have it done to me, in regard to my sins." When an acquaintance betrayed an Anabaptist peddler to the authorities, the arrested man assured him that he would "gladly and from my heart forgive you for this, and it is my earnest desire that the Lord may have mercy upon you." Sisters-in-law Maria and Ursula van Beckum echoed Jesus' words on the cross, "Forgive them, for they know not what they do," and another martyr, Jan Watier, even asked his executioners to forgive *him,* in case Watier had inadvertently wronged them.

Others awaiting execution wrote to their families with directives to forgive those who were about to take them from their loved ones. From his prison cell Jan Wouters sent word to his wife to pray for and forgive the person who had captured him. Refusing to forgive would place her in divine danger, he feared, because it would "prevent the Lord . . . from forgiving your debt; hence I beseech you to forgive it from the heart. And pray for them that afflict you . . . for we daily need forgiveness, because we are frail."

Nonresistance, humility, and forgiveness blend together in the Old Order spirit of *Gelassenheit*. "Forgiving the persecutors at the moment of death was the final act of following Christ during one's lifetime," according to the Amish study guide. "Christ did not use the sword during his life, nor did He resist with the sword at the time of His death. Rather, He forgave His enemies." In the Amish mind, to love one's enemies, as Jesus taught, surely means forgiving them as well.

The Dramatic Witness of Dirk Willems

As we asked Amish people about examples of forgiveness, many of them mentioned a story "about the guy who ran across the ice." Although not everyone could recall the story's details, all knew the general outline—and the Amish moral—of this dramatic *Martyrs Mirror* account of self-sacrificing love for one's enemy.

The guy who ran across the ice was Dirk Willems, a Dutch Anabaptist from the village of Asperen who was arrested in 1569 for being baptized as an adult and allowing forbidden religious gatherings to be held in his home. Jailed in a palace-turned-prison, Willems escaped by knotting rags into a rope and lowering himself out a window of the castle. But his getaway would not be easy. A guard noticed the prisoner's flight and began pursuing him, apparently with the mayor in tow. As they ran, Willems came to a frozen pond, and although he made it safely across, the ice was beginning to break up with the spring thaw. The hapless guard fell through the ice, however, and began to sink. Fearing he would drown, the guard cried out for Willems to turn back and rescue him.

Here Amish storytellers often pause for effect: listeners are to consider Dirk Willems's options and reflect on their own ethical instincts. Did the guard's fall through the ice provide a path of escape, a providential means of saving Willems, for which the Anabaptist escapee should praise God? Should Willems keep running and leave the mayor to save his employee from the icy waters? Was it even practical for Willems to try to help his pursuer, since the pond's surface might easily collapse under his weight and leave them both to drown?

The narrative tension only increases as the story continues. Willems stopped, turned around, and went back to save his pursuer's life. Willems literally extended his hand to his enemy and carefully pulled him to safety. Unlike stories commending soldiers who sacrifice their lives for their comrades or parents who forfeit health and wealth for their children, this story lauds a man for risking his life for his mortal enemy.

The story's conclusion drives the point home: no sooner had Willems saved the guard than the mayor caught him and insisted on having him burned at the stake. The execution was bungled—a strong wind briefly blew the flames away from Willems's upper body—but that only made his death more torturous. *Martyrs Mirror* reports that the wind carried Willems's voice to the next village, where residents heard him cry out more than seventy times. "Seventy times!" the *Martyrs Mirror* study guide underscores. "Peter asked Jesus if he should forgive one who sinned against him seven times, and Jesus said not seven times, 'but seventy times seven.' Dirk forgave his enemies many times."

This striking story of forgiveness and love for one's enemy has become the classic Amish martyr story, memorialized not only in *Martyrs Mirror* but also in the Amish periodical *Family Life*. An embellished version titled "Dirk Willems and the Thief Catcher," in the curricula of Amish schoolchildren, implicitly asks students to identify with the man who turned back to do good to the one who was trying to harm him.

Forgiveness in Amish Schoolbooks

The Bible and *Martyrs Mirror* are the primary forgiveness texts in Amish life, but children learn stories of forgiveness from their schoolbooks as well. The vast majority of Amish children attend Amish schools, where teachers reinforce the church's values through curricula that parents have helped to shape. Many schools use Pathway Readers, a set of textbooks published by an Old Order Amish press that bear titles such as *Living Together* and *Seeking True Values. Our Heritage,* the last volume in the series, is used in the eighth grade, the final year of Amish education.

The cover of *Our Heritage* features a drawing of chains and shackles, an image of imprisonment and an allusion to martyrdom. Dozens of stories, arranged in sections such as "The Way of Love" and "People Who Served," explicitly teach nonresistant love and encourage the practice of forgiveness. For example, "Peter Miller's Revenge" tells the tale of a nonresistant Christian named Peter Miller who lived during the time of the American Revolution. "Miller and his friends could not conscientiously take part in war, nor could they take sides," the story explains. "They strongly believed war was wrong but they never refused to help a man in need, whether he was a British soldier or an American." The narrative then introduces readers to Michael Whittman, a man who considered Miller "a stupid fool" for his nonresistant position and repeatedly harassed him.

One day, as Miller was tending to a "half-starved" deserter from George Washington's army, he learned from the runaway that Whittman was about to be hanged as a turncoat. Immediately Miller set out to intercede for his harasser, walking three days through deep snow to appeal directly to General Washington. The general patiently listened

110

to Miller but then explained that Whittman had received a fair trial and a just sentence. Had that not been the case, Washington replied calmly, "I would be happy to pardon your friend." "My friend?" exclaimed Miller. "He is my bitterest enemy!"

Washington was shocked, unable to comprehend Miller's desire to request leniency for his enemy. Nonetheless, Washington issued a pardon and Miller delivered it to the place of execution in the nick of time. The story ends with another Amish lesson: the priority of action over talk. "'Oh, Peter,' Whittman sobbed, 'How could you ever forgive me after the way I treated you?' Dumbly Peter shook his head. He could not speak. And words were not needed."

Not all the girls enrolled at the West Nickel Mines School would complete their lessons in the eighth-grade Pathway Reader. Yet they had already absorbed Amish values from their families, churches, and school—sources of teaching, example, and encouragement that reinforced one another.

On Sunday, October 1, children in Amish households around Nickel Mines would have heard Jesus' parable of the servant who begged his master for forgiveness but then turned and refused to forgive a fellow servant (Matthew 18:21–35). This story, which is part of the Amish lectionary for the weeks prior to their autumn communion service, suggests that Christians withhold forgiveness at their peril. Families attending church that day would have heard sermons on forgiveness, along with allusions to the sacrificial love of martyr ancestors. Because church districts gather for worship only every other Sunday, families who did not have church that day would have read and discussed the Matthew 18 text at home. When the parents of a ten-year-old girl who would be wounded in the shooting asked her the meaning of the parable, she responded, "We must forgive others."

The next day, when thirteen-year-old Marian asked Charles Roberts to shoot her first, apparently hoping to absorb his anger and

111

save her classmates, her first response in the face of unprecedented risk was to sacrifice herself to save others. As an eighth-grader, she had already acquired the habits of *Gelassenheit,* habits that were so deeply ingrained that she could face her death with a courage that characterized the martyrs whose stories she had so often heard. Those values, deeply embedded in Amish consciousness, sprang into practice during the course of Roberts's rampage—and in the forgiveness that flowed in its wake.

CHAPTER NINE

The Practice of Forgiveness

We are not always able to forgive. We have struggles too.

—AMISH MINISTER

T o many observers, the swift and gracious response of the Amish at Nickel Mines made forgiveness look easy. The Amish people we spoke with, however, said that forgiveness is hard work that never ends. They also admitted that it is often more difficult to extend grace to those inside the church than to outsiders. Gid, a minister, admitted as much. "The hard part with forgiveness that bothers me is all the grudges that we have against each other in the church," he said. "Sometimes it's harder to forgive each other than it is [to forgive] someone like [Charles] Roberts. We have our own petty grudges."

The Amish recognize two things about forgiveness. First, they believe that God's forgiveness of them is tied to their ability to forgive others. Second, they know that extending forgiveness to an offender is not easy. For both of these reasons, they devote significant energy to training their children in forgiveness and to learning how to practice it themselves.

Train Up a Child

A remarkable thing about Amish society is its relative lack of formal religious education. While a few subgroups have Sunday schools, there are no Amish summer church camps, vacation Bible schools, colleges, or seminaries. Even Amish schools like the one at Nickel Mines do not teach doctrine in any formal way. True, the school day does include Bible reading and the recitation of the Lord's Prayer, and the reading books include stories that teach Amish values. But there is no explicit instruction in the Amish faith. Leaders place the responsibility for religious education primarily on the parents, not on the school or the church.

Because Amish parents have no formal curriculum to follow (only the Bible, prayer books, and various Amish magazines), we asked the obvious question: How do Amish people learn to practice forgiveness? The answer we received was a simple one: "That's just the way we are taught." When we probed for details, parents had no single answer. Typically they turned to examples about resolving sibling conflicts. Mary, a thirty-eight-year-old mother of young children, said, "My children learn forgiveness when they are fighting. If they are fighting, I teach them to say 'I'm sorry' and 'I forgive you.' It's just our routine."

Other mothers emphasized the importance of teaching their children submission and self-control from an early age. "Children need to know that they cannot wiggle around when you are changing their diapers," explained one. Some parents stressed the importance of children learning to fold their hands and keep them still for the silent prayers before and after meals. One grandmother said, "It's important they learn [to do] that while they're still on your lap [and] before they sit in a high chair." With sizable families and a half dozen children eyeing the same piece of apple pie, a lot of yielding and forgiving is learned around the kitchen table.

The importance of deferring to others is also learned through singing. During the Christmas season children at the West Nickel Mines School sometimes sang a song called "Joy," to the tune of "Jingle Bells." The lyrics are "J-o-y, J-o-y, / J-o-y for Joy, / Jesus first, / Yourself last, / And Others in between."

For the most part, however, learning the habits of yielding and forgiving happens through cultural osmosis, in which stories and examples are more important than formal instruction. It's what educators sometimes call "the hidden curriculum": values that are not often verbalized but are taught by example in daily living. A writer in an Amish periodical recalled the hidden curriculum from his own childhood. "When I was growing up," he wrote, "my parents taught me by example to think of others before myself." In particular, "my father and mother always tried to make sure the other person got the best end of the deal." With God's help, the writer concluded, "we hope to pass this [attitude] on to the next generation."

Giving Up Self

Parents generally suggested that the first step in the practice of forgiveness is learning to yield to authority. Learning to accept the collective wisdom and authority of the church is a major challenge of living in community. In contrast to mainstream American culture, where the rights of individuals are esteemed and even celebrated, Amish culture emphasizes the primacy of the community over the individual. "*Uffgevva* means giving up self and accepting God's will," said Mose, a cabinetmaker. "That's what our life is all about. It's the biggest thing about being Amish." In the words of a young mother, "*Uffgevva* is the opposite of 'me, myself, and I.' It means letting go of self-will."

115

Minister Amos described the tension between self-denial and self-assertion: "It's like two forces at war. It's always a struggle to give up [to accept the community's authority]." Comparing the Amish way with that of other churches, he noted, "A lot of churches don't have anything to give up [have no rules]. Each [person] is on his own, and there's nothing to give up. The giving up is the bottom line." For most Americans, who relish their array of choices, it seems a strange bottom line. But Amos was thankful that he was "brought up to learn to give up myself."

If the Lord's Prayer motivates the Amish to forgive, and their martyr heritage inspires them to forgive, *Uffgevva* orients them toward forgiveness as a way of life. The father of a girl who died at Nickel Mines linked forgiveness directly to *Uffgevva:* "Forgiveness means giving up your right to revenge."

Uffgevva undergirds all of Amish life, ensuring its survival from generation to generation. In their late teens and early twenties, Amish youth face a monumental decision: will they join the church or not? This voluntary decision is central to Amish theology. Those who decide to join the church must humble themselves at the time of baptism. Kneeling before God and their fellow church members, they vow to serve Jesus Christ and to uphold the *Ordnung* for life, a vow that subjects their personal desires to the authority of the church.

In most Amish communities, 90 percent or more of young adults join the church, pledging to turn from sin, from the Devil, and from the world. The decision to be baptized and to join the church is the ultimate *Uffgevva:* giving up self to God and the church, forever.

Preparing for Communion

Twice each year, during their spring and fall communion seasons, Amish church members renew their pledges to submit to church authority. The month-long communion season, consisting of four Sundays, culminates in Communion Sunday. In this eight-hour service, church members listen to sermons and participate in the Christian ritual of eating bread and drinking wine in remembrance of Jesus' death. Following the command of Jesus in John 13:14, they also wash one another's feet as a ritual of humility and servanthood. In Sylvia's words, "I don't think there is anything comparable to the sacredness and holiness of our communion service."

Unlike most Protestant and Catholic observances of communion, which focus on an individual's standing before God, the Amish observances carry a deep communal dimension. For the Amish, communion is essentially a celebration of the unity of the church as the people of God. For that reason, the communion season stresses the importance of forgiveness and right relationships within the church, which the Amish consider necessary for personal harmony with God.

On the second Sunday of communion season—two weeks before Communion Sunday itself—the Amish participate in a worship service they call Council Meeting.* This important service marks the beginning of preparation for the holy moment when Amish church members will drink from a common cup of wine, eat from a common loaf of bread, and wash one another's feet. In Council Meeting, ministers admonish members to forgive those who have wronged them and to abandon grudges so that the community can celebrate the Lord's Supper in unity.

The centerpiece of Council Meeting is Matthew 18, a chapter containing thirty-five verses. In the first cluster of verses (1–14), Jesus reminds his disciples that in order to enter the kingdom of heaven they

---

*Districts hold services every other Sunday, so the first and third Sundays of the communion season are "off-Sundays." On the first off-Sunday, Amish families stay at home and read Matthew 18 in preparation for Council Meeting; on the second off-Sunday (the third Sunday of communion season), families read scripture passages in preparation for Communion Sunday.

must humble themselves and become like small children (Matthew 18:3). Bishop after bishop we talked with underscored this verse, which is one of several that the Amish cite for their belief that humility is a key virtue of Christian faith.

The second section of verses (15–17) outlines a four-step process for resolving disputes within the church. First, the offended member is to confront the offender privately. If that is not possible or does not result in reconciliation, then the offended person should take two or three others to meet with the transgressor. If that fails, the church is to call the offender before the entire church for public reproof. If the wayward member still shows no remorse, the church, according to Jesus, is to consider that person a "heathen" and outside the community of faith. We explore the Amish application of this section of Matthew 18 in Chapter Eleven.

The last fifteen verses of Matthew 18 focus explicitly on the theme of forgiveness. First, the disciple Peter asks Jesus if forgiving a person seven times is enough. Jesus replies that forgiveness should be offered "seventy times seven." Jesus then tells a story, as noted earlier, about an unforgiving servant who refuses to extend mercy (vv. 23–35). When the king learns about his servant's lack of grace, the king hands the servant over to "the tormentors" (v. 34). The chapter ends on this somber note: Jesus warns that the unforgiving servant's fate describes anyone who does not forgive others their trespasses.

With these scripture passages providing the biblical basis for Council Meeting, it is hardly surprising that forgiveness is a central concern in Amish faith. "Forgiveness is *always* the theme of Council Meeting," Bishop Eli told us. "If anyone has an unforgiving attitude, they can't partake in communion." Even ordained leaders, setting an example for others, ask to be forgiven for their shortcomings and invite their fellow members to show them where they have erred. The leaders also urge members to seek forgiveness for any shortcomings through the love of Christ. Using a metaphor he hoped an outsider might understand, one leader explained it this way: "The emphasis on forgiveness in the Council Meeting is like a search engine, searching for any unforgiven thing."

These biannual Council Meetings are not empty rituals. In fact, they are taken so seriously that a church district will sometimes delay communion for weeks or months until it can achieve unity. A delay of the communion service could happen for a number of reasons—for example, disagreements over an *Ordnung* regulation or a dispute over how to discipline a member with a rebellious attitude. A delay typically happens only when serious discord occurs. If only one or two members disagree with the rest, they may attend the service but not participate in the Lord's Supper, thus enabling the rest to proceed. The goal, of course, is for everyone to participate in unity.

Council Meetings encourage deep soul-searching as church members ponder the heavy teachings and as leaders encourage them to forgive one another and purge their hearts of bitterness. Members are urged to confess their sins, to forgive others, and to give themselves up completely to God and the church so they can celebrate harmony in the communion service two weeks later.

The Struggle to Forgive

Despite all the teaching and preaching on the topic, forgiveness within Amish communities is sometimes like forgiveness in the non-Amish world: more of an ideal than a reality. Living within a mile of fellow church members presents a special challenge for the Amish; with that proximity, everyone's foibles and transgressions are well-known. No one is easily avoided either, because everyone is expected to attend every worship service in their district. In fact, some Amish people attend Sunday worship in the same church district with the same people for their entire lives.

In these tightly knit communities, indifference to ordinary dis-agreements is hardly an option, and grudges often linger. An Amish shop owner reflected on the suicide of his father-in-law: "It was very hard for us to forgive, but each of us decided that we have to forgive him for committing suicide. That's the only way we could go on, and so all the family members forgave him. It was a big relief, and we realized it was the only way for healing and for us to move on."

"Sometimes it's easier to forgive the big issue, but you might have a little issue that you just can't forgive," said Mose, a grandfather sur-rounded by stacks of Amish newspapers in his spacious kitchen. "We have our own petty grudges," a minister admitted. "We can forgive Roberts in a heartbeat, but we can't always forgive our [Amish] neigh-bor." "Some Amish people have a hard time forgiving," a retired farmer explained. "We have a battle with forgiveness. It's hard to forgive, but we can't be forgiven if we don't forgive, so we really try hard to over-come that. We're very human, you know." These words were repeated time and again in our conversations with Amish people: "We try to forgive, but we are human too."

A mother whose daughter died in the shooting also acknowledged that forgiveness is an ongoing struggle. "Forgiveness stretches out over time, but you have to start out with the will to forgive. But the bitter-ness may reenter your mind from time to time, and then you have to think about forgiveness again."

As we asked Amish people about the *reality* of forgiveness in their lives and in their churches, we heard many stories about failed grace. One man noted, "I have a brother-in-law who harbors grudges against other people. . . . He just won't let the grudges go." One of the slain girls' parents found it harder, in some ways, to forgive a family mem-ber who fed information to the media than to forgive the killer. Family feuds, sour marriages, and disputes over inheritances emerged as other examples of failed forgiveness.

Still, despite their ongoing and very real struggles to forgive, the Amish work hard to keep personal disagreements from severing relationships. Indeed, the ritual greetings before the beginning of each church service keep everyone, even adversaries, in touch. As the women gather in a circle, they greet one another with a kiss. The men, gathering in a separate circle, shake hands. These rituals help to maintain relationships that may otherwise rupture. "It's rare," said Mary, "for Amish people to stop talking to each other" even if they strongly disagree or are at odds.

Fasting and Communion

A day of fasting and prayer falls between Council Meeting and Communion Sunday. Again, forgiveness is an important theme in this final ritual before the bread and the wine are shared. Having been admonished at Council Meeting to let go of grudges they might be holding against fellow church members, many people pray on fasting days for God's help in the work of forgiveness.

The Amish take very seriously the Apostle Paul's warning against those who "eateth and drinketh unworthily" (1 Corinthians 11:29)—in other words, those who participate in communion without first mending relationships with fellow members. It is not unusual for church members, heeding Paul's warning and the advice of Matthew 18, to seek out other members during communion season for the purpose of reconciliation. Both at Council Meeting and again on Communion Sunday, each member is asked to affirm that he or she is at peace with everyone and therefore ready to proceed with communion. On both days, the response needs to be unanimous, or nearly so, for the service to proceed.

The observance of communion begins at about 8:00 A.M. and continues until 4:00 P.M. without a formal break. During the lunch

121

hour, people quietly rotate out of the main worship area in small clusters to eat in an adjoining room. The service, which includes songs, prayers, and several long sermons, comes to a climax when the minister retells the suffering of Christ and the congregation shares the bread and the wine. The bishop breaks a piece of bread from a loaf and offers it to each member as a symbol of Jesus' body broken on the cross. The congregation then drinks wine from a single cup to commemorate the blood of Jesus Christ.

Throughout the service, the sacrifice and bitter suffering of Christ are emphasized and held up as models for members. When speaking of the bread and wine, the bishop stresses the importance of each member being crushed like a grain of wheat to produce a loaf of bread and pressed like a small berry to make a bottle of wine. One bishop explained, "If one grain remains unbroken and whole, it can have no part in the whole. . . . If one single berry remains whole, it has no share in the whole . . . and no fellowship with the rest." These metaphors encourage individuals to yield their wills for the welfare of the larger body.

The service culminates in footwashing as the congregation sings a familiar hymn from the *Ausbund*. Segregated by gender and arranged in pairs, the members wash one another's feet in basins of warm water as a symbol of service and humility.

Having again affirmed their right relationships with God and with their fellow members, the Amish are prepared for another six months of life together. The rituals of communion and footwashing, and the season of self-examination and reconciliation that precedes them, serve to remind the Amish of the importance of forgiving others and asking to be forgiven. These solemn practices do not make forgiveness easy or painless; they do, however, make forgiveness not simply an option but an enduring expectation.

Part Three

CHAPTER TEN

Forgiveness at Nickel Mines

The acid of hate destroys the container.

—AMISH FARMER

To err is human; to forgive, divine." These well-known words from the English poet Alexander Pope strike many as the right way to think about forgiveness: as something good but almost impossible to do. For that reason, many people found the Amish almost saintly for their expressions of forgiveness at Nickel Mines. A local dentist, expressing Pope's idea without the poetic refinement, put it like this: "Those Amish people—they impress the bejeebers out of me!"

Although forgiveness earned the Amish high praise, it also brought them criticism. The act of forgiveness did not take the crime seriously enough, said some. It was offered too quickly, said others. It repressed natural and necessary emotions, claimed a third chorus of voices.

These complaints raise important questions: What exactly is forgiveness? How do we know if someone has really forgiven someone else? Do the words *I forgive you* mean that forgiveness has happened, or is more required? What are the conditions, if any, for granting forgiveness? Is it

125

possible to forgive someone who does not apologize—like a gunman who shoots your children and then takes his own life?

What Is Forgiveness?

Forgiveness is a concept that everyone understands—until they're asked to define it. Many Christians say that people should forgive because God forgave them. The Amish say that people should forgive so that God will forgive them. But those statements point to *theological* motivations for offering forgiveness; they do not define what forgiveness is. Others argue that forgiveness brings emotional healing to the forgiving person, but this *psychological* motive for forgiveness also fails to define forgiveness.

In recent years, psychologists such as Robert D. Enright and Everett L. Worthington Jr. have helped to define forgiveness and examine its effects. As a result of their clinical research, both Enright and Worthington have come to believe that forgiveness is good for the person who offers it, reducing "anger, depression, anxiety, and fear" and affording "cardiovascular and immune system benefits." To make that claim, however, they've needed to clarify what forgiveness is—and what it is not.

Enright, in his book *Forgiveness Is a Choice,* uses philosopher Joanna North's definition of forgiveness: "When unjustly hurt by another, we forgive when we overcome the resentment toward the offender, not by denying our right to the resentment, but instead by trying to offer the wrongdoer compassion, benevolence, and love." In Enright's view, this definition highlights three essential aspects of forgiveness: that the offense is taken seriously ("the offense was unfair and will always continue to be unfair"), that victims have "a moral right to anger," and that for forgiveness to take place, victims must "give up" their right to anger and resentment. In sum, forgiveness is "a gift to our offender," who may not necessarily deserve it.

Forgiveness, then, is both psychological and social: psychological because the forgiver is personally changed by the release of resentment, and social because forgiveness involves another person. That other person, the wrongdoer, may or may not change as a result of the forgiveness. In fact, Enright and many other scholars argue that forgiveness does not and should not depend on the remorse or apology of the offender. Rather, forgiveness is *unconditional,* an unmerited gift that replaces negative feelings toward the wrongdoer with love and generosity. "In spite of everything that the offender has done," writes Enright, forgiveness means treating the offender "as a member of the human community."

There are certain things, however, that forgiveness does not mean. Partly in response to their critics, forgiveness advocates have developed a long list of things that forgiveness is not: it is not pretending that a wrong did not occur, it is not forgetting that it happened, and it is not condoning or excusing it. To the contrary, "forgiveness means admitting that what was done was wrong and should not be repeated." Similarly, forgiveness is not the same thing as *pardon.* In other words, granting forgiveness does not mean that the wrongdoer is now free from suffering the disciplinary consequences of his or her actions (for example, legal or other forms of discipline).

Finally, forgiveness should not be confused with *reconciliation*— the restoring of a relationship. That's because "reconciliation requires a renewal of trust, and sometimes that is not possible." Forgiveness may open the door to reconciliation, and in some ways is a prerequisite for reconciliation, but a victim may forgive an offender without reconciliation taking place. For instance, a victim of domestic abuse may forgive her abuser but at the same time seek legal means to keep him at a distance. Forgiveness advocates such as Enright even argue that forgiving a dead person is both possible and appropriate, even though reconciliation cannot take place in such cases.

These ideas suggest that some of the reactions to Amish forgiveness at Nickel Mines resulted from mistaken, or at least questionable, assumptions about forgiveness. For instance, when one columnist asked, "Why Do the Amish Ignore Reality?" she assumed something that all forgiveness advocates would challenge: that forgiveness means pretending an evil did not occur. Anglican Bishop N. T. Wright likewise challenges the notion that forgiveness implies indifference. "Forgiveness doesn't mean 'I didn't really mind' or 'It didn't really matter,'" says Wright. "I did mind and it did matter; otherwise there wouldn't be anything to forgive at all."

Other critiques of the Amish response were more formidable than the suggestion that they "ignored reality." The problem wasn't that the Amish offered forgiveness, some remarked; it was that they offered it too quickly. Others suggested that the speed with which forgiveness was offered stifled healthy emotions. For instance, one observer reduced the Amish reaction to one sentence: "They have responded to the massacre of their innocents by repeating that the Lord giveth and the Lord taketh away"—charging the Amish with substituting trite theological mantras for heartfelt grief. In reality, however, the Amish emotional response was much more complex than this one-sentence summary. Similarly, their gift of forgiveness was not as quick or as easy as some commentators thought.

Amish Anger?

It hardly makes sense to talk about forgiveness unless anger or other negative emotions arise from an offense. Did the Amish feel anger toward Charles Roberts? Did they feel anger toward his family and friends? Some commentaries implied that they did not. "I would not want to be like them, reacting to terrible crimes with dispassion," wrote Jeff Jacoby of the *Boston Globe*. "How many of us would really want to live in a society in which no one gets angry when children are slaughtered?"

Jacoby's critique was more spirited than most, but it was not unique. Moreover, he did not make up this notion of a mild Amish response. On Wednesday morning, two days after the shooting, a Mennonite nurse-midwife close to some of the grieving families told NBC's *Today Show* that one of the slain girls' mothers had already forgiven Roberts. "She holds no ill will toward the shooter," reported Rita Rhoads. "Even last night [Tuesday night] there was no anger toward the shooter." An Amish woman living in Georgetown said, "I just shiver when I think what would have happened if we had been angry at the firehouse, the funerals, or the burials. It was not a choice we made at the time to *not* be angry. The emotions of deep hurt and sadness along with the tears of grief snuffed out the feelings of anger. Love was something I felt a lot more than anger."

Is it possible that some of the families most affected by the shooting felt absolutely no anger? Some of our interviews suggest that this may have been the case. "There was never a time that I felt angry," the father of one slain girl told us. "It's been a very hard experience, but I don't hold any hard feelings against anyone, not against the killer or anybody in his family." Citing a newspaper article he read about a non-Amish family that "spouted hateful things" for years after a family member's murder, this grieving parent concluded that "anger helps no one and simply makes the bearer of the anger feel worse."

In other interviews we did hear Amish people admit to angry feelings at the time of the shooting and in the months that followed. Typically, however, the killer was not identified as the target of the rage. Sylvia, for instance, spoke of the anger she felt when she attended the

viewing for Naomi Rose, the youngest victim. "She was just so beautiful. It really made me angry. I wasn't angry at Charles; I was mad that
she was dead, just mad at the evil." Her husband concurred: "I am angry
at the evil and at how much suffering the evil caused because of sin."
The couple went on to tell of a time, several months after the shooting,
when the father got mad at his son for failing to clean up some tools
in the shop. "You were really angry," said his wife, "and I think it was
because of October 2nd." In fact, she said, "I think sometimes you get
more angry now because of all the emotion related to the shooting."

These comments illustrate what psychologists call displacement:
the redirection of one's feelings to an alternate target. It's a coping
mechanism that is hardly unique to the Amish. As these comments
show, some anger was part of the Amish experience, but it was often
deflected or otherwise constrained. In some cases, Amish persons we
interviewed did connect the offense and the person who committed
it. Still, compared with the way many Americans express their rage,
Amish anger was always carefully controlled. And it was expressed in
a uniquely Amish manner, as in one elder's refusal to use the term *evil*
to describe the gunman. "It would be better to say he was overcome
by evil," he told us, speaking softly and with no visible hint of anger.
"He was overcome by Satan, by evil, but he was not an evil man."

Psychologists have long observed that both the experience and the
expression of emotions are shaped by cultural conditioning. This is true
even of anger. "People get angry and interpret [anger] according to
the culture in which they live," write scholars Eric Shiraev and David
Levy in their book *Cross-Cultural Psychology*. In collectivist cultures,
which stress the goals and identities of communities at the expense of
individual freedoms, anger "is seen as an emotion of disengagement
from the society" and is therefore discouraged. In individualist societies,
on the other hand, tolerance for anger is much higher because people
"recognize other people's rights to independence and self-expression."

This description helps to explain why some outsiders considered the Amish community's emotional response inappropriately mild. Judging Amish emotions by American cultural norms, they found the restrained Amish response unnatural and therefore inappropriate.

Unnatural or not, the Amish restraint at Nickel Mines reflected typical Amish views of anger. For the Amish, anger is a dangerous emotion. In fact, one Amish magazine illustrated a series of essays on anger with a diamond-shaped warning sign containing the words "Danger Zone." Of course, to call anger dangerous does not say whether or not it is acceptable to feel angry. Although every Amish person we interviewed admitted that Amish people *do* get angry, we received mixed responses when we asked whether it was *OK* to be angry. Mary told us, "Feelings of anger are not a bad thing," a view that's supported by *Putting Off Anger,* a popular booklet in some Amish communities. The booklet's author, John Coblentz, describes anger as an involuntary emotion that is "part of the human experience." Citing Jesus, Moses, and other biblical figures who experienced anger, Coblentz says the Bible forbids only the "destructive words and actions provoked by anger," not anger itself.

But not every Amish person we interviewed was so willing to condone angry feelings. Demonstrating the literalism with which the Amish approach the Sermon on the Mount, Bishop Eli reminded us that, in Matthew 5, Jesus equated anger with murder. "Anger is not OK," he concluded, "but it does happen. The main thing is not to carry a grudge."

Indeed, the most consistent Amish view of anger is that nursing grudges is wrong. Scholars who study forgiveness often make the distinction between *anger,* the first response to hurt, and *resentment,* continually "re-feeling the original anger." The Amish make the same distinction. They may disagree among themselves about whether initial angry feelings are acceptable, but they agree that angry reactions are

131

wrong, as is resentment and harboring bitterness in one's heart. Sylvia's husband put it this way: "We say, 'It's OK to get angry, but don't hit the horse or kick the dog or punch your brother.'" Gid spoke for many about the problem of nursing angry feelings: "If I hold a grudge for one day, it is bad. If I hold it for two days, it's worse. If I hold a grudge for a year, then that man [Roberts] is controlling my life. Why not just let go of the grudge now?"

Gid's question is a good one, though even Amish people will admit it is not easy to release a grudge. "Forgiveness is something that's easier said than done," Mary confessed. "We know we're supposed to do it. In the Bible it says we should do it. But when we're tested and tried, it's not always easy to forgive." A retired farmer used warfare metaphors to describe how hard it is for some Amish to forgive. "We have a battle with it," he told us. "We have to really fight the tendency not to forgive." Of course, the Amish have a very strong theological motivation to move beyond resentment, a point he quickly added: "We can't be forgiven if we don't forgive, you know, so we really try hard to overcome that."

Instant Forgiveness?

Some reports suggested that the Nickel Mines Amish were not angry after the shooting, and indeed some of our conversations, even with parents who lost daughters, confirmed that fact. On the other hand, some Amish people continued to wrestle with bitter feelings months later. Given the horrible nature of the killer's actions, it's not surprising that these feelings lingered. But it does raise a crucial question: Did the Amish *really* forgive the killer after the shooting? That's what the media suggested. Did the media get it right?

As we consider that question, it's important to highlight once again the collectivist nature of Amish society. Most studies of forgiveness take an individualistic approach to it: an individual victim gets hurt, experiences negative feelings, and has a choice to forgive. This is how most Americans think about forgiveness: it's something the victim does, or does not do, to his or her offender. In fact, some who have pondered the meaning of forgiveness argue that *only* the victim can forgive the evildoer.

This raises an important issue. All of our references to Amish forgiveness at Nickel Mines pertain to Amish adults. Because we did not seek access to the surviving schoolchildren, we know relatively little about their response to the horror they faced on October 2. We do know that Amish families sought help from English mental health professionals to talk with their children about the trauma they experienced. Even so, the challenge of navigating the emotional fallout remains. "We're not sure what to tell our boys," confessed one parent. "We don't really talk with them about forgiveness."

Implicit in this parent's confession is an important truth: the responsibility to forgive Charles Roberts was not assigned to the schoolchildren or even to their families but was embraced by the entire Amish community. Indeed, because of their collectivist nature, the Amish would never place the responsibility to forgive an offense of this magnitude on the principal victims alone. Clearly the primary victims at Nickel Mines were the persons Roberts accosted in the schoolhouse, but the Amish of Nickel Mines also knew that their entire community was wounded in Roberts's rampage; they understood forgiveness as a community responsibility, not as the exclusive task of the individuals most directly affected. Mose confirmed this when he responded to one of our questions. "When the men went to see Amy Roberts on the evening of the shooting, were they extending forgiveness on behalf of the entire Amish community or just speaking for themselves?" we asked. His answer was clear: "They were speaking for the whole community." Other Amish people agreed.

This is one more example of mutual aid among the Amish. As anyone who has seen the movie *Witness* can attest, barn raisings are a striking example of Amish mutual aid: dozens of people complete a project that would take an individual family weeks or even months. But mutual aid happens in far less visible ways too as church members help one another through difficult times. In the case of the shooting, the Amish helped one another forgive Charles Roberts. At the very least, they helped one another tell the Roberts family their *intention* to forgive.

Therefore, did the media get it right? Did the Nickel Mines Amish *really* forgive Roberts within twenty-four hours of the shooting? If forgiveness is defined as forgoing the right to revenge, the Amish clearly forgave Roberts immediately. If forgiveness also includes overcoming resentment and replacing it with love, then the answer must be yes and no. As we've noted, some bitter feelings lingered. Nonetheless, the community's commitment to forgive had been set long before Charles Roberts entered the schoolhouse, and therefore the Amish could declare immediately their intention to forgive.

Their verbal declaration was soon accompanied by small but noteworthy acts of grace: hugs between Amish people and members of the Roberts family, the presence of Amish families at Roberts's burial, and Amish contributions to the Roberts Family Fund. Of course, these gracious actions were expressed not to Roberts directly but to his surviving family. Still, they were an outgrowth of forgiving Roberts himself. Gracious words came first, quickly followed by gracious acts—words and acts offered in good faith that kind feelings would eventually replace bitter ones.

All of this falls in line with the research of Everett L. Worthington, who has identified two types of forgiveness: decisional and emotional. Decisional forgiveness is a personal commitment to control negative behavior, even if negative emotions continue. "Decisional forgiveness," writes Worthington, "promises not to act in revenge or avoidance, but it doesn't necessarily make a person feel less unforgiving." Worthington, a Christian, connects decisional forgiveness to two biblical passages that are central to Amish thinking about forgiveness: the Lord's Prayer in Matthew 6 ("forgive us our debts, as we forgive our debtors") and the parable of the unforgiving servant in Matthew 18. Emotional forgiveness, on the other hand, happens when negative emotions—resentment, hostility, and even hatred—are replaced by positive feelings. Thus, forgiveness is both a short-term act and a long-term process, but as Worthington points out, the two are connected. The initial decision to forgive may spark the emotional change. A decision to forgive does not mean a victim has erased bitter emotions, but it does mean that emotional transformation is more likely to follow.

The Amish at Nickel Mines would not use academic phrases such as *decisional forgiveness* to name what they did after the shooting, but we think the term helps to explain the media reports of that week. An Amish man, interviewed less than forty-eight hours after his granddaughters had been shot, was asked if he had forgiven. "In my heart, yes," was his simple reply. With these four words, a grieving Amish grandfather expressed his commitment to do something that God expected him to do, a commitment embedded in the history and spirituality of the Amish church. Still, as Gid told us, this commitment to forgive was only the first step. "I'm concerned these families will struggle with the forgiveness issue for a long time. They will have to forgive again and again and again, and accept [the loss] again and again."

Gid was actually struggling with resentment himself, which surfaced because his twelve-year-old son had recently dreamed of an armed intruder entering their home. The boy's nightmare "really torqued me up again about the Nickel Mines shooting," the minister confessed. "I had to forgive Roberts all over again." His wife concurred: "Regardless of how many times you forgive, forgiveness must be practiced again and again." For the Amish, this insight comes not from clinical research but rather from experience—and also from the Bible. Invoking Jesus' instructions to Peter to forgive his brother seventy times seven,

135

one Amish writer counseled his readers to forgive their offenders "repeatedly, unceasingly." Only then, he concluded, can "the broken relationships that threaten to destroy our families, our churches, our communities, and ourselves" be healed.

"Forgiving" the Killer's Family

As we recounted in Chapter Four, the Amish forgave not only the killer but the Roberts family as well in the days following the shooting. Like other observers at the time, we found these particular references to forgiveness perplexing. The Roberts family was not responsible for the shooting; in fact, they were victims of the gunman's actions too. They were casualties of a different sort than the schoolgirls, to be sure, but they were victims nonetheless. We later learned that the killer's wife found the reports about "forgiving the family" cause for some chagrin. "She had no culpability," one of her friends told us. "She was a victim and didn't do anything to harm anyone."

What meanings were embedded in the forgiveness the Amish offered to the Roberts family? First, some Amish people used forgiveness as a blanket term—something they wanted to express toward the killer. With Roberts dead, they transferred some of their forgiveness, which they felt duty-bound to extend, to the family, which became a surrogate recipient of their forgiveness for the killer. Second, many Amish people realized that the Roberts family would feel shame for what their family member had done. A parent of a slain child said, "The pain of the killer's parents is ten times my pain. You would just feel terrible if you were the parent of a killer." Thus some used the words *we forgive you* to mean "we feel sorry for you." In that respect, *we forgive you* doubled as an expression of sympathy for a grief- and shame-stricken family that was also victimized by the school shooting.

There was one additional meaning of the forgiveness granted to the Roberts family by their Amish neighbors. It was, we believe, the primary meaning: *despite the evil your family member enacted on our children, we will do our best not to hold a grudge against you.* Strictly speaking, the gift of forgiveness can be given only to someone who has perpetrated a wrong. As we've noted, however, the most widely held understanding of forgiveness—in the Amish world and beyond—is refusing to hold a grudge. Realizing that tragedies can quickly spawn bitter feelings, and knowing how easily bitterness can be heaped onto scapegoats, the gift of forgiveness to the Roberts family was the Amish way of saying they would seek to keep bitterness at bay.

In sum, the Amish response to the Roberts family was about tending relationships. In the small-town world of southern Lancaster County, relationships between the Roberts family and their Amish neighbors had existed long before the October 2006 shooting. The words *we forgive you* were a promise to the Roberts family that, in the aftermath of this horrific event, the Amish community would seek to maintain those relationships and not focus their feelings of anger on the gunman's family. It may be too early to know whether that promise will be fully kept, but the gracious acts that followed their words indicated that many Amish people would work hard to make it happen.

The Question of Self-Respect

Our final reflection on Amish forgiveness extends far beyond the events at Nickel Mines and far beyond the Amish themselves. Some critics have suggested that forgiveness can be a self-loathing act wrapped in sentimental garb. Jeffrie G. Murphy, for instance, has argued that vindictiveness, while a dangerous passion, has too often received "bad press."

Murphy contends that some vindictive feelings reflect a healthy degree of self-respect.

This critique goes to the heart of forgiveness. If forgiveness means giving up resentment that one has every right to feel, then forgiveness is by definition self-renouncing. The question Murphy raises, then, is really this: When does self-renunciation become emotionally damaging to a forgiving person? This complicated question cannot be answered in a few short paragraphs. Suffice it to say that Murphy's observations are important, and that we agree that there are times when self-renunciation is an improper response to evil.

There have been times in Amish life when the church's understanding of forgiveness has led to sad consequences and multiplied the pain of victims. In 2005, the periodical *Legal Affairs* published an account of sexual abuse in several Amish communities, abuse typically perpetrated by the fathers and brothers of young girls. In addition to detailing the abuse, author Nadya Labi records the actions—or in many cases the inactions—of Amish church leaders. In particular, Labi cites the leaders' willingness to "forgive" the abusers, which in Labi's article means pardoning offenders who acknowledge their sins and verbalize remorse. In these cases, Labi writes, the Amish "ethic of forgive and forget" often enables offenders to continue their abusive practices.

We explore disciplinary procedures within the Amish church in more detail in Chapter Eleven. Ideally, church sanctions should punish wayward behavior and bring it to a halt. In reality, Amish disciplinary procedures are often ineffective with chronic behaviors related to alcohol abuse or sexual abuse. Moreover, some Amish leaders are reluctant to report illegal behavior to outside authorities, and women, taught to submit to church authority, may fear reprisals if they contact police themselves. In these situations, perpetrators may go unpunished and return to their abusive behaviors. Because church decisions to pardon remorseful offenders must be endorsed by church members, victims may feel enormous pressure to swallow their pain and get on with life.*

This problem of pressured forgiveness is not unique to the Amish, of course. In *The Cry of Tamar,* Pamela Cooper-White decries the widespread tendency of Christian churches to pressure victims of sexual abuse to forgive their offenders too quickly. "All too often," asserts Cooper-White, "survivors of violence are retraumatized by pastors and other well-meaning helpers who press forgiveness upon them." In these cases, "if the survivor tries to forgive, she can only fail, and her failure will reinforce all the self-blame and shame of her original abuse." This tendency is especially strong in Christian communities that, like the Amish, place a heavy emphasis on forgiveness.

Although the Amish girls and boys who survived the school shooting are not victims of domestic violence, some observers may wonder if these children have felt a similar pressure from their families and church to forgive Roberts before they were ready. We cannot answer this question definitively, but our impression is that no, they have not. When we inquired about her surviving children and their thoughts about Roberts, one parent told us, "We explain to them what forgiveness is, but we don't make them forgive." Continuing, she said, "You can't make someone forgive. It takes time." Perhaps because of her conversations with English mental health professionals, perhaps for other reasons, this Amish woman seemed attuned to the counsel of mainstream psychology: those who care for the abused, especially abused children, should not force them to arrive at any place of emotional resolution before they are ready.

---

*In recent years, some Amish communities have enlisted the help of outsiders to confront the problem of domestic and sexual abuse. One Amish publisher has distributed nine thousand copies of a resource book titled *Strong Families, Safe Children,* which provides guidance on recognizing and reporting instances of abuse. Written by social service professionals, the book's publication indicates the desire of some Amish to address the issue more effectively.

Of course, it is also important to recognize the differences between situations of domestic abuse and the Nickel Mines school shooting. Unlike domestic violence, the evil perpetrated at Nickel Mines ended when the gunman took his own life. Also, because of Roberts's suicide, there was no pressure on victims to reconcile quickly with their offender. In fact, when we pressed Amish people on how they could forgive Roberts so quickly, some of them noted that it was easier because he was dead.

Did this swift forgiveness include an element of self-renunciation? Of course, it did. Forgiveness involves giving up feelings that one has a right to feel. Still, we believe that the Amish willingness to give up the right to be bitter about the shooting was not self-loathing. It may, in fact, be the opposite. In *Forgive for Good,* Fred Luskin, director of the Stanford University Forgiveness Project, writes that forgiveness means becoming "a hero instead of a victim in the story you tell." Granted, we heard no claims of heroism when we listened to Amish people talk about forgiving Charles Roberts, but given their understanding of the Christian life, we do see some parallels with Luskin's assertion. In Amish life, offering forgiveness places one on the side of the martyrs, indeed, on the side of God. It is the spiritually courageous thing to do.

This does not mean, as we've noted, that the Amish of Nickel Mines found forgiveness easy. Still, forgiveness probably comes easier for the Amish than it does for most Americans. Genuine forgiveness takes a lot of work—absorbing the pain, extending empathy to the offender, and purging bitterness—even *after* a decision to forgive has been made. Amish people must do that hard work like anyone else, but unlike most people, an Amish person begins the task atop a three-hundred-year-old tradition that teaches the love of enemies and the forgiveness of offenders. An Amish person has a head start on forgiveness long before an offense ever occurs, because spiritual forebears have pitched in along the way. Like a barn raising, the hard work of forgiveness is easier when everyone lends a hand.

CHAPTER ELEVEN

What About Shunning?

Some outsiders think that shunning is barbaric.

—AMISH CARPENTER

D espite the widespread acclaim for the grace displayed at Nickel Mines, some observers thought they saw a glaring inconsistency in the Amish way of life. "Forgiveness—but Not for All," proclaimed a newspaper editorial four days after the shooting. The writer described a woman's decision to leave her Amish community to marry an outsider, only to be ostracized by her own family and friends. "A terrible killer might be forgiven," the writer observed, but "a woman in love with an English man could not be." The commentary then asked a pointed question: "Where is forgiveness for her?"

It's an important question to consider. Many non-Amish people are troubled by the Amish practice of shunning, which stigmatizes offenders in the community. How can the forgiving Amish be so judgmental of their own people? The answer lies in the distinction between *forgiveness* and *pardon*.

Amish forgiveness, like forgiveness in the outside world, can be offered regardless of whether an offender confesses, apologizes, or expresses remorse. Extended by the victim to the offender, it is an *unconditional* gift. Pardon, on the other hand, at least in the Christian tradition, requires repentance. The Amish believe that the church is responsible to God to hold members accountable to their baptismal vows. When a member transgresses the *Ordnung,* the church's regulations, he or she is given several chances to repent. Upon making a confession and accepting discipline, a member receives pardon from the church and is restored to full fellowship. If the person does not confess, the Amish, drawing on particular New Testament texts, practice shunning, with the goal of restoring an offender to full fellowship. Although shunning may seem inconsistent with forgiveness, it logically follows from the Amish view of spiritual care.

Members Meetings and Pardon

In addition to their semiannual Council Meetings, Amish church districts periodically hold Members Meetings at the conclusion of regular Sunday services. These meetings also encourage forgiveness, but their primary focus is on pardoning wayward members. If someone confesses a sin and accepts the church's discipline, the other members reinstate him or her into fellowship. Unlike unconditional forgiveness, pardon has conditions: confession and discipline. Members Meetings emphasize the church's authority to restore a member to full communion within the church—if the member shows remorse. Drawing on Matthew 18:18–20, the Amish see the decision to pardon as one of the church's key responsibilities. In some ways, this authority parallels that of a Roman Catholic priest, who can pardon, or *absolve,* a repentant parishioner of sin.

The Amish believe that in Matthew 18 Jesus authorizes the church to make binding decisions about religious matters, decisions that will be endorsed in heaven. To paraphrase verse 18, whatever the church decides about membership on earth will be ratified in heaven. The sacred nature of church decision making is also underscored in verse 20, when Jesus says, "For where two or three are gathered together in my name, there am I in the midst of them." Given the importance of verses 18–20 in Anabaptist beliefs, historian C. Arnold Snyder says that the *gathered church,* meeting in the presence of Christ, is the only real sacrament in the Anabaptist tradition. This view of the church, which for the Amish consists of the thirty or so families in their local district, infuses Members Meetings with moral gravity.

The moral order of Amish life has two dimensions. Some ethical understandings flow directly from scripture: prohibitions against lying, cheating, divorce, sexual immorality—even "beating a horse, which is forbidden in the Old Testament," according to an Amish historian. Other moral guidelines, however, are derived from biblical principles that need to be interpreted and applied to daily life. For instance, *Ordnung* regulations on matters such as clothing, technology use, and leisure activity emerge from the church's discernment of the principle of "separation from the world." The church disciplines members both for violating direct biblical teaching, such as that against adultery, and for spurning guidelines such as those that forbid purchasing a car or wearing fashionable clothing.

Although the Amish view Members Meetings with solemn respect, most of them are also aware of the fallibility of their church. They realize it consists of people who are prone to sin yet sincerely seek to carry out the will of God on earth. Violations of the *Ordnung* are always seen as sinful, but not because the *Ordnung* is perfect or an exact replication of divine will. Transgressions of the *Ordnung* are

143

considered sinful because, to the Amish, they indicate self-centeredness and rebelliousness—in short, a disobedient heart.

The Amish view of the *Ordnung* in some ways parallels athletes' views of sports uniforms. Although athletes would never claim that the specific colors of their uniform make them better players or that wearing the uniform is a substitute for skillful play, they do believe that in order to avoid confusion it is absolutely necessary that team members wear their assigned uniforms and not those of the opposing team. Players cannot ignore the uniform requirement, even though they would not say that the uniform itself is necessary to win. What is important, in athletes' minds, is that all sides respect the distinctions that the uniforms represent.

Similarly, the Amish do not equate the *Ordnung* with divine law. The sin in any given violation relates not to owning a prohibited item (a television, for example) but to the fact that only a self-centered person would flout the *Ordnung*. The self-centeredness, not the television itself, is seen as the sin. Minister Amos said, "I know it doesn't make sense to outsiders; they think, 'What's the matter with a car?' Well, nothing. It's the giving up part. *That's* what's important." A bishop explained, "A car is not immoral; the problem is, where will it lead the next generation?"

The Amish emphasis on giving up things not explicitly forbidden in the Bible might surprise many religious people. Indeed, many outsiders would see some violations of the *Ordnung* as signs of free thinking, not self-centeredness, of healthy individuality, not sinfulness. Such a difference simply points to the deep distinction between Amish culture and mainstream American values. For most Amish, it is not particularly important what the *Ordnung* prohibits, or even if the prohibitions were to change next year. The obedience or disobedience revealed by a person's attitude is the issue, not the infallibility of the church.

The church demonstrates its authority at Members Meetings in a variety of ways. In some instances, a wayward member may confess a transgression of the *Ordnung*. In other instances, an out-of-order member who refuses to confess a wrong may be "subpoenaed," in the words of one member, to give an account of his or her questionable behavior. After an individual confesses and submits to the church's discipline, the congregation pardons the wayward person and restores him or her to full fellowship by a vote of all members. Offenders unwilling to express remorse, to give themselves up to God and the gathered community, may face excommunication.

The frank discussions and binding decisions in Members Meetings are strictly confidential. Ministers urge church members to *fuhgevva und fuhgessa* (forgive and forget—or more precisely, pardon and forget). Members are forbidden from talking about others' confessions or circulating them as gossip. "This 'forgive and forget' really means to let back what is back, to not bring it up again," explained one church member. In the words of an Amish historian, "A confessed sin may never be held against a person again—it is dead and buried." In fact, if a member does leak information from the meeting, he or she could be censured for breaking the silence.

The pardon in Members Meetings is quite different from the forgiveness that happens when an individual erases a personal grudge or bitterness from his or her heart. The forgive-and-forget policy focuses on the confidentiality following Members Meetings but does not mean that Amish people are expected to forget painful events of victimization or repress all feelings about them. Everyone we spoke with agreed that no one would forget—or be expected to forget—the shooting at the West Nickel Mines School. Of course, the fact that the shooting was perpetrated by an outsider also makes it quite different from offenses discussed in a Members Meeting. Even if Charles Roberts had not taken his own life that day, the fact that he was not

145

Amish meant that the Amish would have had no authority to punish or pardon him.

Excommunication

The Anabaptist view of the church emphasizes the accountability of members to one another and to the collective authority of the church. The tie between pardon and church discipline rests on several key assumptions. First, Amish members emphasize that forgiving an offender does not mean releasing that person from disciplinary action. "Just because there's forgiveness doesn't mean there's no consequences," said Minister Gid.

Second, the Amish see a spiritual difference between church members and outsiders. Members of the church have made a voluntary pledge on their knees at baptism to support the church's *Ordnung* for the rest of their lives. This vow before God and the gathered community is viewed very seriously, because the Amish believe it was uttered in the presence of Christ and ratified in heaven. Thus, baptized members fall under the authority of the church; outsiders do not.

Third, the Amish hold to a two-kingdom theology in which the church, a manifestation of the kingdom of God, operates under a different ethical standard than "the world." Based on their reading of Romans 13, the Amish believe that God ordained the state with authority to reward those who do good and to punish troublemakers. Thus, the Amish assume that the government will use coercion and even lethal force if necessary to impose its will. At the same time, the church, as a part of the kingdom of God, espouses nonresistance and nonviolence. For this reason, activities such as participating in the military, serving jury duty for capital offenses, holding political office, and filing legal suits are forbidden for members. Although the Amish respect the state and pray for its leaders, they will not participate in state-sponsored activities that involve the use or threat of force.

When an outsider (such as Charles Roberts) wrongs an Amish person, the Amish consider themselves responsible to forgive but not to punish or pardon, for that is the state's responsibility. However, when a member wrongs another member or affronts the church as a whole, both forgiveness *and* pardon fall within the jurisdiction of the church. For minor and interpersonal offenses, this distinction between the church and the world works quite simply: the church alone handles the disciplinary process. But if a member breaks the law, then he or she will face not only discipline from the church but also punishment from the public system of justice.

If Amish church members break their baptismal pledges, they are confronted and invited to confess their sins and mend their ways. As a minister explained, "If a person makes an error, according to Matthew 18 we go to them three times before they are excommunicated." At any one of these three encounters the offending party may repent, at which point the church pardons the member and commits itself not to talk about the matter again. Indeed, almost all transgressions are absolved with this sort of simple confession, discipline, and promise to change behavior.

Occasionally, however, church members may balk and refuse to confess their errors. Those who refuse to confess face excommunication. This happens, for instance, if a member who buys a car refuses to sell it, shows no remorse, and refuses to respond to the church's "subpoena."

Excommunication, a long-standing practice of the Catholic Church and many Protestant churches, is similar in some ways to firing an employee who violates company policy. Among the Amish, excommunication is affirmed by a vote of church members, but it is done only after many attempts by leaders to invite the wayward member to repent and uphold his or her baptismal vow. Restoration is always the goal, but because repentance by the wayward person is the key to restoration, the goal is not always achieved.

The Amish church makes a sharp distinction between baptized members and those who choose not to join the church. (Baptism and joining the church occur simultaneously.) Only *members* of the Amish church can be excommunicated and shunned. Amish youth typically make a decision about baptism in their late teens or early twenties. Those who leave the community before joining the church are not disciplined by excommunication and shunning.

Shunning

Because the Amish believe that church membership is not just an individual spiritual matter, leaving the church or otherwise forfeiting church membership carries significant social implications. The stigma that accompanies excommunication is commonly known as shunning. Shunning follows excommunication and involves rituals of shaming designed to remind all sides of the broken relationship, and hopefully to win the wayward one back into full fellowship. It is precisely this practice that so many outsiders find judgmental and unforgiving.

Contrary to popular notions, shunning does not involve severing all social ties. Members may talk with ex-members, for example. But certain things are forbidden, such as accepting rides or money from ex-members, and eating at the same table with them. "Remember," said a farmer, "we still help ex-members. If an ex-member's barn burns down, we go and help to rebuild it. We will help them if their wife is sick. . . . [But] generally we don't invite them to social events or to weddings or to things like school meetings." Members are expected to shun ex-members even within their own household, and those who refuse to do so may jeopardize their own standing within the church. Although shunning is a widely accepted practice within the Amish faith, the strictness with which it is applied varies greatly from family to family and from church district to church district.

The Amish cite at least four reasons for the practice of shunning. First, shunning is supported by more than a half dozen New Testament passages. A key scripture passage read at every Council Meeting reminds participants of the church's authority over each member. In 1 Corinthians 5, the Apostle Paul urges church members to clean out the "old leaven" of "malice and wickedness" before they eat the Lord's Supper (v. 8). In a pointed admonition, Paul tells the Corinthian church to remove a wicked person from its midst and "deliver such an one unto Satan" so that his or her spirit will eventually be saved (v. 5).

Second, the practice finds support in Article 17 of the Dordrecht Confession of Faith, an early-seventeenth-century Anabaptist statement of belief that the Amish use in the instruction of baptismal candidates.

Third, the Amish believe that shunning is the most effective way to maintain the integrity of the church. In the words of Bishop Eli, "It helps to keep our church intact" by removing rebellious and disobedient people who would stir up dissension.

Last, and most important, shunning serves to admonish offenders and remind them of their broken vows in hopes that they will confess their errors and return to the church. Ex-members are not enemies of the church, Amish leaders are quick to say, but brothers and sisters who must be treated with love. They are always welcome to come back into fellowship upon confession of their sin. In the words of the Dordrecht Confession, "Such persons should not be considered enemies but should be admonished as brethren . . . to bring them to acknowledgment, contrition, and repentance of their sins . . . reconciled to God and again received into the church . . . [so that] love can have its way with them."

In the Amish view, shunning is a form of tough love for backsliders. An elderly bishop called it "the last dose of medicine that you can give to a sinner. It either works for life or death." Another bishop explained that a church without shunning "is like a house without doors or walls, where the people just walk in and out as they please."

An Amish woman drew from her experience as a mother to explain the basis for shunning. "Shunning and spanking go side by side," she told us. "We love our children. When we spank them, it's a discipline to help them control their minds. When spanking, we don't get angry at them, and the same is true for shunning." The comparison of spanking and shunning may not be a perfect analogy, but for the Amish, healthy churches, like good parents, should mete out discipline with love. Parents and churches both seek to protect those under their care from their own frailties. Because the Amish believe that each person's eternal soul is at stake, they contend that communal discipline is the loving thing to do.

Although the church views shunning as a tough form of Christian love, Amish church leaders are as susceptible as leaders in other churches to abusing power. In some cases, bishops and ministers have wielded their authority in oppressive ways. A domineering leader may at times use excommunication and shunning as a tool of retaliation.

Some ex-members become bitter at the church and denounce shunning as an unloving practice. Ex-members can, however, return to the fold anytime and receive pardon—if they are willing to confess their deviance. "I have a brother who is excommunicated," explained Mose. "We have forgiven [but not pardoned] him. But the back door is always open. He can come back if he wants to, but it's up to him." Although most ex-members never return, some do. One ex-member, touched by the grace at Nickel Mines, asked church leaders what she would have to do to return.

Shunning and Forgiveness

Some onlookers point to shunning and ask how the Amish can forgive people like Charles Roberts and yet be so unforgiving of their own members. Is grace extended only to outsiders who do horrific things?

A carpenter summed up these sentiments when he told us bluntly, "Some outsiders think that shunning is barbaric."

Are ex-members forgiven? To answer this question, it is important to note once again the distinction between forgiveness and pardon. Erasing feelings of resentment toward a wrongdoer is different from pardoning a culprit of his or her sins. Letting go of a grudge does not require remorse from an offender. Pardon, however, does require repentance. This is certainly the case in the Amish church, where pardon and restoration of fellowship are available to wayward souls who confess their wrongdoing.

These distinctions between forgiveness and pardon help to clarify Amish responses to the question, "Are ex-members forgiven?" Defining forgiveness as "not holding a grudge," Gid answered the question with a carefully qualified yes. Ex-members can and should be forgiven, he said, though church members often fall short of that ideal. "Some people shun others and don't forgive them," he told us. "Many, however, forgive and also shun." Another Amish person put it this way: "People who are shunned feel like they are not forgiven, but we *do* forgive them. But they need to be reminded of their sin until they repent." Mose explained it by saying, "We do try to forgive those that leave. We don't hold a grudge against them. When someone is shunned, it does not mean they are not forgiven. It's just a reminder of where they stand [in their relationship to the church]."

An Amish leader explained the necessity of judgment—the reason for withholding pardon from unrepentant church members—in this way: "People don't understand how we can seem to forgive outsiders so easily and not [forgive] among ourselves. . . . But really there is a difference. When we see wrong in the world, we can't judge that. We leave it up to God to judge. But since God ordained the church to watch over Christians, we have to judge [our own members] out of concern for each other's souls. That's what it comes down to: with church discipline we're concerned about their souls."

The Amish believe that they have a divine responsibility to judge those who break their baptismal vows, to remind them of what the Amish believe to be the eternal consequences of their negligence, and to preserve the purity of the church. But their view that the church is distinct from the world also means that they can be remarkably non-judgmental toward outsiders who have not taken a vow of obedience before God and the Amish church. This two-kingdom view, when combined with clear definitions of forgiveness, helps unravel the paradox of Amish grace. In other words, it shows us how Amish people around Nickel Mines could forgive their children's killer even as an Amish church elsewhere could not pardon an unrepentant member who left the community in search of romantic love.

Two Sides of Love

Like most people we know, the Amish place a high value on love. They draw their inspiration to love from Jesus' command to love others and, more generally, from the idea that the God they worship is a loving and gracious Father. They do not love one another perfectly and, like many non-Amish people, they do not always know what the most loving response should be. Still, they value the ideal of love and, for the most part, they pursue that ideal in their families and their churches.

Love, like forgiveness, is a complicated concept. What does it mean to love another person? Endlessly debated by philosophers, poets, and heartsick college students, this question has no simple answer. We can say this, however: Amish views of love, like many of their beliefs, are not always the same as those of their English neighbors.

Is forgiveness always the loving thing to do? Most Amish people would probably say yes—if forgiveness means replacing bitterness in one's heart with compassion for one's offender. The Amish would point to God's work in Jesus Christ as the clearest example of this link between love and forgiveness. "Herein is love," notes one Amish writer on the topic of forgiveness, quoting 1 John 4:10, "not that we loved God, but that he loved us, and sent His Son . . . for our sins."

But if forgiveness means pardoning an unrepentant member, then the Amish believe that forgiveness is *not* the loving thing to do. Because they consider the sinner's eternal soul to be at stake, their understanding of love in this situation is akin to parents disciplining a child. To fail to discipline would not only neglect their God-given responsibility, it would, in fact, be the unloving thing to do. If, however, the sinner expresses remorse for his or her actions, pardon and restoration of fellowship would be the loving response.

This is not a common notion of love in twenty-first-century America, at least as it pertains to the church. From the outside, Amish-style discipline may appear harsh, judgmental, and even cruel. Those who have experienced shunning by their Amish churches often agree. Indeed, like the media critics who accused the Amish of hypocrisy when they forgave Charles Roberts, ex-Amish members may wonder how the Amish can forgive outsiders and still shun their own religious offspring.

The Amish answer to this question will never satisfy all the critics, but at least their answer is clear. It is also quite logical, at least from a perspective that considers life to be short, eternity to be long, and heaven and hell to be real. For a people who believe choices have eternal consequences, there are two sides of love, and to forgo one or the other would bring spiritual tragedy to everyone involved.

CHAPTER TWELVE

Grief, Providence, and Justice

"Do your people ever ask, 'Why did God let this happen to us?'"

Yes, probably a million times!

—AMISH MAN, in response to the question

I n the days that followed the Nickel Mines shooting, the Amish grieved their children's deaths and committed them to God at their funerals. They believed that the girls who died were now in heaven, a conviction that made it easier to navigate the terrible loss. Still, religious faith in no way makes the death of a child *easy*. Make no mistake: many tears were shed in Amish homes. Despite what some outsiders thought, Amish parents grieve the death of children as deeply as non-Amish parents do.

The Nickel Mines Amish, like nearly all people coping with trauma, pondered the meaning of their loss. As a people with a deep and abiding faith in God, the Amish often cast their questions in terms of God's involvement in the tragedy. Was the shooting part of some larger, mysterious plan? Did it carry a divine imprint or message? Was it something that God hated but would nonetheless use for good? All of these questions gained a hearing in the Nickel Mines Amish community, and no single answer carried the day. As with their commitment to forgiveness, however, the answers to these questions drew from a wellspring of distinctive Amish resources.

Amish Grief

The grief of the Amish parents and community members at Nickel Mines exhibited a particularly Amish flavor. Like many aspects of Amish life, their public grief was restrained, not marked by uncontrolled weeping or anguish. The funerals were quiet, solemn affairs, but they were hardly emotionless. Shedding tears in public is not uncommon, and friends and family who gathered at the viewings and funerals cried freely, if often silently. And tears continued for months afterward. Mary, who was not closely related to any of the victims, admitted that she continued to cry every day for several months after the shooting.

And it wasn't just women who wept. One Amish minister recounted his first effort at preaching after the tragedy. Given the rotation of preachers in the Amish church, this man had not had to deliver a sermon until six weeks after the shooting. Even then, his pain was still raw. "I stood up [to preach], but I just couldn't get started," he told us. Standing in front of the congregation, "I just cried and cried, until finally I was able to say Psalm 23."

An Amish grandmother who lives close to the school said, "We felt a deep sadness. It overshadowed anger in a real way. Our hearts were bleeding, sadness filled our eyes, we were in shock and disbelief and felt overwhelmed with grief for the families." Another woman, knowing the depth of her anguish and that of her Amish friends, wondered if Amish people grieve more intensely or more willingly than non-Amish people. After all, she said, "The English can just turn up the radio and try to forget it."

It would be difficult to establish that the Amish grieve *more* than the non-Amish. They do, however, allow more structure, space, time, and silence for grief than most Americans do after the death of a loved one. Apart from the personal emotions of grieving, the Amish have four rituals of mourning that tap into the resources of their community and aid the grieving process.

In the Lancaster settlement, after a death, grieving families typically have visitors every evening for the first two or three weeks, followed by a year's worth of Sunday afternoon visits. On Sunday afternoons in the first weeks after a burial, it's not unusual for twenty to thirty visitors to be seated in a circle of chairs at one time in the living room of a bereaved family.

A second ritual that facilitates the Amish grieving process is dress. Women wear black when they are in mourning. One of them explained, "We dress completely in black whenever we go to public or social gatherings." This includes, of course, church services and the times when visitors come to their home. The length of time women wear black varies by their relationship to the deceased: six weeks for the death of a cousin; three months for an aunt or uncle, a niece or nephew; six months for a grandparent or a grandchild; and an entire year for a child, brother, sister, or spouse. This ritual reminds others in the community of the death so they can respond with appropriate care for the bereaved.

Another common grieving ritual involves writing memorial poems to express gratitude for the deceased person's life and anguish for his or her death. These poems, typically written by the adult children of the deceased, may be fifteen verses or more in length. Sometimes published in Amish newspapers, the poems are also printed on card stock and distributed to family and friends. When one Amish minister died of natural causes on his eighty-first birthday, his children composed a thirteen-verse poem that included the following lines:

Oh, Daddy, dear Daddy; how can it be
That you are now in eternity?
It was so hard to let you go
For Daddy you know we loved you so.
Happy Birthday we sang; did you hear us, Dad
As we were standing around your bed?
We prayed, we pleaded, we sang through our tears
We wondered, yes wondered, if our Dad still hears.
But time passes on, and if we would be true
We must keep on singing, even tho' we miss you.
And hope to some day all sing together again
With that happy band, where time knows no end.

This poem demonstrates the depth of grief felt when someone dies under ordinary circumstances. These survivors were not mourning the death of a child, but they clearly felt real pain, real grief. Although the poem reveals confidence in an afterlife, it does not express a stoic, unemotional acceptance of death, even of the elderly.

So much greater, then, was the grief felt after the schoolhouse shooting. These heart-wrenching deaths produced poetry as well. The sister of a boy who was in the schoolhouse wrote a song a few weeks afterward. The lyrics recount the good things: "People helping, people praying / God is touching lives of people near and far." But in the midst of these affirmations, the pain wells up: "We miss them so much it hurts. / When will the pain just go away? / They were our friends and sisters too."

A fourth distinctive ritual of grieving involves "circle letters." Amish people in different states who share a common experience— anything from raising twins to having open-heart surgery to caring for children with a particular disability—contribute to a letter that is mailed from family to family. The writers in the "circle" often keep in contact for many years. Some circle letters connect people who are grieving: widows, widowers, parents who have lost children to sudden infant death syndrome, or parents who have lost children in accidents.

On occasion, Amish people who experience loss find additional help outside their tradition, such as through grief support centers in their communities. One such center in northern Indiana facilitates support groups that include both Amish and English participants. An Amish couple volunteers for the center as trained group facilitators; the center also provides Pennsylvania German translators for groups that include Amish preschoolers who cannot speak English. Amish participants easily bond with English people who have experienced similar losses, according to center staff. The non-Amish social worker who directs the program stresses the universal nature of grief, but also notes a difference: "It's clear when you listen to them [the Amish participants] that their faith gets them through. And they'll talk about it—not evangelistically but matter-of-factly. They turn things over to God—they'll say that—more than the other participants."

Other Amish people develop their own, more private rituals. Some write in diaries or compose memoirs. Said one, "I felt the need to express my feelings on paper in order to dispose of my thoughts and get them out of my system, for they were like poison inside me. Writing down my feelings has done the work of a psychiatrist for me." Some of the parents of the Nickel Mines children also found writing to be helpful therapy for their grief. Nonetheless, a father who lost a daughter said, "The best counseling happened when we parents got together and talked. That's where we got our most support."

God's Providence and the Reality of Evil

Communal care, mourning rituals, bereavement groups, and belief in God: as valuable as these are, they do not stop grieving members from asking hard questions about suffering. The Amish join people of faith throughout the ages in pondering one of the most disturbing theological questions: why does God allow bad things to happen? In fact, when a questioner in a public forum in the fall of 2006 asked an Amish man, "Do your people ever ask, 'Why did God let this happen to us?'" the man's response was immediate: "Yes, probably a million times!"

Providence, the idea that God "unceasingly cares for the world, that all things are in God's hands, and that God is leading the world to its appointed goal," holds an important place in the Christian faith. Indeed, all three Abrahamic faiths—Judaism, Christianity, and Islam—have traditionally claimed that God cares for and sustains the world in an ongoing way.

God's providence has both miraculous and everyday dimensions. Christian author Philip Yancey says that apart from miracles, the Bible also "emphasizes an ongoing providence of God's will being done through the common course of nature and ordinary human activity: rain falling and seeds sprouting, farmers planting and harvesting, the strong caring for the weak, the haves giving to the have-nots, the healthy ministering to the sick."

Still, it is one thing to say that God sustains and cares for the world; it is another thing to know what that means in a world in which bad things happen—in a world where little girls are shot in the head.

160

The overwhelming evidence of evil in the world has produced almost endless theological reflection. How does the notion of God's providence fit with the problem of evil?

Generally speaking, Christians have proposed three answers to this question. One is that God's decision to grant human freedom—to allow humans to do both good and evil—may sometimes require God to take a hands-off approach in order to fully respect that freedom.

A second perspective holds that while God has given humans freedom of choice, God retains ultimate control and sometimes wills or allows certain things to happen for particular purposes. Although these purposes may not be obvious at the moment, if one were to have God's big-picture perspective, one could see how something bad in the present will eventually be part of a greater good.

A third approach to this problem is similar to the second but wrapped in more ambiguity. It basically says this: evil happens in the world under God's watch, and human beings will never know why. This view draws on the biblical book of Job. In it, a suffering man named Job listens to three friends explain to him why he is undergoing adversity. In the end, God scoffs at their explanations and challenges Job to consider his finite status relative to the One who created the universe. Job can respond with only, "Behold, I am vile; what shall I answer thee?" (Job 40:4).

There are of course other solutions to the problem of evil. The most prominent of these is an outright rejection of God's existence. Many atheists have cited the problem of evil as grounds for their unbelief, asserting that a God who allows suffering is not God in any meaningful sense. We do not wish to belittle the objections of those who, after wrestling with the problem of evil, find belief in God impossible. Nevertheless, the Amish have not found that conclusion thinkable, let alone attractive. In all our conversations after the shooting, not one Amish person questioned the existence of a loving God.

161

What then did the Amish say about God's providence in the face of this horrific event?

Amish Views of Providence

Unlike some religious traditions, the Amish do not place a high priority on systematic theological reflection. They do affirm the Dordrecht Confession of Faith, an Anabaptist statement written in 1632. This confession, reviewed by bishops with those preparing for baptism, says that "there is one eternal, almighty, and incomprehensible God." The confession also asserts that God "continues to rule and maintain his creation by his wisdom and by the power of his word." By confessing that God governs the world and yet is ultimately incomprehensible, Dordrecht provides some clues to the Amish view of providence, yet the ideas it expresses are hardly unique to the Amish tradition.

To gain more insight into the Amish view of God's providence, we interviewed people and read their letters in two Amish correspondence newspapers, *The Budget* and *Die Botschaft*. To this vexing question about God's providence, Amish people offered various answers, many of which were similar to other Christians' responses to tragedy. At the same time, the Amish emphasized the Old Order view of God's providence, a view that facilitated the Amish ability to forgive the killer.

Affirmations, Questions, and Struggles

If there was one overriding theme that emerged in the correspondence newspapers, it was this: God was in charge. "What can one say?" asked a woman in her letter to *Die Botschaft* less than a week after the shooting. She answered confidently: "God is still in control." "We trust him, yes," said another writer, even though "what happened that Monday was enough to shake a person up, nerves and all."

Despite the affirmations, the Nickel Mines shooting brought hard questions into sharp focus. In a discussion we had with several people around a kitchen table in an Amish home, one person suggested that the shooting was part of God's plan. That assertion set off a vigorous debate between two brothers in their sixties about whether God causes things to happen or just allows them to happen: "Can angels stop things?" "If everything is preplanned, why pray?" "Do our prayers change God's mind?" "Was this a battle of good and evil that touched down at Nickel Mines like a violent tornado?" The wide-ranging discussion produced no conclusions as they struggled with the questions. But even the person who thought the tragedy was part of a "plan" was not ready to say that God had *willed* it. In fact, a preacher at the funeral for one of the slain children was very clear: "It's not God's will that people kill each other," he declared.

Human choice was a theme that emerged in circles of conversation across the Amish community as members searched for answers to explain the nagging questions. A middle-aged Amish mother was emphatic: "It wasn't God's will. God doesn't intervene and stop all the evil in the world. God doesn't stop people from making evil choices." "We have free will," offered a grandfather, "and the Devil also has things in his mind too." Others underscored that point but often added, "But God doesn't make mistakes."

A Greater Good

How could these two views—God did not will the killing but God was in control—be reconciled? Many Amish believe that God allowed the shooting to occur but then brought some greater good out of it. Bishop Eli recounted a conversation he had with one of the families who lost a daughter at Nickel Mines: "I have no idea what good will come from the event, but perhaps some." Many others agreed that God could bring good from dreadful circumstances. "It wasn't His will that someone would do such an awful thing," wrote a correspondent in *Die Botschaft,* "but He only allowed what He chose to allow, and hopefully it can be used for our spiritual good."

As they sought to solve the riddle of divine providence, Amish people frequently cited the example of Jesus' death on the cross. "Where was God when the school shooting happened?" asked one bishop. "I like to say he was at the same place he was when Jesus died on the cross." A building contractor explained it this way: "When Jesus died for us, it was a bad thing, but he did it to help us. Look how much good came out. The shooting was evil, but the good that came out touched a lot of people."

One Amish woman found a parallel in the New Testament book of Matthew. Recalling that King Herod had slaughtered "little children . . . in Bethlehem long ago," an act that "God allowed to happen," this woman wrote, "We don't know why, but [we] do believe He can make good come out of all such happenings." Amish elders concurred: "[God] will not force everyone to be good. But He will bring good out of every situation, if we allow Him to do so—no matter how evil the deed." A letter in *Die Botschaft* suggested that family members' deaths were God's way of turning the minds of survivors heavenward. "If our precious family circle never was broken here below," offered the writer in rhyming verse, "would we truly long for heaven where our loved ones we shall know?" Someone else cited the fact that two outsiders who had been embroiled in a conflict were reconciled by the story of forgiveness.

A few Amish people, revealing a somewhat more evangelical bent than most of their fellow church members, advanced more specific reasons for why God might allow such an evil event to transpire. Pointing to the way the story of Amish forgiveness had been reported around the world in the shooting's aftermath, one man observed, "The Lord works in mysterious ways. Is this his way of spreading the Word?" Another man told us that "an atheist wrote to us and wanted to know more about forgiveness."

A mother who lost a daughter in the shooting summed up her own feelings, and likely those of many other Amish people, in these words: "Knowing that the forgiveness story has touched so many lives around the world has helped the healing process for me because we know the girls didn't die in vain. It might have been a lot harder to accept all of this if the forgiveness story hadn't happened."

A Wagon Without Wheels

Despite searching for answers to the problem of evil, every Amish person with whom we spoke deferred in the end to divine mystery. With typical Amish humility, they all recognized that they did not know why this event had happened or, with certainty, what good might come from it. "Every religion has mystery," said an Amish craftsman. "I like to say a religion without mystery is like a wagon without wheels."

Indeed, although the Amish wrestle with questions of providence, they are not inclined toward endless speculation and do not expect to find answers to the theological questions they have. Not only do they wish to avoid the spiritual perils that sometimes come with theological speculation, but their willingness to give up questioning—another form of *uffgevva,* of giving up—also, in fact, fits their notion of God's providence. "We must stop asking questions," said one Amish person. "We will never have all the answers." Some Amish ministers made the point even more emphatically: "We should not put a question mark where God puts a period."

A mother of school-age girls told us that the minister who gave the main sermon at one of the funerals compared the Amish community to Job, who early on in his suffering demanded an explanation from God. The minister acknowledged that it is only human to want explanations for suffering, but he urged his listeners to "stop asking questions," for "we will never have all the answers for why it happened." A man writing later in *Die Botschaft* echoed the minister's counsel: "Some things in life we may never understand [so] let's leave it all where it belongs, to a Higher hand." He concluded his correspondence with these thoughts: "Death is in the Lord's hands. The shooting was in the Lord's hands. There's a higher power and we simply need to bow down to it."

We Don't Pray for Rain

It was not surprising that Amish attempts to find purpose in tragedy or to decipher why God might stop, permit, or endorse evil ended at the door of mystery. Not only did Job of old end up at that same door, but so do the learned theologians of today. What was different about the Amish response was not that they were willing to place their confidence in a higher power to manage the mysteries of the universe, but that they were willing to "bow down to it" so quickly. Like the swift forgiveness itself, they were quick to say, "Thy will be done." These words in the Lord's Prayer flash across Amish minds frequently, especially when they face situations in which they are vulnerable. A seventy-year-old grandmother said that the phrase "is on my mind all the time. If I go on the road in the carriage I say it subconsciously all the time."

Uffgevva, in the words of one bishop, means "submitting to God's perfect will." It means not fighting or striving against God. One bishop paraphrased a few lines from one of his favorite German hymns to explain submission to God's will: "God, you let it be so. Who are we to strive against you? Even if the tears fall, let it be so." Another Amish elder emphasized the importance of submitting to God's will quickly: "The quicker you give up, the better things go. In our way of life it takes a lot of giving up."

Despite their simple trust in God's will, the Amish are not mired in fatalism. For example, Amish women who own craft shops make strategic decisions every day. They plan, organize, and seek new markets for their products. Nevertheless, in the religious realm of life they exercise patience, and are willing to live without demanding answers from God. In a letter to one of us, an Old Order woman described *Gelassenheit* this way: "It's a yieldedness to whatever God sends. Especially an untimely death of a loved one or a long-term sickness, but also the weather—drought, floods, extreme heat or cold, crop failure, missing the market, disease in animals, hail, fire [and so forth]." She concluded, "We don't pray for rain. We wait for rain, and when it comes, we thank God for it."

Salvation and Final Judgment

The Anabaptist emphasis on nonretaliation, love for the enemy, and defenselessness places the responsibility for punishment squarely on God rather than on humans. The sixteenth-century martyrs could die unjustly—and without attempts by others to avenge their deaths—precisely because they believed that ultimate justice lay on God's desk. This long-term view of justice is in part what frees the Amish to forgive on earth. The Amish cite a passage in the New Testament book of Romans in which the Apostle Paul writes that we should not avenge ourselves but leave vengeance in God's hands. In fact, Paul takes it one step further: we are to feed our enemies if they are hungry and give them something to drink if they are thirsty. "Be not overcome of evil, but overcome evil with good," he writes (Romans 12:17–21).

Amish humility and their willingness to turn justice over to God sharply diverges from some hungry calls for revenge by outsiders. One English observer said he wanted Roberts's ashes tossed into a dumpster. Never once in our conversations with Amish people did we hear calls for vengeance—not even God's vengeance—against Charles Roberts. This stands in stark contrast to a parent's response to a college dormitory fire in New Jersey in which three students died. Speaking at the sentencing for the young men who set the fire, the parent of one of victims warned the arsonists, "You will face a higher court one day, and when that day comes, the sentence of that court will be that you both rot in hell together."

Even if some Amish people privately thought that the deceased gunman was condemned to eternal punishment, we never heard expressions of satisfaction or vindication about it. The people we spoke with expressed typical Amish humility on this point. "I am overcome with sadness that Roberts's life ended without the opportunity for repentance," said the mother of one of the slain girls. "I can't say anything about Roberts in eternity," said an Amish craftsman. "Only God knows. I wish him [Roberts] the same as I wish for myself." When a Canadian Amish minister was asked by an English acquaintance shortly after the shooting, "Don't you think the killer is burning in hell?" the minister was similarly noncommittal. "I don't know," he replied. "Only God can judge. All I can tell you is that I would not want to stand before God having done what that man did. But how God has judged him, I can't say."

Interestingly, the Amish apply the same humility to their own eternal destiny that they applied to Roberts's eternal fate. They are loathe to speculate on both salvation and damnation, and unwilling to insist either that they are saved or that Charles Roberts went to hell. Amish people speak of having a "living hope" of salvation. Unlike many evangelical Christians who openly pronounce assurance of salvation, the Amish resist declaring that they are saved. Such proclamations of human certainty are, in the Amish mind, an offense to God, for only God knows the mysteries of salvation. Our task, they would say, is to follow faithfully the way of Jesus in daily life and not to presume to know the mind of God. Nevertheless, they have hope and confidence that God will be a just and merciful judge.

This understanding of salvation reflects the Amish focus on practice rather than doctrine, on acting rather than speaking. One young Amish father made a direct connection between forgiveness and the Amish view of salvation, pointing to Jesus' words that God will forgive us by the same measure we forgive others. "That means that if in the future you don't forgive, you will lose your salvation. You can't say 'once saved, always saved.'" An Amish deacon also linked forgiveness and salvation together. The two, in his words, "are one and the same; they're pretty close together. Every sin can be forgiven, but to be saved, you need to forgive. To enter into a holy place [Heaven] your sins must be forgiven, but if you don't forgive, your sins can't be forgiven. . . . If we do not forgive, there will be dire consequences."

This view of salvation elevates the importance of forgiveness in the Amish faith, making forgiveness essential for eternal salvation. Some Christians may find such understandings of eternity disturbing. While many would agree that God is the final judge, Amish humility about eternal security and their fusion of behavior and salvation counter the ideas of many Christians. Indeed, these convictions about salvation represent the most striking application of *Gelassenheit:* the willingness to yield certainty about eternal outcomes to the providence of God.

Earthly Justice

Beyond the questions of long-term justice and divine providence lies the issue of earthly justice here and now. For the Amish, forgiveness does not mean condoning bad behavior or erasing its consequences. "If Roberts had lived, we would have forgiven him, but there would have been consequences," explained a minister. Yet the Amish do not believe that worldly justice rests in the hands of the church.

As mentioned in Chapter Eleven, the Amish subscribe to a two-kingdom theology, shaped by their history of religious persecution in Europe. The churchly kingdom of God operates with a pacifist ethic that avoids force to achieve results. The ethics that Jesus taught—love for enemy, nonretaliation, and forgiveness—guide this spiritual kingdom.

In contrast, the worldly kingdoms—the governments of this world—rely on force, or at least the threat of force, to achieve their goals. The Amish accept the state's authority to use force, and the Dordrecht Confession of Faith instructs obedience to the state as long as its demands do not conflict with God's. For example, the Amish flatly refuse to participate in the armed forces, press charges in court, or sue those who wrong them. They do pay all taxes except Social Security, which they consider a form of insurance that undermines the church's responsibility to care for the needs of its members.

Nonetheless, because they believe that the state is ordained by God to maintain order in the larger world, they expect that the state will organize a police force, imprison lawbreakers, and conduct war. "We fully expect a killer to go to jail," said an Amish elder. "We're not naïve. We would never want a killer turned loose," added a deacon. "It's the government's job to punish evildoers." As the tragedy unfolded in Nickel Mines, the Amish readily accepted the intervention of the state police and thanked them profusely for their help. They saw the events of that October morning as an intrusion of worldly violence into their community, and they expected worldly authority to counteract it.

The boundaries between church and world are not always that tidy, of course, and the Amish have occasionally faced perplexing questions of justice when worldly and churchly authorities overlap. In 1994, for example, a Pennsylvania jury found a twenty-eight-year-old Amish man, Ed Gingerich, guilty of involuntary manslaughter but mentally ill after he brutally killed his wife in front of two of the couple's young children. Testimony revealed that he had been diagnosed with schizophrenia and had occasionally been hospitalized in the past, but that his family and church neighbors had helped him substitute homeopathic alternatives for his prescribed medication.

The case exposed conflicting views of justice, responsibility, and punishment. Jurors later said they blamed the church for creating conditions that made the murder likely, while a criminal justice professor charged that prosecutors had not done enough to secure a first-degree murder conviction. Meanwhile, the Amish bishop, who was also an uncle of the victim, was quoted as saying that he was dismayed that the court handed down only a five-year sentence: "We thought he would be put away for a long time, maybe ten or fifteen years." Indeed, when Gingerich was released from prison, having paid his debt in the eyes of secular society, his church in northwestern Pennsylvania would not allow him to return, continuing to shun him and separate him from his children and most other relatives. Gingerich instead found a home in two midwestern Amish settlements whose members considered his punishment sufficient and supported his return to psychological care. Gingerich's case demonstrates the sometimes complicated and overlapping boundaries of the worldly and churchly kingdoms in Amish life.

This World Is Not Our Home

The Amish belief in miracles is part of their understanding of God's providence, and it is woven into their affirmation that God is closely and directly involved in the world. Many Amish people spoke of miracles in the wake of the shooting. Some believed angels were hovering above the roof of the school that day. As we noted earlier, the girl who escaped the building before the shooting said she heard a voice tell her to run—a voice that many ascribe to an angel. In addition, Amish people often described the healing of the injured girls as miraculous.

The poem written by a sister of one of the boys in the Nickel Mines
school included these lines:

> Some days we think we can't go on
> When so many of our friends are gone.
> But we just hold on to the good things,
> We're surrounded by miracles.

Certainly, as we have seen, the Amish conviction that God
intervenes in miraculous ways does not mean the Amish have solved
age-old questions about God's providence. It doesn't mean they never
wrestle with questions of how a loving God is involved not only in
"the good things" mentioned in the poem but also in the terrifying and
tragic things in life. Nor does it mean they skirt questions of justice.

But accepting miracles, like accepting mystery, goes hand-in-hand
with Amish humility, submission, and patience with life. This combination
of values provides them with an enormous capacity to absorb adversity,
forgo revenge, and carry on—gracefully.

CHAPTER THIRTEEN

Amish Grace and the Rest of Us

True forgiveness deals with the past, all of the past, to make the future possible.

—DESMOND TUTU, SOUTH AFRICAN ARCHBISHOP

A s we began writing this book, we soon faced a challenge: what should we title it? We settled on the main title, *Amish Grace,* quickly, but the subtitle, *How Forgiveness Transcended Tragedy,* took much longer. The problem was the verb between *forgiveness* and *tragedy.* To put it simply, we couldn't quite decide what the act of forgiveness had done to the tragic events of October 2, 2006.

We discussed the word *redeemed.* Had Amish forgiveness redeemed the tragedy that befell their community? For a book about the Amish, the word *redeemed* had the advantage of carrying Christian connotations. It also suggested, as many Amish people told us, that good is more powerful than evil. Still, the more we thought about it, the less comfortable we became with the notion that forgiveness had redeemed the tragedy at Nickel Mines. The tragedy remains. Five girls died, others carry scars, and one remains semicomatose. Amish families continue to grieve, Amish children still have nightmares, and Amish parents pray for their children's safety with an urgency they didn't know before. The expressions of forgiveness that flowed in the aftermath of Roberts's rampage brought healing, but they didn't bind up all the wounds of the shooting. The word *redeemed* claimed too much.

We settled on *transcended,* for two reasons. First, *transcended* conveys very well how the Amish of Nickel Mines rose above—far above—the evil that visited their schoolhouse. Whether good is more powerful than evil may be a matter of philosophical debate, but who can dispute the fact that the Amish responded to absolute horror with an amazing generosity of spirit? Second, the story of Amish forgiveness quickly eclipsed the story of the shooting itself. Devastating violence visits our world every day, but rarely is violence greeted with forgiveness. In Nickel Mines it was, and that response became the big story to emerge from a small village in Lancaster County.

But what should we make of that story? Like some of the Amish people we interviewed, we are glad that the story of Amish forgiveness received wide play after the shooting. At the same time, we have reservations about the way the story was used and celebrated. As much as we were impressed, even inspired, by the Amish response in Nickel Mines, we wondered: Is there anything here for the rest of us? The longer we worked on this book, the more vexing that question became.

The Amish Are Not Us

If there's one thing we learned from this story, it's this: the Amish commitment to forgive is not a small patch tacked onto their fabric of faithfulness. Rather, their commitment to forgive is intricately woven into their lives and their communities—so intricately that it's hard to talk about Amish forgiveness without talking about dozens of other things.

When we first broached the subject of forgiveness with Amish people, we were struck by their reluctance to speak of forgiveness in abstract ways. We did hear forgiveness defined as "letting go of grudges." More frequently, however, we heard responses and stories with *forgiveness* interspersed with other terms such as *love, humility, compassion, submission,* and *acceptance.* The web of words that emerged in these conversations pointed to the holistic, integrated nature of Amish life. Unlike many of their consumer-oriented neighbors, the Amish do not assemble their spirituality piecemeal by personal preference. Rather, Amish spirituality is a precious heirloom, woven together over the centuries and passed down with care.

To hear the Amish explain it, the New Testament provides the pattern for their unique form of spirituality. In a certain sense they are right. The Amish take the words of Jesus with utmost seriousness, and members frequently explain their faith by citing Jesus or other New Testament texts. But the Amish way of life cannot be reduced simply to taking the Bible—or even Jesus—seriously. Rather, Amish spirituality emerges from their particular way of understanding the biblical text, a lens that's been shaped by their nonviolent martyr tradition. With the martyrs hovering nearby, offering admonition and encouragement, the Amish have esteemed suffering over vengeance, *Uffgevva* over striving, and forgiveness over resentment. All Christians can read Jesus' words in Matthew's Gospel—"forgive us our debts, as we forgive our debtors"—but Amish people truly believe that their own forgiveness is bound up in their willingness to forgive others. For them, forgiveness is more than a *good* thing to do. It is absolutely central to the Christian faith.

All of this helps us understand how the Nickel Mines Amish could do the unimaginable: extend forgiveness to their children's killer within hours of their deaths. The decision to forgive came quickly, almost instinctively. Moreover, it came in deeds as well as words, with concrete expressions of care for the gunman's family. For the Amish, the test of

175

faith is action. Beliefs are important, and words are too, but actions reveal the true character of one's faith. Therefore to *really* forgive means to act in forgiving ways—in this case, by expressing care for the family of the killer.

In a world where the default response is more often revenge than forgiveness, all of this is inspiring. At the same time, the fact that forgiveness is so deeply woven into the fabric of Amish life should alert us that their example, inspiring as it is, is not easily transferable to other people in other situations. Imitation may be the sincerest form of flattery, but how does one imitate a habit that's embedded in a way of life anchored in a five-hundred-year history?

Most North Americans, formed by the assumptions of liberal democracy and consumer capitalism, carry a dramatically different set of cultural habits. In fact, many North Americans might conclude that certain Amish habits are problematic, if not utterly offensive. Submitting to the discipline of fallible church leaders? Forgoing personal acclaim? Constraining intellectual exploration? Abiding by restrictive gender roles? Declining to stand up for one's rights? Refusing to fight for one's country? Could any set of cultural habits be more out of sync with mainstream American culture?

Many observers missed the countercultural dimension of Amish forgiveness, or at least downplayed it, in the aftermath of the Nickel Mines shooting. Outsiders, typically impressed by what they saw, too often assumed that Amish grace represented the best in "us." Few commentators did this as crassly as the writer who equated the faith of the Amish with the faith of the Founding Fathers. In his mind, the Nickel Mines Amish were not acting counterculturally; they were simply extending a long American tradition of acting in loving, generous, and "Christian" ways. Other commentators, eager to find redemptive lessons in such a senseless event, offered simple platitudes. Rather than highlighting the painful self-renunciation that forgiveness (and much of Amish life) entails, they extolled Amish forgiveness as an inspiring expression of the goodness that resides in America's heartland.

We are not suggesting that the Amish response to the shooting was not praiseworthy. We contend, however, that the countercultural value system from which it emerged was too often neglected in the tributes that followed in the wake of the shooting. As if to drive home the depth of this cultural divide, ministers in one Ohio Amish community forbade a member from giving public lectures on Amish forgiveness. Ironically, the very value system that compelled the Nickel Mines Amish to forgive Charles Roberts constrained a member's freedom to talk about forgiveness with curious outsiders. No, the Amish response at Nickel Mines was not so much the "best of America" as it was an expression of love by a people who every day challenge many of the values the rest of us hold dear.

The Perils of Strip Mining

If some observers detached Amish forgiveness from its countercultural weave, others severed it from its social context—drawing dubious lessons the Amish could teach the world. For instance, numerous writers cited the Amish example at Nickel Mines to score points against the violence so prominent in U.S. foreign policy, particularly the Bush administration's war on terror. Many of these critiques contrasted the Christianity of President Bush with the faith of the Amish and then asked readers which one Jesus himself would endorse. From a rhetorical standpoint, the contrast worked well, though its proponents failed to mention that the two-kingdom Amish would never expect the government to operate without the use of force. Even as the Amish use their own disciplinary procedures to prune unrighteousness within their churches, they expect the government to restrain evildoers in the larger society, often by force. For that reason, it's unlikely the Amish would encourage a U.S. president to pardon someone like Osama bin Laden.

Of course, it's possible that these commentators were talking not about *pardoning* terrorists (releasing them from punishment) but rather about *forgiving* them (replacing rage with love). Still, in their quick application of Amish forgiveness to complex, entrenched conflicts, many pundits neglected a key point: the schoolhouse shooter was dead and his offenses were in the past. As horrible as the shooting was, it was a single event that dawned unexpectedly and ended quickly. Contrast this, for instance, with the centuries-long history of oppression of African Americans, the calculated extermination of six million Jews, or the fear that families living amid ethnic conflict experience every day. Offering forgiveness is much more complicated, and much more challenging for ongoing offenses. Even minor offenses—demeaning comments from a supervisor, for instance—can obstruct forgiveness when they continue day after day.

Other factors made this forgiveness story distinct, even within Amish life. The Nickel Mines Amish had neighborly ties with the gunman's family, relationships they hoped to mend and keep. In this small-town environment, extending grace quickly was both practical and uncomplicated, for the Amish knew exactly whom to approach and could even walk to their homes. Furthermore, the scale of the offense meant that no one person or family had to bear the burden of forgiveness alone. The wider Amish community, in a spirit of mutual aid, carried one another along. Moreover, the enormity of the evil made the Amish more open to the possibility that the shooting might have a place in God's providential plan. Together these factors help to explain why some Amish people suggested that forgiving Charles Roberts was easier than forgiving a fellow church member for a petty, run-of-the-mill offense.

Again, we are not minimizing Amish generosity in the face of this horrific shooting. We are suggesting, however, that the uniqueness of Amish culture—and the details of the tragedy—should chasten us as we apply the Amish example elsewhere. The Amish do not simply tack forgiveness onto their lives in an individualistic fashion, nor do they always forgive as quickly and as easily as media reports seemed to suggest. For these reasons, Amish-style forgiveness can't be strip-mined from southern Lancaster County and transported wholesale to other settings. Rather, the lessons of grace that the rest of us take from Nickel Mines must be extracted with care and applied to other circumstances with humility.

Extracting Lessons from Nickel Mines

Although the Amish approach the task of forgiveness with rich cultural resources, they also approach the task as fallible human beings. In that respect the Amish *are* like the rest of us, and we are like them. This point should be obvious, but some people assume the Amish have access to otherworldly resources that the rest of us have not found. To be sure, that assumption contains some truth: the God the Amish worship *fully expects* human beings to love their enemies and forgive their debtors. Nevertheless, the ability to forgive is not restricted to the Amish, or to Christians, or to people who believe in God. To forgive may be divine, as the poet Alexander Pope suggested, but if so, it's a divine act that is broadly available to the human community.

Indeed, in the course of writing this book, we encountered stories of forgiveness that were every bit as moving as the Nickel Mines story: stories of people shot and left for dead, people whose children were abducted and harmed, people whose marriages were shattered by unfaithfulness, people whose reputations were destroyed by so-called

179

friends. Most of these people had no connection to the Amish and few of the cultural resources the Amish bring to bear when they face injustice. Yet they forgave—not quickly or easily, but eventually and for the good of all involved.

Psychologists who study forgiveness find that, generally speaking, people who forgive lead happier and healthier lives than those who don't. The Amish people we interviewed agreed, citing their own experience of forgiving others. Some said they were "controlled" by their offender until they were able to forgive; others said the "acid of hate" destroys the unforgiving person until the hate is released. Coming from members of a religious community that emphasizes self-denial, these comments show that the Amish are nonetheless interested in self-care and personal happiness. Forgiveness may be self-renouncing in some respects, but it is not self-loathing. The Amish we interviewed confirmed what psychologists tell us: forgiveness heals the person who offers it, freeing that person to move on in life with a greater sense of vitality and wholeness.

Still, if the Amish provide evidence that forgiveness heals the forgiver, they provide even more evidence that forgiveness benefits the offender. Forgiveness does not deny that a wrong has taken place, but it does give up the right to hurt the wrongdoer in return. Even though Charles Roberts was dead, opportunities to exact vengeance upon his family did not die with his suicide. Rather than pursuing revenge, however, the Amish showed empathy for his kin, even by attending his burial. In other words, the Amish of Nickel Mines chose not to vilify the killer but to treat him and his family as members of the human community. Amish forgiveness was thus a gift to Charles Roberts, to his family, and even to the world, for it served as the first step toward mending a social fabric that was rent by the schoolhouse shooting.

These acts of grace astounded many people who watched from afar. Living in a world in which religion seems to nourish vengeance more often than curb it, the Amish response was a welcome contrast to a barrage of suicide bombings and religiously fueled rage. What is less clear is whether the rest of us saw the Amish response as something to emulate, or as just a noble but impossible ideal.

Perhaps the answer to that question lies somewhere in the middle. Perhaps we were awed and truly impressed that the Amish sought to counter evil with a loving and healing response. At the same time, we may know that had *our* children been the ones gunned down in the West Nickel Mines School, our response would have been rooted in rage rather than grace. It's an honest perspective, but also a problematic one, because it assumes that revenge is the natural response and forgiveness is reserved for folks like the Amish who spend their lives stifling natural inclinations.

We often assume that humans have innate needs in the face of violence and injustice. For instance, some who said that the Amish forgave Roberts "too quickly" assumed that Amish people had denied a basic human need to get even. But perhaps our *real* human need is to find ways to move beyond tragedy with a sense of healing and hope.

What we learn from the Amish, both at Nickel Mines and more generally, is that how we choose to move on from tragic injustice is culturally formed. For the Amish, who bring their own religious resources to bear on injustice, the preferred way to live on with meaning and hope is to offer forgiveness—and offer it quickly. That offer, including the willingness to forgo vengeance, does not undo the tragedy or pardon the wrong. It does, however, constitute a first step toward a future that is more hopeful, and potentially less violent, than it would otherwise be.

How might the rest of us move in that direction? Most of us have been formed by a culture that nourishes revenge and mocks grace. Hockey fans complain that they haven't gotten their money's worth if the players only skate and score without a fight. Bloody video games are everywhere, and the ones that seemed outrageously violent ten years ago are tame by today's standards. Blockbuster movie plots revolve around heroes who avenge wrong with merciless killing. And it's not just the entertainment world that acculturates us into a graceless existence. Traffic accidents galvanize hoards of lawyers who encourage victims to get their "due." In fact, getting our due might be the most widely shared value in our hyperconsumerist culture. "The person who volunteers time, who helps a stranger, who agrees to work for a modest wage out of commitment to the public good . . . begins to feel like a sucker," writes Robert Kuttner in *Everything for Sale*. In a culture that places such a premium on buying and selling, as opposed to giving and receiving, forgiveness runs against the grain.

Running against that grain, finding alternative ways to imagine our world, ways that in turn will facilitate forgiveness, takes more than individual willpower. We are not only the products of our culture, we are also producers of our culture. We need to construct cultures that value and nurture forgiveness. In their own way, the Amish have constructed such an environment. The challenge for the rest of us is to use *our* resources creatively to shape cultures that discourage revenge as a first response. How might we work more imaginatively to create communities in which enemies are treated as members of the human family and not demonized? How might these communities foster visions that enable their members to see offenders, as well as victims, as persons with authentic needs? There are no simple answers to these questions, though any answer surely will involve the habits we decide to value, the images we choose to celebrate, and the stories we remember.

In fact, forgiveness is less a matter of forgive and forget than of forgive and *remember*—remembering in ways that bring healing. When we remember we take the broken pieces of our lives—lives that have been *dismembered* by tragedy and injustice—and *re-member* them into something whole. Forgetting an atrocious offense, personally or corporately, may not be possible, but all of us can and do make decisions about how we remember what we cannot forget.

For the Amish, gracious remembering involves habits nurtured by memories of Jesus forgiving his tormentors while hanging on a cross and of Dirk Willems returning to pull his enemy out of the icy water. When thirteen-year-old Marian said "shoot me first" in the schoolhouse, and when adults in her community walked over to the killer's family with words of grace a few hours after her death, they were acting on those habits. And just as surely their actions at Nickel Mines will be recounted around Amish dinner tables for generations to come, creating and renewing memories about the power of faith to respond in the face of injustice—even violence—with grace.

In a world where faith often justifies and magnifies revenge, and in a nation where some Christians use scripture to fuel retaliation, the Amish response was indeed a surprise. Regardless of the details of the Nickel Mines story, one message rings clear: religion was used not to justify rage and revenge but to inspire goodness, forgiveness, and grace. And that is the big lesson for the rest of us regardless of our faith or nationality.

AFTERWORD (2 0 1 0)

Our narrative of Amish grace came to a close in November 2006. Since then, the Nickel Mines community has returned to "a new normal" that includes joy, sadness, occasional fears, expressions of courage, and moments of grace.

By Christmas 2006, four of the five injured girls had returned to school and were functioning well despite their serious injuries. One of the girls successfully completed all the homework she had missed in the weeks after the shooting. Although some of the girls faced additional reconstructive surgeries and months of rehabilitation, by spring 2009, two of them had completed their eighth-grade studies and graduated from school. In the words of an Amish leader, "The four of them will be able to live [physically] normal lives, even the one with seven bullet wounds."

The recovery of the most seriously injured girl continues very slowly. She remains in the care of her parents, at home, and shows small signs of improvement. Fed by a tube, she is not able to walk or talk but does smile and recognize certain people despite suffering some seizures. She attends a non-Amish public school for special-needs children.

The healing process has also been slow for some of the older boys who were taken hostage in the schoolhouse and then expelled by the gunman. Several experienced the feelings of survivors' guilt—including blaming themselves for not stopping the shooting that took the lives of some of their sisters and friends. The one who suffered the most was hospitalized in summer 2007 for anorexia and other symptoms of emotional trauma.

School itself resumed very quickly after the shooting, first in a temporary facility on a nearby Amish property. By late February 2007, Amish carpenters had a new school under roof. Located about a half mile from the old school, the new building sits in a more secluded spot, close to several homes and away from the road. The pupils moved into New Hope School, on Monday, April 2, exactly six months after the tragedy. The ratio of girls to boys gradually rebalanced as some pupils transferred from a nearby Amish school, the older boys graduated, and new families moved into the area.

Emma continued to teach at New Hope School for two years but stopped at the close of the school year in May 2008 because she thought a change would be best for the students and herself. A year later, in fall 2009, she began teaching again at the nearby Wolf Rock Amish School. The young woman who replaced her at New Hope School in fall 2008 had graduated from the Nickel Mines School a few years before the tragedy.

The forgiveness and grace of October 2006 were first steps in an ongoing, sometimes awkward, but always insistent effort at reconciliation—at mending the relationships so strained by the shooting. The emotional meeting at the Bart Firehouse at the end of October between Charles Roberts's relatives and the Amish families was not their final contact. For example, Roberts's widow, Amy, drove one of the mothers to visit her injured daughter, recovering in a hospital, and at Christmastime, the Amish schoolchildren went to the Roberts home to sing carols. Amy and members of her family also visited New Hope School in spring 2007. Eventually, Amy remarried and moved a few miles away from Georgetown. She spoke publicly about her healing and spiritual journey for the first time at a community-wide ecumenical gathering in October 2009.

Charles Roberts's parents visited the temporary school, attended an Amish school Christmas program, and in winter 2007 visited in the homes of the Amish parents involved in the tragedy. In addition, the gunman's parents hosted a picnic and swimming party at their home for the surviving children and parents that summer. Since then, Roberts's mother has hosted teas for the mothers and grandmothers of the children who died or were injured. In an extraordinary act of grace, she also visits the most severely injured girl weekly, reading and singing to her and sometimes bathing her. One Amish parent, reflecting on the graceful response of the Roberts family, said, "Their kindness has helped us a lot in the healing process."

The pain from the trauma has faded but the memories linger. "The half-year mark was pretty rough on some of us," observed one Amish woman. Certain images, sounds, and words still provoke anxious thoughts and reactions. Some adults still flinch at the sound of helicopters flying in the area. Finding a new normal has taken time and hard work. Several new babies born to parents who lost children in the shooting have helped the quest to return to normal living.

The parents of the schoolchildren have found meaningful support among Amish and English friends and particularly among one another. The mothers meet periodically to share their grief and find encouragement. Some of the fathers get together too, but on a less regular schedule. A father who lost a daughter said, "We get our most support just meeting and talking with the other parents." Most of the families and surviving children received support and guidance from professional counselors in the aftermath. About six months after the shooting, one church leader noted, "We are still processing some anger, but we are moving in the direction of forgiveness."

At the first anniversary, in October 2007, the school was closed and one of the parents who lost a child hosted a gathering for families involved in the tragedy as well as the state police commissioner, police officers, and some of the first responders. Later anniversaries were quietly observed by informal gatherings and visiting in some of the homes.

In keeping with Amish sentiments of humility, no ongoing public commemoration has been established or historical markers erected to memorialize the tragedy. Nonetheless, the memory of the story is often retold in the oral traditions of Amish communities across the country. Some of the parents have been invited to meet with and console Amish victims of various tragedies in other Amish communities.

Members of the broader Nickel Mines community continue to support one another and their Amish neighbors in many ways. In summer 2007, a picnic, or what locals called a reunion, was held for police officers, fire company personnel, emergency responders, Amish parents and families, and the Roberts family. An Amish artist crafted a large wooden plaque for the event, with messages of gratitude for the state police. Pupils from the West Nickel Mines School used a wood-burning pen to inscribe their names on the plaque, which was presented to the police at the reunion. Amish families have been keenly grateful for the continuing support and presence of the state police in the Nickel Mines area, which has helped them regain a sense of security in their daily lives.

Financial gifts still trickle in to the Accountability Committee, which has now received some $4.7 million from donors around the world. The committee supervises a trust fund that supports therapy for the physical and psychological needs of the victims and their families.

Beyond its initial reverberations around the world, the Nickel Mines forgiveness story continues to touch and inspire many people. Educators, pastors, and victims of violence from Russia, Israel, Switzerland, Brazil, South Africa, Lebanon, Argentina, and elsewhere have come to Nickel Mines to learn about forgiveness and reconciliation. For several months, a patchwork comfort quilt hung in the local firehouse. Made by students in Ohio for the children of 9/11 victims in New Jersey, the quilt had been sent to survivors of Hurricane Katrina and then to Nickel Mines. In August 2007, a bus of Amish people took the comfort quilt to Virginia Tech University, where they shared it with family and friends related to the shooting on that campus in April 2007.

Whether the Amish witness in Nickel Mines has made the world—even small corners of it—more forgiving is difficult to assess. Many people remain interested in the Amish response, some continue to be inspired by it, and still others publicly praise it when they have the chance. Of course, the Amish in and around Nickel Mines would be the first to remind us that their expressions of grace in the face of tragedy were not performed to elicit responses from others. Rather, as one Amish leader remarked at the time, their extension of forgiveness was simply "the right thing to do." Four years later, the Nickel Mines Amish still believe that to be true.

INTERVIEW WITH
TERRI ROBERTS

Terri is the mother of Charles Carl Roberts IV, the man responsible for the tragedy at the Nickel Mines Amish School on October 2, 2006. She was interviewed by Donald B. Kraybill in 2010.

What were your initial reactions?

"Why, Lord? Why did this have to happen? Why now? Why me?" The kind of storm that hit me I pray that nobody else ever has to face; it was like a Katrina, a tsunami. It's the kind of a storm that takes your life, and changes it forever, in ways you could never anticipate. So it's the kind of storm that just rocks the whole world you live in, that you feel secure in, and it makes you question, "How, how could something like this happen? How could you allow this, Lord?"

Where were you when you learned of the tragedy?

October 2, 2006, was a beautiful day. My friend and I were eating lunch on the patio at work as we did every day. We heard sirens, helicopters. Even when I'm driving down the street and I hear a siren, I always offer a short prayer: "Whoever's involved in this, Lord, just be with them, bring healing," which I did that day. We finished our lunches, walked back into the office, and the phone was ringing. It was my husband, "I need you to come down to Charlie's house right away."

As I drove there, I turned on the radio and heard there'd been a shooting at the Nickel Mines School. I knew that my son parked his truck down near there. "Wow," I thought, "don't tell me Charlie was around when this was happening and tried to help with the rescue or something and got shot!" I arrived to learn that not only was my son not living anymore, but he was the perpetrator of the crime. This couldn't be! This was not the man that we knew, the wonderful dad, the wonderful husband. Our lives were shattered in a way that no one can prepare for. There's nothing that could have prepared me for it, except God knew that it was going to happen, and as best as could be, He walked us through this. We take our sorrows, and we ask God to restore our joy.

How did the Amish community respond to your family?

On the day it happened, Henry, our Amish neighbor up on the hill, whom I call an "angel in black," came to our house. My husband provided transportation for the Amish when they needed to travel by car, and he was just devastated. All day long, my husband couldn't lift his head. He kept taking a towel and wiping it over his head—he just kept wiping the tears away and couldn't lift his head up at all. And then Henry came, and he was the first sign of healing for my husband. He put his hand on my husband's shoulder, just stood there and comforted and consoled him for an hour. Henry said, "Roberts, we love you," and just kept affirming and assuring him. The acceptance we have received from the Amish community is beyond any words. To be able to have a community of people that have been hurt so much by what our son did and yet to have them respond to us the way that they have has been an incredible journey.

How do you think about your son since the tragedy?

A piece of advice from a counselor was so helpful to me. And
I think anyone going through a tragedy or a hard time can use
some aspect of this. The counselor asked me, "How old was your
son?" I said, "He was thirty-three years old." And she said, "From
what I'm hearing from you, he was a wonderful son." I said,
"Yes, he was an absolutely wonderful son. We never knew that
our son was suffering. We never knew that he was angry after
losing his first child; I never knew that he was angry with God."
Then the counselor said, "What happened that day was a tiny
slice of your son's life. When your mind goes there, take it back
to the thirty-three years of wonderful memories that you have."

That has been such a help to me, such a consolation to me,
and that is what I do. When my mind goes to the events at the
school, I don't ever stop it from going there. I can never ignore
what happened. It will never go away because it was so devastating and lives are still being lived in hurt, sorrow, and suffering.
But it's helpful when I remember that day and still shed tears, to
then go back to the other years of my son's life and flood it with
wonderful memories because that's what we had! He wasn't perfect, but he was a wonderful son. And I just want to encourage
anybody that's going through a trial or a struggle to do that—to
use that longer perspective because it's been so helpful to me.

Have you been able to forgive your son?

Unforgiveness leads to self-pain, and I believe the Bible com-
mands us to forgive. There was no doubt in my mind that I
would forgive Charlie. However, the anguish I experienced was

not easy to deal with. Comprehending what he had done took days and weeks to absorb. However, I knew that his actions came from unforgiveness. And seeing what others experience without forgiving—I knew this was not an option for me. He was my son, so full of love but blinded to the love of our heavenly Father. I cannot comprehend how this happened and we did not see it. Yes, I forgave my son.

What happened at the burial?

The funeral was, oh, my goodness, a sorrowful and sad day. And then to see the Amish community as we walked over to the gravesite, to see them come out and encircle us was such a blessing. And the first people to greet us, to greet Marie [Amy], (Charlie's widow) and us, were the parents of the two little sisters who lost their lives that day. How could anyone have the courage to do that? Amish people have built relationships with us and us with them—relationships that have been just incredible. It's just wonderful to have their lives intertwine with ours. And that's not an easy thing to do.

Were there other meetings with the Amish community?

I remember when they got all of our families together at the Bart Firehouse, and that included grandmas and grandpas and every-body. I remember sitting next to an Amish couple who had lost their little girl that day, and we, both couples, we sat there and the tears just kept coming. The love in that room mingled with the sorrow, and there was so much love there, despite what we had been through. It was just wow! We have an awesome God. And if we are truly living for Jesus, we are to forgive, because God has forgiven us for our sins, we are to forgive, and that *is* how we are to live; that *is* to be our testimony. It *is* to be what resonates from us. We've experienced that in a magnificent way in our family.

Did the initial response of the Amish influence how you responded to them?

Since the response came so quickly, it is hard to say how I may have reacted had they not offered forgiveness. I just know that their immediate expression had a tremendous impact on my husband and me. The immediate visits and attendance at the funeral were the beginning of the healing process. It's amazing to me that the Amish refer to the incident simply as "the Happening." Whenever they refer to it, that is the term they use. I count that response, that language, as a blessing. It softened the focus of that day and made a world of difference to me. What a blessing that has been to us.

Did you visit later with the Amish families?

I think it helps to allow other people to participate in our sorrows and to share them with us. So after the tragedy, my husband and I decided that we would visit with all the families, and that is something we started doing in January three months after the Happening. So we went and visited the families, and I'll never forget how just getting to know them was a wonderful experience. Scary, yes, of course. But God doesn't want us to refrain from scary things. What happened in our lives, just through those visits, building those relationships, has been so incredible.

Did you ever visit the school?

I went to the temporary school along with a group of Japanese students who came to share their origami cranes with the Amish children. It's what the Japanese do when they want to help somebody with healing. They fold these origami cranes, and then they take them to the person that's going through suffering. I was invited to go along, and I said, "Oh, I would love to go." Well, I wanted to go along as a fly on the wall; I didn't want the Amish children to know who I was. I didn't want them to think, "Oh, that's Charlie's mother."

But when we arrived, we were all asked to introduce ourselves. And I thought, "Oh, not me! I don't want to do that." But I did, and I walked around the classroom as the Amish children were making their own paper cranes. The Japanese students showed them how to do it. But just the stark reality of being in that classroom was very, very difficult to deal with. To see all the boys and just three girls, that was very hard. But God's grace is sufficient. As I was talking to the children, one boy said, "You've gone to visit almost all the families. Are you coming to visit our family?" And I said, "We sure are." And it was just so healing to have a child look at me and want us to be a part of his life after what my son did.

Did you do things with the families?

In the first summer [2007], we had all the families to our home for a picnic, and it was just really neat seeing everybody get off of a bus at our front yard. They actually rented a bus and all came in a yellow school bus. One of the boys at the picnic, who had been in the schoolhouse the day of the tragedy, was still struggling with guilt because he hadn't tried to stop my son that day. And it was still creating emotional problems for him, and there was counseling and all. And then, at the end of the picnic, he came up to me, and he looked at me and said, "Mrs. Roberts, thank you so much for having us to your home. I had so much fun." Oh! What that did for me. Despite all the work and everything, just that one comment, it was worth the whole picnic! It was just so awesome to be building these relationships and to have that acceptance.

Were there other things you did with the families?

When I had cancer, I had a bald head, and a friend had a tea for me. She had a tea at her home and told me to invite eight friends. We all picked out teacups and hats, and we all wore hats. And you know, when people do things like that, it really helps to lighten the seriousness of what you're going through. So that touching, warm, tea time inspired me to have the surviving girls for a tea.

So now all the little girls come to my house for tea every August, and we have our tea and I take them swimming at my sister's pool next door. So it's just a wonderful way to open doors of communication where there's sorrow and really relate to others. When we take our sorrows and we hold them inside, oh, my, they become such a burden. So I think the Lord wants us to do things for others when we're going through rough times. So for me, it's through teas. I had teas for the moms and grandmoms of the children who died. So I just try to do things that really bring a lot of healing.

A root of bitterness never brings peace. A root of bitterness is worse than any cancer in our body. If we hold any bitterness inside, it's important talk to someone about it and get it released from within our spirit. Choose to praise God, and the bitterness will not take root. Look for those things that can bring healing in difficult situations; that's what we tried to do. There should be permanent gullies in my cheeks from the amount of tears that I have shed, and yet we can go from the pit of despair to the heights of joy. It's a determination in our spirit, of saying, "Lord, you have given me your Word. You have given me a foundation, an anchor." Now we need to use that anchor and build on that joy and make that choice. We need to choose to forgive; it doesn't happen automatically. It's a choice that we make. And we need to choose joy when we're going through trials and struggles.

Have you stayed in touch with the seriously disabled girl?

I had been drawn to reaching out to Rosanna. One year after the Happening, I had a tea for the mothers at our home. As I listened to Rosanna's mother speak of her daughter's challenges, I knew that I wanted to offer to spend time with Rosanna. So on Thursday evenings I go to her home for several hours. It has been both challenging and healing to be accepted in her home and by her precious family. As we reach out in ways that bring a touch, we can find great healing.

Any final thoughts?

The son that we knew acted on his present thoughts. Light dispels darkness. How do we share light to disrupt and obliterate the darkness when it tries to overwhelm us? I knew Philippians 4:6–8 by heart; that was so much a part of me. When this happened, I so wished my son would have known Philippians 4:8, because had he been repeating that verse daily, his mind would have never gone into the darkness as it did. "Do not be anxious about anything, but by prayer and petition, with thanksgiving, present your requests to God. And the peace of God that passes all understanding will guard your heart and your mind in Christ Jesus." Think on these things. "Whatever is true. Whatever is noble. Whatever is right. Whatever is pure. Whatever is lovely. Whatever is admirable. If anything is excellent or praiseworthy, think on such things." When our minds go to darkness, refocus on Philippians 4:8; that takes us to the light!

APPENDIX: THE AMISH OF NORTH AMERICA

Anabaptists, Amish, and Mennonites

The Anabaptist movement emerged in sixteenth-century Europe at the time of the Protestant Reformation. Sometimes called the radical wing of the Reformation, the Anabaptists emphasized an often literal interpretation of the teachings of Jesus, especially the Sermon on the Mount. They rejected infant baptism, arguing that baptism should signify a voluntary adult decision to follow Jesus—and on that basis they proceeded to baptize one another into the movement. Because these radicals had all been baptized in the state church years earlier as infants, their detractors called them *Anabaptists,* meaning "rebaptizers."

The Anabaptist call for a voluntary church separate from government oversight infuriated Catholic and Protestant religious leaders as well as civil officials and brought severe persecution. During the movement's first century as many as twenty-five hundred were executed, often burned at the stake or decapitated. Hundreds more were tortured or imprisoned. This persecution fortified the Anabaptist view that the true church would always be a minority, and it produced a countercultural ethic of separatism. Small, scattered groups with diverse interpretations of faith and practice characterized the early Anabaptist movement.

In 1536 a Dutch Catholic priest, Menno Simons, converted to Anabaptism and eventually became a prolific writer and influential leader. In time many of his followers became known as *Mennonites.* A century and a half later, in the 1690s, another Anabaptist convert named Jakob Ammann led a renewal movement in Switzerland and the Alsatian region of France. According to Ammann, Anabaptists in his area had become enamored of their social standing; he therefore encouraged stricter Christian practices enforced by vigorous church discipline. Ammann's followers eventually became known as *Amish*. Sharing a common Anabaptist heritage, the Amish and Mennonites have been separate groups within the Anabaptist family since 1693.

Amish and Mennonites migrated separately to North America but often settled in the same areas. The Amish migrated in several waves, first in the mid-1700s and again in the 1800s. They established settlements in Pennsylvania, Ohio, and Indiana and eventually spread to other states. In the latter half of the nineteenth century, the Amish struggled with how to respond to changes produced by the Industrial Revolution, evangelical revivalism, and the encroachments of a mass, consumer-oriented society. During this time some of the Amish joined various Mennonite groups. The Amish who held to the older customs eventually became known as *Old Orders*.

In the twenty-first century there are numerous Mennonite groups as well as Amish groups in North America. Although some Old Order Mennonites use horse-and-buggy transportation, many Mennonites drive cars, wear contemporary clothing, support higher education, and use modern technology. Almost all Amish groups reject these things, and for that reason they have become renowned in the United States and beyond for their distinctive way of life.

Family, District, Settlement, and Affiliation

The key building blocks of Amish society are the extended family, the church district, the settlement, and the affiliation. Large extended families are the basic unit of Amish society. It's not unusual for an

Amish person to have seventy-five first cousins and for grandparents to have fifty or more grandchildren. Amish men and women assume traditional and well-defined gender roles. Husbands are considered the religious leaders in their families. Wives typically devote themselves to housekeeping and motherhood. Women with young children almost never work outside the home, although some manage at-home stores, greenhouses, or bakeries. Most Amish women share in household decision making and child discipline, even as they affirm the man's role as the religious head of the home.

Amish society is organized into self-governing local church *districts*. With geographic boundaries marked by such things as roads and streams, the district is the socioreligious home for twenty-five to forty households. The Amish do not have church buildings but instead gather every other Sunday for worship in members' homes, rotating from home to home around the district. The close physical proximity encourages face-to-face interaction in daily life.

Each church district has its own leaders—always men—typically a bishop, two or three ministers, and a deacon. The bishop provides overall leadership for the district, assisted by the ministers. Deacons coordinate mutual aid and determine how the members will share the costs of an expensive medical bill. None of the leaders has formal theological training. Living a consistent Amish way of life is their most important credential. Ordained for life, they receive no payment for their church work and must support themselves in other occupations.

A cluster of districts in a particular region is known as a *settlement*. A settlement might contain only one district or might encompass more than a hundred districts. Holmes County, Ohio, the center of the largest settlement, includes some two hundred districts. The Lancaster settlement is the oldest surviving Amish settlement in North America. About twenty-eight thousand Amish children and adults live in the Lancaster settlement, which currently has about 180 church districts.

Church districts that have similar practices and whose leaders cooperate with one another are known as *affiliations*. Unlike districts and settlements, which are geographically defined, affiliations are based on shared lifestyle regulations and church practices. Members within an affiliation fellowship together, often intermarry, and permit their ministers to preach in one another's services. There are more than two dozen affiliations of Amish in North America, each with its own unique practices. No central organization or national church authority holds the subgroups together. Most districts in an affiliation have similar practices, but even so, the ultimate authority for Amish life and practice lies in the local district.

Growth and Diversity

There are some 425 Amish settlements spread across twenty-seven states and the Canadian province of Ontario. All told, these settlements include some seventeen hundred church districts. Nearly two-thirds of the Amish population lives in three states: Ohio, Pennsylvania, and Indiana.

One might expect a traditional group that rejects higher education, car ownership, and the Internet to be on the wane. Surprisingly, the Amish population is doubling about every twenty years. Counting adults and children, they currently number nearly two hundred forty thousand. Large families and strong retention rates propel their growth. On average, families have about seven children, but it's not unusual to have ten or more. Typically, about 90 percent or more of their youth join the church. Although the Amish do not seek converts, outsiders may join if they comply with Amish guidelines.

The North American Amish may all look alike to outsiders, but practices vary quite widely from affiliation to affiliation. Most groups have battery-powered lights on their carriages, but the most conservative affiliations use only kerosene lanterns. The vast majority of Amish homes have indoor bathrooms, but members in the most traditional groups walk to the outhouse. Power lawn mowers are permitted in some regions of the country but not in others. The women in one affiliation may use only treadle (foot-powered) sewing machines, but those in another group may power their sewing machines with batteries. Some communities are wealthy, and others are rather poor. Even within affiliations and local church districts, diversity abounds.

Ordnung

Biblical principles are applied in daily practice through the *Ordnung*, a German word that means "order." The *Ordnung* consists of district-specific regulations, usually unwritten, that are passed on by practice and oral tradition. The regulations apply the biblical principle of "separation from the world" to issues such as clothing, use of mass media, technology, and leisure activities. Church leaders update the regulations as new issues arise, usually with input from district members. Controversial issues—the use of cell phones, computers, fancy furniture, or immodest dress—receive attention at Members Meetings. Disagreements over the details of the *Ordnung* can sometimes become contentious. Members of each congregation affirm their district's *Ordnung* twice a year, before the spring and fall communion services.

All Amish groups expect men and women to wear prescribed clothing. Married men are expected to grow a beard but not a mustache and to wear an Amish-style hat and vest. Women are expected to wear a head covering and usually a three-piece dress that includes a cape and an apron. Unlike the broader American culture, where dress is often used to express personal preferences, dress among the Amish signals submission to the collective order and serves as a public symbol of group identity.

As part of their *Ordnung,* Old Order Amish forbid owning an automobile; tapping electricity from public utility lines; owning a television, radio, or personal computer; attending high school or college; joining the military; and initiating divorce. Members agree to obey the *Ordnung* at the time of baptism, with the clear understanding that they will be subject to church discipline, and perhaps excommunication, if they break that vow.

The Amish generally do not join public organizations or service clubs in their communities. Some of them, however, are members of local volunteer fire companies and emergency medical units. Although they do not develop intimate relationships with outsiders or marry them, they are usually good neighbors who enjoy many friendships with non-Amish people.

Youth and Rumspringa

Although children learn their district's *Ordnung* by careful observation, Amish youth are not expected to adhere to the *Ordnung* until they are baptized. Young people eagerly await their sixteenth birthday, the traditional age when they begin *Rumspringa,* a time of "running around." During this period they spend more time with their peers, especially on weekends, and often begin dating. *Rumspringa* ends at marriage, which typically occurs between the ages of nineteen and twenty-two.

Rumspringa is a period when some Amish youth, boys more than girls, experience greater freedom. Betwixt and between, they are no longer under the tight control of their parents, but because they are not baptized they are not yet under the authority of the church. During this time, many Amish youth adhere to traditional Amish behavior. Others, however, experiment with "worldly" activities—buying a car, going to movies, wearing English clothes, buying a television or a DVD player. In the larger Amish settlements, an adolescent's behavior often depends on the peer group he or she chooses to join. Amish parents often worry about which group their child will join because the choice will influence the teen's behavior. The practice of *Rumspringa* varies greatly from community to community. Some church districts provide adult supervision, but others do not.

Traditional youth activities may include volleyball, swimming, ice skating, picnics, hikes in a state park, and large outdoor "supper" parties. The most typical gatherings are "singings." Groups meet in a home and sing German hymns and English gospel songs for several hours and then enjoy a time of conversation and food. The "faster," more rebellious groups sometimes drive cars, rent a building for parties, or go to bars and nightclubs in nearby towns. Given the chasm between adult Amish life and the rowdiest of Amish youth parties, *Rumspringa* provides fascinating material for the news media. For most Amish youth, however, *Rumspringa* consists of some newfound freedoms that are expressed in moderate ways.

A fling with worldliness reminds Amish youth that they have a choice regarding church membership, and indeed they do. However, most of the forces of Amish life funnel them in the direction of joining the church. Knowing they have a choice likely strengthens their willingness to obey church standards and, in the long run, the authority of the church itself.

Changing Occupations

Until the 1960s, most Amish people, regardless of the state in which they resided, lived on family farms. Amish farms were small, diversified operations with a dozen cows, some chickens, and a few beef cattle. Although many continue this tradition, Amish farms have grown more specialized, with dairy cows and, in some cases, chickens or hogs. Specialized farms tend to be more mechanized, but still less so than neighboring non-Amish farms. Farmers with more than twenty cows typically use mechanical milkers and bulk cooling tanks. The more traditional farmers milk by hand and ship their milk in old-fashioned cans to cheese plants.

Despite popular mythology, most Amish farmers do not practice organic farming. Many of them use insecticides, herbicides, and chemical fertilizers. A growing trend toward small specialty operations that produce vegetables, herbs, and flowers has emerged in some settlements. Some of these specialty operations do, however, use organic methods to target specific urban markets.

Although farming continues to hold a revered place in Amish life, the majority of Amish people in many settlements have abandoned their plows. In some of the larger communities, fewer than 10 percent farm. This shift to nonfarm work is the biggest change in Amish society in the last century. Still, despite their growing involvement in business and commerce, the Amish remain a distinctly rural people, living along country roads and on the outskirts of small villages. Many families combine off-farm work with hobby farming.

In recent decades, hundreds of Amish-owned shops have sprung up in some communities. Most of these are small family businesses with fewer than ten employees and are usually, but not always, overseen by men. The bulk of these businesses produce wood products—household and outdoor furniture, gazebos, small barns, and lawn ornaments—though quilt shops, greenhouses, and bakeries have also been very successful. With low overhead and an ample supply of family labor, the small home-based shops tend to be very profitable. The annual sales of the larger businesses may exceed $5 million.

Construction work also provides employment for many Amish men in some states. In certain communities, dozens of construction crews travel considerable distances to build homes and commercial buildings for non-Amish people. In other settlements, the majority of Amish men work in English-owned factories located in rural areas or small towns. In northern Indiana, for instance, many Amish work in factories that assemble recreational vehicles.

The growth of nonfarm employment has brought new wealth to many Amish communities. Some leaders worry that the new jobs bring too much "easy money" and will eventually erode a work ethic built on generations of farming. Others fear that fringe benefits, such as medical insurance, that accompany outside factory employment will undermine the commitment to mutual aid within the church. For this reason, many Amish communities prefer home-based shops to "lunch pail jobs" away from home. "What we're trying to do," said one shop owner, "is to keep the family together."

Technology

Many outsiders mistakenly think the Amish reject technology. It is more accurate to say that they use technology selectively. Televisions, radios, and personal computers are rejected outright, but other types of technology are used selectively or modified to fit Amish purposes. Amish mechanics also build new machines to accommodate their cultural guidelines. Moreover, they readily buy much state-of-the-art technology, such as gas grills, shop tools, camping equipment, and some farm equipment.

Why do the Amish fear technology? They do not consider technology evil in itself, but they believe that technology, if left untamed, will undermine worthy traditions and accelerate assimilation into the surrounding society. "It's what it will do to the next generation," said one bishop. Mass media technology in particular, they fear, would introduce foreign values into their culture. A car is seen not as immoral but as a harmful tool that would pull the community apart. Horse-and-buggy transportation keeps the community anchored in its local geographic base. Cars would bring greater mobility that would erode local ties.

Most Amish groups forbid using electricity from public utility lines. "It's not the electricity that is so bad," said one member. "It's all the things we don't need that would come with it." Electricity from batteries is more local, controllable, and independent from the outside world. In some settlements, for example, Amish use batteries to power lights on buggies, calculators, fans, flashlights, cash registers, copy machines, and typewriters. Solar energy is sometimes used to charge batteries, operate electric fences, and power household appliances.

Amish use of technology often perplexes outsiders. Why would God frown on a telephone? What sense does it make to keep a tractor at the barn but not take it to the field? Is it not inconsistent, if not outright hypocritical, to hire English taxi drivers but refuse to own cars? And what could be the difference between 12-volt electricity from batteries and 110-volt current from public utility lines? These distinctions may look silly to an outsider, but within the context of Amish history they are important cultural compromises that have helped slow the pace of social change and keep worldliness at bay.

All of these adaptations reflect Amish attempts to balance tradition and change. Economic viability often factors into their decisions about technology, but convenience for convenience's sake is not a high priority. The Amish seek to master technology rather than become its slave. Like few other communities, they have shown the tenacity to tackle the powerful forces of technology in order to preserve their traditional way of life.

Government Relations

Contrary to some misperceptions, the Amish do pay taxes: state and federal income taxes, sales and real estate taxes, and public school taxes. They are exempt from paying Social Security taxes, however, because they consider Social Security a form of insurance and refuse its benefits. The Amish believe that the Bible instructs them to care for church members who have special needs, including the elderly. To rely on commercial or government insurance would mock their faith that God will care for them through the church.

The Amish are taught to respect and pray for governing authorities according to biblical admonitions. However, when caught in a conflict between their conscience and civic law, they cite the scripture verse "Obey God rather than men" (Acts 5:29). From their reading of the New Testament, particularly the Sermon on the Mount, they believe that Jesus' followers are to be nonviolent, and they forbid self-defense as well as entering the armed forces. They generally avoid holding public office and engaging in political activism. They are, however, permitted to vote. The rate of voting is typically low unless a local issue is on the ballot.

In recent years, numerous conflicts have pitted the Amish against the growing regulatory power of the state. The points of friction have included military service, education, Social Security, health care, property zoning, child labor, photo identification, and the use of slow-moving-vehicle signs. To cope with these various conflicts, the Amish have formed a national steering committee with representatives in various states to work with public legislators when issues arise. In general, however, the Amish have

fared rather well in a political system that respects and protects their freedom of religious expression.

Blemish and Virtue

The Amish are far from perfect. Amish hearts sometimes swell with
greed, jealousy, and anger. Parents worry about their children, and
some Amish youth rebel against their parents, their churches, and even
the law. Although the Amish forbid divorce, some marriages do sour.
Church leaders have been known to abuse their power, and sexual
and physical abuse occurs in Amish families as it does in other North
American families. Disagreements sometimes debilitate a church district, forcing the local church to split into factions.

Despite their blemishes, the Amish have developed a remarkably
stable society. With little government aid they provide care and dignity
for elderly and disabled members. Apart from occasional arrests for
alcohol or drug abuse among their youth, Amish communities have
avoided many of the blights of modern life. With only a few exceptions,
they have no homeless or unemployed members and no one living on
government subsidies. Virtually no Amish people sit in prison, and only
occasionally do Amish couples divorce. Thus, all things considered, they
have created a humane society despite their lack of high school education, professional training, and a full embrace of technology.

The Amish have learned to live with limits. Indeed, they would
argue that setting and respecting limits on almost everything is one
of the foundations of wisdom. Limits, for the Amish, are a necessary
requirement for human happiness. Without limits, the Amish believe,
individuals become arrogant, conceited, and self-destructive. To be
sure, restraints diminish individual freedom, personal choices, and various forms of self-expression. At the same time, some would say, they

grant greater dignity and security to the individual than the endless choices afforded by modern life. To the Amish way of thinking, a respect for limits builds community, brings a sense of belonging, and shapes identity—three important keys to human satisfaction and happiness.

ENDNOTES

Chapter 1:   *The Nickel Mines Amish*

4   *The "southern end":* For a history of the Amish south of "the ridge" in the Lancaster settlement, see John S. Kauffman, Melvin R. Petersheim, and Ira S. Beiler, comps., *Amish History of Southern Lancaster County, Pennsylvania, 1940–1992* (Elverson, PA: Olde Springfield Shoppe, 1992; available from Masthof Press, Elverson, PA). For a social history of the Lancaster Amish settlement in the twentieth century, see Donald B. Kraybill, *The Riddle of Amish Culture,* rev. ed. (Baltimore: Johns Hopkins University Press, 2001). For a history of the Amish in Europe and North America, see Steven M. Nolt, *A History of the Amish,* rev. ed. (Intercourse, PA: Good Books, 2003).

10   *This occurs, the manual explains: Standards of the Old Order Amish and Old Order Mennonite Parochial and Vocational Schools of Pennsylvania* (Gordonville, PA: Gordonville Print Shop, 1981), 2.

Chapter 2:   *The Shooting*

18   *At about 3:00 on Monday:* Our sources for this chapter include interviews with Amish and non-Amish people familiar with the tragedy, letters and commentary in Amish newspapers, media accounts, and police reports. One of the best summaries of the shooting is "Lost Angels: The Untold Stories of the Amish School Shootings," a three-part series that appeared in the *Lancaster New Era* on December 13, 14, and 15, 2006. This series, from which our account is adapted, was reprinted as a twenty-eight-page booklet in January 2007. The material in this section relies heavily on pages 11–18.

21   *"Consider, Man! the End": Unpartheyisches Gesang-Buch: Translations and Lessons* [Impartial Songbook: Translations and Lessons], 2nd ed. (East Earl, PA: Schoolaid, 1997), 171. Translation used by permission of the publisher.

21   *In quiet solitude: Unpartheyisches Gesang-Buch*, 151. Original translation used by permission of the publisher. Revised translation 2007 by David Rempel Smucker, Ph.D., Akron, PA. Used by permission.

28   *The old martyr stories:* The complete title of the English edition, which is 1,158 pages long and kept in print by Herald Press, is *The Bloody Theater or Martyrs Mirror of the Defenseless Christians Who Baptized Only upon Confession of Faith, and Who Suffered and Died for the Testimony of Jesus, Their Saviour, from the Time of Christ to the Year A.D. 1660*, (Scottdale, PA: Herald Press, 1968).

Chapter 3:   The Aftermath

31   *"I can't put into words":* "Georgetown, PA," *Die Botschaft,* October 16, 2006, 43.

33   *In a public statement released:* The full statement of the Nickel Mines Accountability Committee appeared in the *Lancaster New Era* as a letter to the editor; see Herman Bontrager, Nickel Mines Accountability Committee, letter to the editor, *Lancaster New Era,* October 11, 2006. The letter was also distributed by the Associated Press on October 10, 2006.

33   *The front-page headline:* "THANK YOU," *Die Botschaft,* October 16, 2006, 1.

34   *"We will never forget the feelings":* Mr. and Mrs. Amos K. Ebersol, letter to the editor, *Lancaster Intelligencer Journal,* October 18, 2006.

34   *"Our perceptions of 'worldly'":* Benuel Riehl, letter to the editor, *Philadelphia Inquirer*, October 8, 2006.

34   *"We are thankful":* "THANK YOU," 1.

36   *I was a little child:* Mary M. Miller, comp., *Our Heritage, Hope, and Faith* (Shipshewana, IN: privately published, 2000), 342. Original translation, by John B. Martin, used by permission. Revised translation 2007 by David Rempel Smucker, Ph.D., Akron, PA. Used by permission.

Chapter 4:   The Surprise

44   *"He stood there for an hour":* Mark Scolforo, "Police: Gunman at Amish School Told Wife He Molested 2 Little Girls 20 Years Ago," Associated Press, October 3, 2006.

45   *"Do you have any anger":* "Victims' Grandfather Talks to News 8," WGAL. com, October 4, 2006, http://www.wgal.com/news/9997465/ detail.html.

45   *"We have to forgive":* "Grief-Stricken Community of Nickel Mines Trying to Deal with Deaths of Five Amish Girls, Shot in Schoolhouse," *The Early Show,* CBS News transcripts, October 4, 2006.

45   *"We shouldn't think evil":* David Cox, "Grief of the Amish," *Sunday Mirror,* October 8, 2006.

45   *"I hope they [Roberts's widow and children]":* Michael Rubinkam, "Amish Community Prepares to Bury Victims, Urges Forgiveness," Associated Press, October 5, 2006.

47   *"Your compassion has reached":* "Statement from the Roberts Family," *Lancaster Sunday News,* October 15, 2006.

51   *"It is only through our faith":* Mr. and Mrs. Amos K. Ebersol, letter to the editor, *Lancaster Intelligencer Journal,* October 18, 2006.

Chapter 5:   The Reactions

54   *Perhaps too the media hoped:* Carolyn Kitch, "Who Speaks for the Dead? Authority and Authenticity in News Coverage of the Amish School Shooting," in Carolyn Kitch and Janice Hume, *Journalism in a Culture of Grief* (New York: Routledge, 2007).

55   *"I am profoundly moved":* Joan Uda, "At the Water's Edge," *Helena* (MT) *Independent Record,* October 7, 2006.

55   *"What wonderful people they are":* Joan Eshleman, letter to the editor, *Lancaster Intelligencer Journal,* October 10, 2006.

55   *A writer in Philadelphia concurred:* Daniel B. Lee, letter to the editor, *Philadelphia Inquirer,* October 9, 2006.

55   *In the* Sacramento Bee: Anita Creamer, "In Wake of Tragedy, Some Can Still Forgive," *Sacramento* (CA) *Bee,* October 15, 2006.

55   *"We should all be that odd":* Marvin Reed, "Believers Who Lead by Example: Nice," *Pueblo* (CO) *Chieftain,* October 14, 2006.

55   *"The Amish have shown the rest of the world":* Dean Frantz, "Amish Forgiveness Teaches Us a Lesson," *Fort Wayne* (IN) *News-Sentinel,* October 9, 2006.

55   *"This is not about being Amish"*: Bob Koehler, "Naked and Afraid," OpEdNews.com, October 12, 2006, www.opednews.com/articles/opedne_bob_koeh_061012_naked_and_afraid.html.

55   *Numerous observers lamented:* E. Ralph Hostetter, "Shoot Me First," Free Congress Foundation, October 12, 2006, www.freecongress.org/commentaries/2006/061012.aspx.

56   *"Modern society's sophisticates sneer"*: Mary Pat Hyland, "A Society So Modern It's Sickening," *Binghamton* (NY) *Press and Sun-Bulletin,* October 9, 2006.

56   *An early and stinging critique:* Jeff Jacoby, "Undeserved Forgiveness," *Boston Globe,* October 8, 2006.

57   *"They have responded to the massacre"*: Cristina Odone, "Why Do the Amish Ignore Reality?" *Observer,* October 8, 2006, http://observer.guardian.co.uk/comment/story/0,,1890309,00.html.

58   *"My Amish neighbors / forgive"*: Denise Duhamel, "June." Used with permission of the author.

58   *"This extreme event needs time"*: Mary Lou Vegh, *USA Today* blog, October 9, 2006, http://blogs.usatoday.com/oped/2006/10/amish_know_how_.html.

58   *For instance, legal scholar Jeffrie G. Murphy:* Jeffrie G. Murphy, preface to *Before Forgiving: Cautionary Views of Forgiveness in Psychotherapy,* ed. Sharon Lamb and Jeffrie G. Murphy (New York: Oxford University Press, 2002), ix.

58   *In Murphy's view:* Murphy, preface to *Before Forgiving,* x.

59   *In most situations of abuse:* Sharon Lamb, "Women, Abuse, and Forgiveness: A Special Case," in Lamb and Murphy, *Before Forgiving,* 156.

59   *"I have longed to talk about"*: Quoted in Simon Wiesenthal, *The Sunflower: On the Possibilities and Limits of Forgiveness,* rev. ed. (New York: Schocken Books, 1997), 54.

60   *"If asked to forgive, by anyone"*: Wiesenthal, *The Sunflower,* 169 (Hesburgh), 129 (Dalai Lama), 226 (Prager), 243 (Shachnow).

61   *"Her story paints a very different picture"*: Emily Smith, "Why I Fled from the Amish Sect," *Sun,* October 7, 2006, http://www.thesun.co.uk/printFriendly/0,11000-2006460644,00.html. See also Samuel Beiler, letter to the editor, *Lancaster Intelligencer Journal,* October 20, 2006.

61   *"Why does a tormented, suicidal adult"*: "Dealing with School Violence," *Scripps News,* October 20, 2006, http://www.scrippsnews.com/ node/14966.

61   *"This shooting . . . and every school shooting"*: "Rendell Admits Gun Laws Could Not Prevent School Shooting," news release from the Citizens Committee for the Right to Keep and Bear Arms, October 3, 2006, http://www.ccrkba.org/pub/rkba/press-releases/CC-RELEASE_ Pennsylvania.html.

62   *The Amish response to Charles Roberts:* Doug Soderstrom, "If Only George Bush Had Been Amish," Axis of Logic, October 15, 2006, http://www. axisoflogic.com/cgi-bin/exec/view.pl?archive=148&num=23236.

62   *"What if the Amish were in charge"*: Diana Butler Bass, "What If the Amish Were in Charge of the War on Terror?" Faithful America blog, October 11,2006,http://faithfulamerica.blogspot.com/search?q=diana+butler +bass.

62   *"You respect people who are true to their words"*: George Diaz, "Lessons from Lancaster County," *Orlando* (FL) *Sentinel,* October 8, 2006.

63   *"The so-called Christian Right"*: Stephen Crockett, "Personal Reflections on the Amish and the So-Called Christian Right," Democratic Talk Radio, October 10, 2006, http://www.DemocraticTalkRadio.com.

63   *Recalling the bravery of the Amish schoolgirls:* David W. Virtue, "Lancaster Murders, Mayhem, and Guns," VirtueOnline.org, October 9, 2006, www.virtueonline.org.

63   *Sister Joan Chittister:* Joan Chittister, "What Kind of People Are These?" *National Catholic Reporter,* October 9, 2006.

Chapter 6:   The Habit of Forgiveness

70   *Although the Anabaptist movement was never large:* James Stayer, "Numbers in Anabaptist Research," in *Commoners and Community: Essays in Honour of Werner O. Packull,* ed. C. Arnold Snyder (Kitchener, ON: Pandora Press, 2002), 58–59.

72   *Still, three years later:* Esther F. Smucker, *Good Night, My Son: A Treasure in Heaven* (Elverson, PA: Olde Springfield Shoppe, 1995), 84. The quotations are from the police officer's recollection of events, which was included as an appendix in this memoir.

72   *Another story that highlights the speed:* Joel A. Kime, "The Freedom of Forgiveness Received," handout (Elizabethtown, PA: Center for Parent/Youth Understanding, 2003).

74   *The case even appeared as a feature:* Hal White, "Terror at the Amish Farmhouse," *True Detective,* November 1957, 16–21, 83.

74   *They were particularly puzzled by the fact:* Alma Kaufman, "Murder Violence Leaves Holmes Amish Bewildered but Not Seeking Vengeance," *Wooster* (OH) *Daily Record,* July 20, 1957.

75   *Mose seemed to express the grief:* "Arguments on State's Use of Alleged Confession on Monday; Father of Victim Is Witness," *Wooster* (OH) *Daily Record,* December 6, 1957.

75   *An Ontario Amish man:* "Aylmer, ON," *The Budget,* March 20, 1958, 6.

76   *"The boys were caught soon after":* "Berne, IN," *The Budget,* September 12, 1979, 11.

76   *Levi Schwartz told a journalist:* Barry Siegel, "A Quiet Killing in Adams County," *Rolling Stone,* February 19, 1981, 62.

76   *"We believe," began a letter:* Simon M. Schwartz, "Death of an Amish Child," *Liberty,* March-April 1981, 3.

78   *The families of sexual assault victims:* Anne Hul, "A Still Life Shattered," *St. Petersburg* (FL) *Times,* July 7, 1996; Meg Jones, "Attorney Calls Defendant 'Seriously Disturbed,'" *Milwaukee (WI) Journal Sentinel,* February 20, 1996.

79   *"It shows that he's not seeking revenge":* Joe Williams, "Buggy Fatality; Amish Man Won't Take the Money," *Milwaukee (WI) Journal Sentinel,* March 9, 1996.

80   *Even so, her written account:* Emma King, *Joys, Sorrows, and Shadows, by One Who Experienced the Joys, Sorrows, and Shadows* (Elverson, PA: Olde Springfield Shoppe, 1992), v, 24, 27, 37, 74.

81   *"We don't believe in pressing charges":* Doug Johnson, "Amish Reach Out to Trucker Following Death of Mother of 13," Associated Press, January 19, 2000.

81   *Similar sentiments marked responses:* Linda L. Mullen, "Amish Forgiving in Wake of Attempted Assaults," *South Bend* (IN) *Tribune,* August 28, 1996.

82   *Eight days before the shooting:* Cindy Stauffer and Janet Kelley, "A Boy's Death, a Family's Forgiveness," *Lancaster New Era,* September 25, 2006; "Woman Charged in Boy's Death in Crash," *Lancaster New Era,* December 22, 2006.

Chapter 7:   The Roots of Forgiveness

86   *From their beginning in the sixteenth century:* The centrality of discipleship to the Anabaptist tradition has been noted by many scholars, including Richard T. Hughes, *How Christian Faith Can Sustain the Life of the Mind* (Grand Rapids, MI: Eerdmans, 2001), 76–85.

87   *During the first twelve weeks:* John S. Oyer, "Is There an Amish Theology?" in *Les Amish: Origine et Particularismes, 1693–1993* [The Amish: Origin and Characteristics, 1693–1993], ed. Lydie Hege and Christoph Wiebe (Ingersheim, France: Association Française d'Histoire Anabaptiste-Mennonite, 1994), 283–286, 301.

87   *"Whoever boasts that he is a Christian":* Menno Simons, "Foundation of Christian Doctrine," in *The Complete Writings of Menno Simons, c. 1496–1561,* ed. J. C. Wenger, trans. Leonard Verduin (Scottdale, PA: Herald Press, 1956), 225.

88   *"Who now would follow":* "Who Now Would Follow Christ," in *Hymnal: A Worship Book* (Scottdale, PA: Mennonite Publishing House, 1992), 535. Revised translation by David Augsburger, 1983, used with permission.

93   *At the same time, some critics complain:* Christopher Lasch, *The Culture of Narcissism: American Life in an Age of Diminishing Expectations* (New York: Norton, 1978).

93   *In fact, in his book* The Saturated Self: Kenneth J. Gergen, *The Saturated Self: Dilemmas of Identity in Contemporary Life* (New York: Basic Books, 1991).

94   *The second prayer is read: Die ernsthafte Christenpflicht* [Prayer Book for Earnest Christians] (Lancaster County, PA: Amischen Gemeinden, 1996). See also Leonard Gross, ed. and trans., *Prayer Book for Earnest Christians* (Scottdale, PA: Herald Press, 1997). An old collection of Anabaptist and Pietist prayers dating back to 1708, *Die ernsthafte Christenpflicht* is used by the Amish in their church services and for family prayers.

95   *In response to a flood:* This undated and unsigned letter written by several church leaders was distributed in late October 2006 to outsiders inquiring about Amish forgiveness.

96   *He had "suffered verbal abuse":* "Set Your Captive Free," *Family Life*, February 2003, 8–9.

96   *"There is perhaps no other factor":* "That Our Hurts May Be Healed," *Family Life*, January 2003, 10.

97   *"Forgiveness is never dependent":* Nicholas Ayo, *The Lord's Prayer: A Survey Theological and Literary* (Notre Dame, IN: University of Notre Dame Press, 1992), 79.

97   *In his commentary on this section of Matthew:* William Barclay, *The Gospel of Matthew,* vol. 1, 2nd ed. (Philadelphia: Westminster Press, 1958), 223.

97   *"The main 'forgiveness'":* "Georgetown, PA," *Die Botschaft,* October 23, 2006, 22.

Chapter 8:   The Spirituality of Forgiveness

100 *The Amish, Cronk says, "see God working":* Sandra Cronk, *"Gelassenheit:* The Rites of the Redemptive Process in Old Order Amish and Old Order Mennonite Communities," *Mennonite Quarterly Review,* 1981, 55, 7–8.

104 *They stretch me: Songs of the Ausbund: History and Translations of Ausbund Hymns,* vol. 1 (Millersburg: Ohio Amish Library, 1998), 168. Used by permission.

105 *Take notice how: Songs of the Ausbund,* 73. Used by permission.

105 *It is not uncommon for sermons:* The English edition of *Martyrs Mirror* is kept in print by Herald Press, Scottdale, PA. Pathway Publishers, Aylmer, ON, issues a 1,004-page German edition of the book, *Der blutige Schauplatz, oder, Märtyrer-Spiegel der Taufgesinnten, oder, wehrlosen Christen, die um des Zeugnisses Jesu, ihres Seligmachers, willen gelitten haben und getötet worden sind, von Christi Zeit an bis auf das Jahr 1660.* The English edition includes fifty-five etchings, produced in the seventeenth century by a Dutch Mennonite artist, that graphically illustrate the martyrdom. The German edition is not illustrated.

106 *From the beginning, the Anabaptists:* Brad S. Gregory, *Salvation at Stake: Christian Martyrdom in Early Modern Europe* (Cambridge, MA: Harvard University Press, 1999), 319.

222

106   *Indeed, in recently published reflections: The Amazing Story of the Ausbund* (Narvon, PA: Benuel S. Blank, 2001), 116–117.

107   *In a study guide:* James W. Lowry, *The Martyrs' Mirror Made Plain: A Study Guide and Further Studies* (Aylmer, ON: Pathway, 2000), 99.

107   *Forgiveness is a regular feature: Martyrs Mirror,* 750, 610, 759, 467.

107   *From his prison cell: Martyrs Mirror,* 914.

108   *"Forgiving the persecutors":* Lowry, *The Martyrs' Mirror Made Plain,* 100.

109   *The story's conclusion drives the point home:* Lowry, *The Martyrs' Mirror Made Plain,* 117.

110   *For example, "Peter Miller's Revenge": Our Heritage* (Aylmer, ON: Pathway, 1968), 433–439.

Chapter 9:   The Practice of Forgiveness
115   *A writer in an Amish periodical recalled:* "Is the Golden Rule Outdated?" *Family Life,* January 2003, 14.

122   *The service culminates in footwashing:* The description of the communion service is adapted from Donald B. Kraybill, *The Riddle of Amish Culture,* rev. ed. (Baltimore: Johns Hopkins University Press, 2001), 127–128.

Chapter 10:   Forgiveness at Nickel Mines
125   *"To err is human":* Alexander Pope, *An Essay on Criticism,* originally published 1711.

126   *As a result of their clinical research:* Everett L. Worthington Jr., *Forgiveness and Reconciliation: Theory and Application* (New York: Routledge, 2006), 272.

126   *"When unjustly hurt by another":* Joanna North, quoted in Robert D. Enright, *Forgiveness Is a Choice: A Step-by-Step Process for Resolving Anger and Restoring Hope* (Washington, DC: American Psychological Association, 2001), 25.

126   *In Enright's view, this definition:* Enright, *Forgiveness Is a Choice,* 25.

127   *"In spite of everything":* Enright, *Forgiveness Is a Choice,* 25–26.

127   *To the contrary, "forgiveness means":* Enright, *Forgiveness Is a Choice,* 28.

127   *That's because "reconciliation requires":* Enright, *Forgiveness Is a Choice,* 31.

128 *For instance, when one columnist asked:* Cristina Odone, "Why Do the Amish Ignore Reality?" *Observer,* October 8, 2006, http://observer.guardian. co.uk/comment/story/0,,1890309,00.html.

128 *"Forgiveness doesn't mean 'I didn't really mind'":* N. T. Wright, *Evil and the Justice of God* (Downers Grove, IL: InterVarsity Press, 2006), 152.

128 *For instance, one observer reduced:* Odone, "Why Do the Amish Ignore Reality?"

129 *"I would not want to be like them":* Jeff Jacoby, "Undeserved Forgiveness," *Boston Globe,* October 8, 2006.

129 *"She holds no ill will":* "Pa. School Shooter Said He'd Molested Relatives," *NBC News,* October 3, 2006, http://www.msnbc.msn.com/id/ 15113706.

130 *"People get angry and interpret":* Eric Shiraev and David Levy, *Cross-Cultural Psychology: Critical Thinking and Contemporary Applications*, 2nd ed. (Boston: Allyn & Bacon, 2004), 178.

131 *In fact, one Amish magazine:* "Anger," *Family Life,* February 2002, 10.

131 *The booklet's author, John Coblentz:* John Coblentz, *Putting Off Anger: A Biblical Study of What Anger Is and What to Do About It* (Harrisonburg, VA: Christian Light Publications, 1999), 7–8.

131 *Scholars who study forgiveness:* Enright, *Forgiveness Is a Choice,* 33.

134 *Decisional forgiveness is a personal commitment:* Everett L. Worthington Jr., *Forgiving and Reconciling: Bridges to Wholeness and Hope,* rev. ed. (Downers Grove, IL: InterVarsity Press, 2003), 53.

135 *Emotional forgiveness, on the other hand:* Worthington, *Forgiving and Reconciling,* 41–42.

135 *Invoking Jesus' instructions to Peter:* "Nine Principles for Mending Broken Relationships," *Family Life,* November 2001, 8.

137 *Jeffrie G. Murphy, for instance:* Jeffrie G. Murphy, "Two Cheers for Vindictiveness," *Punishment and Society,* 2000, *2*, 131–143.

137 *In 2005, the periodical* Legal Affairs: Nadya Labi, "The Gentle People," *Legal Affairs,* January-February 2005, 25–32.

139 *"All too often . . . survivors of violence are retraumatized":* Pamela Cooper-White, *The Cry of Tamar: Violence Against Women and the Church's Response* (Minneapolis: Fortress Press, 1995), 253.

224

140 *In* Forgive for Good*, Fred Luskin:* Fred Luskin, *Forgive for Good: A Proven Prescription for Health and Happiness* (San Francisco: HarperSanFrancisco, 2002), 45.

Chapter 11:   What About Shunning?

141 *"A terrible killer might be forgiven":* Ellis Henican, "Forgiveness—but Not for All," *Newsday,* October 6, 2006.

143 *Given the importance of verses 18–20:* C. Arnold Snyder, *Anabaptist History and Theology: Revised Student Edition* (Kitchener, ON: Pandora Press, 1997), 370–373.

149 *The Amish cite at least four reasons:* For more in-depth views of Amish shunning, see *The Amazing Story of the Ausbund* (Narvon, PA: Benuel S. Blank, 2001), 109–112, and "Shunning," *Family Life,* April 1970, 18–21.

149 *First, shunning is supported:* The primary biblical texts that support shunning include Matthew 18:15–18; Romans 16:17; 1 Corinthians 5; 2 Thessalonians 3:6, 14–15; 2 Timothy 3:2–5; and Titus 3:10.

149 *Second, the practice finds support:* "The Shunning of the Excommunicated," Article 17 in the Dordrecht Confession of Faith, in Irvin B. Horst, ed. and trans., *Mennonite Confession of Faith* (Lancaster, PA: Lancaster Mennonite Historical Society, 1988), 35. The Dordrecht Confession is used by the Amish even though it was written originally by Dutch Mennonites in 1632, before the Amish emerged as a distinct group. A more accessible text of the Dordrecht Confession is available at http://www.mcusa-archives.org/library/resolutions/dordrecht/index.html.

153 *"Herein is love":* "The Need of Forgiving," *Family Life,* October 1985, 9.

Chapter 12:   Grief, Providence, and Justice

156 *"Like many aspects of Amish life":* Expression of emotion is culturally formed. Amish weeping, which is marked by the quiet, public shedding of tears by both men and women, bears some similarities to eighteenth-century European custom and differs from later notions of crying as primarily a private or feminine activity. See Anne Vincent-Buffault, *The History of Tears: Sensibility and Sentimentality in France* (New York: St. Martin's Press, 1991).

225

159 *"I felt the need to express my feelings":* Emma King, *Joys, Sorrows, and Shadows* (Elverson, PA: Olde Springfield Shoppe, 1992), v.

160 *Providence, the idea that God:* Daniel L. Migliore, *Faith Seeking Understanding: An Introduction to Christian Theology,* 2nd ed. (Grand Rapids, MI: Eerdmans, 2004), 421.

160 *Christian author Philip Yancey:* Philip Yancey, *Prayer: Does It Make Any Difference?* (Grand Rapids, MI: Zondervan, 2006), 139.

162 *This confession, reviewed by bishops:* "God and Creation," Article 1 in the Dordrecht Confession of Faith, in Irvin B. Horst, ed. and trans., *Mennonite Confession of Faith* (Lancaster, PA: Lancaster Mennonite Historical Society, 1988), 24.

162 *"What can one say":* "Oxford, PA," *Die Botschaft,* October 16, 2006, 49.

162 *"We trust him, yes":* "Kirkwood, PA," *Die Botschaft,* October 16, 2006, 47.

163 *"It wasn't His will":* "New Holland, PA; Groffdale," *Die Botschaft,* October 23, 2006, 36.

164 *"We don't know why, but":* "Hopkinsville, KY," *Die Botschaft,* October 23, 2006, 10.

164 *Amish elders concurred:* This undated and unsigned letter written by several church leaders was distributed in late October 2006 to outsiders inquiring about forgiveness.

164 *"If our precious family circle":* "Parkesburg, PA," *Die Botschaft,* October 16, 2006, 59.

164 *"The Lord works in mysterious ways":* "Georgetown, PA," *Die Botschaft,* October 23, 2006, 22. For a similar assertion (though in this case the Amish writer attributes the assertion to a non-Amish person), see "Kindardine, ON," *Die Botschaft,* October 23, 2006, 16.

166 *"Some things in life":* "Dry Run, PA," *Die Botschaft,* October 16, 2006, 51.

168 *"You will face a higher court":* Frank Caltabilota, quoted in Ronald Smothers, "Relatives of New Jersey Dorm Fire Victims Lash Out at Sentencing," *International Herald Tribune,* January 27, 2007, http://www.iht.com/articles/2007/01/27/america/web.0127seton.php.

171   *Meanwhile, the Amish bishop:* "Amish to Blame, Jurors Declare," *Pittsburgh Post-Gazette,* March 28, 1994; "Amish Killer's Sentence Criticized; 5 Years Not Enough in Slaying of Wife, Author Says in Book," *Pittsburgh Post-Gazette,* May 30, 2000.

Chapter 13:   Amish Grace and the Rest of Us

176   *Few commentators did this as crassly:* E. Ralph Hostetter, "Shoot Me First," Free Congress Foundation, October 12, 2006, http://www.freecongress.org/commentaries/2006/061012.aspx.

177   *As if to drive home the depth:* For this story, see "Speech Underscores Amish Ways," *Mansfield* (OH) *News Journal,* February 24, 2007, http://www.mansfieldnewsjournal.com/apps/pbcs.dll/article?AID=2007702240326.

181   *What we learn:* Joseph C. Liechty, "Forgiveness," *Vision: A Journal for Church and Theology,* 2007, *8*(1), 47–49.

182   *"The person who volunteers time":* Robert Kuttner, *Everything for Sale* (New York: Knopf, 1996), 62–63.

182   *In a culture that places such a premium:* Miroslav Volf, *Free of Charge: Giving and Forgiving in a Culture Stripped of Grace* (Grand Rapids, MI: Zondervan, 2005), 14.

182   *In fact, forgiveness is less a matter:* Miroslav Volf, *The End of Memory: Remembering Rightly in a Violent World* (Grand Rapids, MI: Eerdmans, 2007).

Appendix: The Amish of North America

191   Portions of the Appendix are adapted from *The Amish: Why They Enchant Us,* by Donald B. Kraybill. Copyright © 2003 by Herald Press, Scottdale, PA 15683. Used by permission.

RESOURCES FOR FURTHER READING

On the Amish

Johnson-Weiner, Karen M. 2007. *Train Up a Child: Old Order Amish and Mennonite Schools*. Baltimore: Johns Hopkins University Press. An introduction to Old Order elementary schools in North America.

Kraybill, Donald B. 2001. *The Riddle of Amish Culture*. Rev. ed. Baltimore: Johns Hopkins University Press. An exploration of why the numbers of Old Order Amish are growing so rapidly in modern society.

Kraybill, Donald B., ed. 2003. *The Amish and the State*. 2nd ed. Baltimore: Johns Hopkins University Press. A series of essays that examines conflicts between the Amish and the state in the twentieth century.

Nolt, Steven M. 2003. *A History of the Amish*. 2nd ed. Intercourse, PA: Good Books. A history of the Amish since their origins in 1693.

Nolt, Steven M., and Thomas J. Meyers. 2007. *Plain Diversity: Amish Cultures and Identities*. Baltimore: Johns Hopkins University Press. An exploration of the origins and meaning of diverse Amish practices in various subgroups.

Stevick, Richard A. 2007. *Growing Up Amish: The Teenage Years*. Baltimore: Johns Hopkins University Press. A definitive study of Amish *Rumspringa* and other rites of passage of Amish teenagers.

Umble, Diane Zimmerman, and David Weaver-Zercher, eds. 2008. *The Amish and the Media*. Baltimore: Johns Hopkins University Press. Essays by a variety of scholars on mainstream media treatments of the Amish and Amish uses of media.

Weaver-Zercher, David. 2001. *The Amish in the American Imagination*. Baltimore: Johns Hopkins University Press. An exploration of outsiders' interest in and perceptions of the Amish throughout the twentieth century.

For additional information on the Amish, visit www.etown.edu/Amishstudies.

On Forgiveness

Doblmeier, Martin. *The Power of Forgiveness.* Documentary film that explores research into the psychological and physical effects of forgiveness in a variety of personal and social contexts.

Enright, Robert D. 2001. *Forgiveness Is a Choice: A Step-by-Step Process for Resolving Anger and Restoring Hope.* Washington, DC: American Psychological Association. An introduction to definitions of forgiveness and steps for extending forgiveness to one's offenders.

Gobodo-Madikizela, Pumla. 2003. *A Human Being Died That Night: A South African Story of Forgiveness.* Boston: Houghton Mifflin. A South African woman's reflections on the atrocities of apartheid, including her thoughts on the problems and possibilities of apology and forgiveness.

Iligabiza, Immaculée. 2007. *Left to Tell: Discovering God Amidst the Rwandan Holocaust.* Carlsbad, CA: Hay House. The memoirs of a Tutsi woman whose family was killed in the 1994 Rwandan massacre; the book recounts her struggle to forgive those responsible for her family members' deaths.

Luskin, Frederic. 2002. *Forgive for Good: A Proven Prescription for Health and Happiness.* San Francisco: HarperSanFrancisco. An overview of how grievances are formed and how forgiveness can happen in appropriate and healing ways.

Minow, Martha. 1998. *Between Vengeance and Forgiveness: Facing History After Genocide and Mass Violence.* Boston: Beacon Press. An examination of varied responses to mass violence around the world and the potential for healing.

Shults, F. LeRon, and Steven J. Sandage. 2003. *The Faces of Forgiveness: Searching for Wholeness and Salvation.* Grand Rapids, MI: Baker Academic. An introduction to the connections between Christian theology and psychological approaches to forgiveness.

Tutu, Desmond. 1999. *No Future Without Forgiveness.* New York: Doubleday. A memoir by the chair of South Africa's Truth and Reconciliation Commission, which responded to the offenses of apartheid.

Volf, Miroslav. 2005. *Free of Charge: Giving and Forgiving in a Culture Stripped of Grace*. Grand Rapids, MI: Zondervan. An exploration of forgiveness from a Christian theologian who connects human forgiveness to God's graciousness.

Wiesenthal, Simon. 1997. *The Sunflower: On the Possibilities and Limits of Forgiveness*. Rev. ed. New York: Schocken Books. A true story of a Nazi's plea for forgiveness to a Jewish prisoner, with subsequent reflections on the prisoner's silent response.

Worthington, Everett L., Jr. 2006. *Forgiveness and Reconciliation: Theory and Application*. New York: Routledge. A clinical-research-based book that combines definitions of forgiveness with clinical theory on how forgiveness can be promoted in practice.

Wright, N. T. 2006. *Evil and the Justice of God*. Downers Grove, IL: InterVarsity Press. An examination of the problem of evil—and the need to forgive in a world where evil exists—by the Anglican archbishop of Durham.

For additional information on forgiveness, visit www.fetzer.org.

ACKNOWLEDGMENTS

Producing this book on a tight schedule demanded a team effort. We are therefore grateful for the kindness and generosity of many people who assisted us with this project. We owe our largest debt to several dozen Amish people who generously shared their time to talk about Amish forgiveness. They patiently answered many questions, some of them painful, all of them probing. This book would have been impossible without their insights.

Many other persons assisted us as well. We especially thank David Rempel Smucker for his historical research and translation of German documents; Florence Horning for her translation of Pennsylvania German and her clerical support; Cynthia Nolt, whose superb copy-editing skills improved our text; Valerie Weaver-Zercher, whose editorial eyes enhanced our prose and the flow of the narrative; and four student assistants—Courtney Fellows, Benjamin Lamb, Megan Memoli, and Kami Tyler—who provided a variety of research and support services.

As always, we benefited from the support of our colleagues at Elizabethtown College, Goshen College, and Messiah College. Some colleagues responded to chapters; others responded to ideas. Charles Seitz at Messiah College and Joe Liechty at Goshen College helped us think through issues related to forgiveness and reconciliation, and the librarians at all three institutions gave generously of their time and energy.

Three nationally recognized scholars of forgiveness—Robert Enright, Fred Luskin, and Everett Worthington Jr.—shared their time and ideas to help us better understand the issues surrounding forgiveness. In addition, their books and articles opened up for us the growing body of scholarship on the topic.

We owe a special debt to the Fetzer Institute for its financial support of our research. We enjoyed the enthusiastic support of Shirley Showalter, Fetzer's vice president for programs, as well as Wayne Ramsey, who kindly spoke with us for hours about forgiveness research.

The text of *Amish Grace* is more accurate because a number of people were willing to read and critique early drafts of the manuscript. In addition to six Amish readers, we appreciate the thoughtful responses and critiques we received from Kimberly Adams, Nancy Adams, Herman Bontrager, Helen Burns, Julie Heisey, Jake Jacobsen, Joe Liechty, Fred Luskin, Wayne Ramsey, Stephen Scott, Richard Stevick, and Everett Worthington. Many of them raised good questions about the nature of forgiveness and Amish life, and though we could not address all their questions, our text is stronger because of their insights.

With warm enthusiasm, Sheryl Fullerton, executive editor at Jossey-Bass, and her team of colleagues turned our manuscript into a polished book. We deeply appreciated their professional expertise throughout the publication process. Our agent, Giles Anderson, guided us through the rapids of the publishing world with uncommon wisdom and insight.

Finally, our hearts are filled with gratitude for our spouses and families. They provided unwavering support to us during the hectic months of our research and writing. They surely learned a lot about forgiveness in the process, sometimes in theory and sometimes through extending it to us. We are blessed to have such gracious people in our lives.

THE AUTHORS

DONALD B. KRAYBILL is distinguished professor and senior fellow at the Young Center for Anabaptist and Pietist Studies at Elizabethtown College in Elizabethtown, Pennsylvania. He has studied and published on numerous Anabaptist communities in North America. His many books on the Amish include *The Riddle of Amish Culture* (rev. ed., 2001), and an edited collection, *The Amish and the State* (2nd ed., 2003), both published by the Johns Hopkins University Press.

STEVEN M. NOLT is professor of history at Goshen College in Goshen, Indiana. He has studied Amish history and culture across many settlements. His books include *A History of the Amish* (rev. ed., Good Books, 2003), *Amish Enterprise: From Plows to Profits* (2nd ed., with Donald B. Kraybill, Johns Hopkins University Press, 2004), and *Plain Diversity: Amish Cultures and Identities* (with Thomas J. Meyers, Johns Hopkins University Press, 2007).

DAVID L. WEAVER-ZERCHER is professor of American religious history at Messiah College in Grantham, Pennsylvania. He has written extensively on mainstream Americans' interest in and perceptions of the Amish. His books include *The Amish in the American Imagination* (Johns Hopkins University Press, 2001), and two edited volumes, *Writing the Amish: The Worlds of John A. Hostetler* (Pennsylvania State University Press, 2005), and *The Amish and the Media* (with Diane Zimmerman Umble, Johns Hopkins University Press, 2008).

For more information, visit www.amishgrace.com.

INDEX

238

DISCUSSION AND REFLECTION GUIDE

Chapter One: The Nickel Mines Amish

1. Prior to the tragedy at Nickel Mines, what were your perceptions of Amish people? What were the sources of those impressions?

2. How did the Nickel Mines tragedy change your views of the Amish?

3. If a shooting of ten schoolgirls had occurred in a suburban or urban setting, do you think it would have attracted as much interest as the shooting at Nickel Mines? In other words, how much of the public interest in this story was related to the "Amish factor"?

4. The authors suggest that the Amish do not explicitly teach religion in their schools or in their churches. How, then, do they pass on their beliefs to their children?

5. Chapter One provides some cultural background on the Amish community. What was your biggest surprise in learning about Amish faith and life?

6. What do you consider the most significant or biggest difference between Amish culture and mainstream American values?

7. It is often said that the Amish are a countercultural people. What are the key Amish values, in your mind, that challenge the cultural assumptions of mainstream society?

8. How do Amish faith and religious practices differ from those of other Protestant groups in North America?

9. At the time of the shooting, many journalists asked if the Amish were prepared for such a tragedy. How would you answer that question? In what ways were they better prepared than other Americans? In what ways were they less prepared?

10. At the end of Chapter One, the authors suggest that the last safe place in America's collective imagination had disappeared with the shooting at Nickel Mines. Do you agree with that assessment? Why or why not?

Chapter Two: The Shooting

1. A number of Amish people compared the school shooting to the September 11 attack on the twin towers in New York City. In what ways were these two events similar? Or is a comparison inappropriate?

2. Some people were surprised to learn that although the Amish are pacifists, some Amish men own guns for hunting. Do you consider the use of guns for hunting inconsistent with pacifist principles? Explain your response.

3. Consider and discuss some of the ironies that emerged from the tragedy. The gunman could not forgive God for the death of his twenty-day-old daughter nine years after her death. He also said he hated himself, suggesting an inability to forgive himself for his own shortcomings.

4. What might be some reasons that Roberts targeted the West Nickel Mines School?

5. How would you describe some of the chief differences between an Amish school and the typical public elementary school in American society?

6. As you reflect on the horror that visited the schoolhouse on Monday morning, October 2, how might you have responded if you had been the teacher? If you had been the parent of one of the children?

7. One of the thirteen-year-old girls told the killer, "Shoot me first." Some observers think she meant "shoot me first before you molest me." Others think she meant "shoot me first" in the hope that her death would satisfy Roberts's anger and he would not shoot the others. What are your thoughts about the meaning of her statement?

8. How was the response of the Amish community on the afternoon of the shooting different from or similar to the response you think non-Amish parents would have had if this tragedy had happened in a public school?

9. At the end of Chapter Two, the authors quote an Amish mother, who did not have children in the schoolroom, as saying that the children were martyrs. Do you agree? Why or why not?

10. What might have been done to prevent the tragedy at Nickel Mines? What might be done to prevent similar tragedies in the future?

Chapter Three: The Aftermath

1. When did you first hear about the shooting? What was your response?

2. What was it about this particular tragedy that brought such a great outpouring of sympathy and support for the Amish community from the outside world?

3. An Amish man who lived near the school said, "We were all Amish this week." What did he mean?

4. What most surprised you about the Amish response to the tragedy?

5. What most surprised you about the larger society's response to the tragedy?

6. Non-Amish people in other communities also reach out to their friends and neighbors in times of tragedy. What did you find unique about how the Amish responded to victims of the tragedy within their own community?

7. The Amish typically have a public viewing of the body of the deceased in their home over several days before the funeral. What does this suggest about Amish acceptance of death?

8. What do we learn about the Amish view of death and children in the song "I Was a Little Child," which was read at one of the funerals?

9. The Amish destroyed the school building soon after the shooting. Would it have been better to save it as a memorial, or at least

create some type of memorial at the site, rather than turn it back into a horse pasture?

10. What do we learn about the Amish view of life and God's providence from their reaction to changing the security in their schools as a result of this tragedy?

Chapter Four: The Surprise

1. People respond in different ways when they are victims of injustice: anger, rage, revenge, silence, acceptance, and forgiveness— or more often a combination of these responses. How might you have responded to the Nickel Mines tragedy if some of the children had been *your* daughters, granddaughters, or nieces?

2. What was unique and distinctive about the Amish response to the shooting?

3. The Amish expressed forgiveness to the widow and her family even though they did not hold any direct responsibility for the injustice. Is it possible or necessary to forgive people who are not directly responsible for a wrong?

4. Although the schoolchildren were the primary victims in this tragedy, were there other victims beyond the ten girls and their families?

5. Why did Amish people who were not primary victims feel responsible to express grace and forgiveness to the killer's family?

6. How did the Amish express forgiveness in ways other than words? What does this say about the Amish understanding of forgiveness?

7. Some people in the outside world were shocked at the speed of Amish forgiveness. Do you think the swift forgiveness was sincere and genuine?

8. The Amish were very uncomfortable receiving recognition for expressing forgiveness. What were the roots of their discomfort?

9. Not only were outsiders surprised by the swift Amish forgiveness, but the Amish themselves were surprised by the worldwide attention and applause received in response to their forgiveness. One Amish man said, "Our forgiveness was just standard Christian forgiveness." What did he mean by that?

10. How did the Amish find meaning and solace in the deep sorrow and pain that they experienced in this tragedy?

Chapter Five: The Reactions

1. Recall your responses when you first heard about the Nickel Mines shooting. What were your feelings and reactions?

2. Why did the Amish forgiveness story become news? Why did anyone care about forgiveness? Why were journalists and their audiences interested in forgiveness?

3. Do you agree with the columnist who wrote, "The Amish show the rest of us what true Christianity is like"?

4. The Amish showed little public anger or outrage over the killings. What is your response to the columnist who asked, in essence, "Do we really want to live in a society in which no one gets angry when children are slaughtered?"

5. Do you think that some injustices or crimes are so horrific that forgiveness is inappropriate? If so, what might be some of those crimes?

6. The authors cite the book *The Sunflower: On the Possibilities and Limits of Forgiveness.* Simon Wiesenthal, a prisoner in a Nazi concentration camp, was asked to forgive a dying SS officer. Wiesenthal responded to the officer's request with silence. What would you have done? What *should* you have done?

7. Should forgiveness be dependent on a perpetrator's saying, "I am sorry," or requesting forgiveness? Or is forgiveness a gift, regardless of the perpetrator's response?

8. In your mind, is it appropriate to forgive someone for evil acts he or she committed against *other* people?

9. We may think we know what forgiveness is until we have to define it. How would you define it?

10. Is forgiveness ever appropriate for men who abuse women? If you think it is, would you place any conditions on it? If you think it isn't, why not?

Chapter Six: The Habit of Forgiveness

1. When you first learned of the Amish expression of forgiveness, did you assume that it was authentic? Offered for the sake of public relations? Naïve? Possible only because the killer had taken his own life and would not have to stand trial?

2. The authors describe the Anabaptist tradition and Amish culture as supplying a repertoire of responses that shape life, particularly

in times of stress or in situations that demand immediate responses. How would you describe your own culture and cultural values? What repertoire shapes your responses to tragedy?

3. Which of the stories in this chapter surprised you? Inspired you?
   Disturbed you? Made you angry?

4. If you have been a primary or secondary victim of crime, are
   you able to identify with the Amish in these accounts? Why or
   why not?

5. If you have not been a crime victim, do you imagine that your
   responses would be different from or similar to those of the
   Amish in this chapter?

6. In two stories, those that occurred in Monroe County and
   Mondovi, Wisconsin, the Amish participated in judicial processes
   through which the state sought to punish criminal wrongdoing
   but then distanced themselves from the outcomes, substituting
   forgiveness as their response. How do you view this distinction
   between consequences and revenge?

7. How did the family—especially female family members—of
   Naomi Huyard struggle emotionally in the aftermath of her
   murder? What factors made forgiveness difficult, according to
   a niece?

8. How do you respond to Amish statements that perhaps a victim's
   "time was up" or that a death was part of God's will?

9. Does forgiveness seem to be easier or more difficult in cases
   where the perpetrator and victim know one another?

10. The stories in this chapter focus on Amish responses to non-Amish aggression. In later chapters, the authors comment on how the Amish handle conflict and wrongdoing within their own community. From what you have read about Amish culture and values thus far, how do you expect the Amish to deal with wrongdoing among themselves?

Chapter Seven: The Roots of Forgiveness

1. Why are the Anabaptists described as having a "discipleship tradition"? What does that mean? From what you know of other Christian traditions, how distinctive are Anabaptist emphases?

2. How similar or different are the Amish approach to and interpretation of biblical texts from those of other Christian traditions with which you are familiar?

3. If you are part of a Christian tradition, how do you view and use the Lord's Prayer? How central is it to your faith? If you are not part of a Christian tradition, how does the theology of the Lord's Prayer compare with your own beliefs?

4. The Amish embrace ritual and prescribed, habitual practices. Do you find such an approach to life familiar or alien?

5. How does the communal nature of Amish life shape Amish religious thought and practice?

6. The authors contend that "the Amish believe if they don't forgive, they won't be forgiven." Does this sentiment surprise you? Resonate with your own beliefs? Trouble you?

7. How do the Amish understand what the authors call "the cross-stitch between divine and human forgiveness"?

8. Why might one say that forgiveness is central to Amish life? Do you see it as more central to the Amish than to people in some other faith traditions?

9. At the beginning of this chapter, the authors ask whether the public's surprise at Amish forgiveness in the wake of the Nickel Mines shooting was because Amish understanding of forgiveness differed from that of other Americans or because the Amish simply practiced something many people believe but few act on. Which do you think was the case?

10. At this point in your reading, has the Amish approach to faith either challenged or reaffirmed your own beliefs and values?

Chapter Eight: The Spirituality of Forgiveness

1. In your own words, describe the concept of *Gelassenheit* or *Uffgevva*.

2. How is *Gelassenheit* different from fatalism?

3. What do you imagine to be some of the implications of *Gelassenheit* beyond those the authors mention as examples?

4. Does the Amish people's understanding of submission clarify your understanding of their gender roles, or does it raise new questions for you?

5. Do you think Jacob Hochstetler was a good father?

6. In twenty-first-century North America, the Amish are not being persecuted as their ancestors were in sixteenth-century Europe. Do you find it surprising that their self-understanding and communal worship are still so heavily indebted to the memory of martyrdom? What memories of historic events shape your sense of self or your community's identity?

7. What is your own understanding of the meaning of martyrdom?

8. What is your reaction to the Dirk Willems story? Do you consider Dirk a moral exemplar or a fool?

9. How do you respond to the Amish inclusion of sometimes graphic stories of death or near-death into their grade school curricula?

10. At the end of the chapter, the authors suggest that Amish school-children have absorbed Amish values to a remarkable degree. Do you agree? What influences shaped—or did not shape—the children of the West Nickel Mines School?

Chapter Nine: The Practice of Forgiveness

1. An Amish minister noted that "sometimes it's harder to forgive each other" than it is to forgive someone like Charles Roberts. Why might this be the case? Have you ever had similar feelings? Or opposite sentiments?

2. Did Amish parental reflections on teaching forgiveness to children surprise you? How do they compare with the way you were raised?

3. The Amish see "giving up self" as central to their faith and life. Do you find the concept appealing or unattractive?

4. How do the religious values of the Amish shape their religious practices, and vice versa?

5. How are the rituals and practices of the Amish "communion season" similar to or different from rituals and practices in other faith traditions with which you are familiar?

6. What are the implications of the communal dimension of Amish worship, as opposed to an approach that views worship as something that simply connects an individual to God?

7. The authors say that "Council Meetings encourage deep soul-searching." Would you appreciate such structured time for reflection in your life, or would you find it morally coercive?

8. Many Amish people described forgiveness as a struggle. Do you see their struggle as uniquely Amish in any way?

9. Community relationships and church rituals keep Amish people talking to one another, even if they are at odds. What social structures in your society encourage people who disagree with one another to remain in conversation? What things discourage such interaction?

10. Do you agree that Amish rituals facilitate forgiveness even if they do not make it easy?

Chapter Ten: Forgiveness at Nickel Mines

1. How would you define forgiveness? Do you agree (with psychologist Robert Enright) that forgiveness does not, and should not, depend on the remorse or apology of the offender?

2. The authors make a distinction between "forgiveness" and "pardon." Do you agree with that distinction, or should pardon always be an aspect of forgiveness?

3. Is it possible to forgive a dead person? In what ways is that process different from forgiving a living person? How might this apply to Charles Roberts?

4. The authors quote the father of a slain Amish girl as saying, "There was never a time that I felt angry." Is that possible? Is that healthy? Is it possible to distinguish anger from resentment in real-life situations?

5. Why would collectivist societies find anger less acceptable than societies that are oriented toward the individual?

6. Does it make sense to talk about forgiveness as a "communal responsibility"?

7. Everett Worthington makes a distinction between "decisional forgiveness" and "emotional forgiveness." Is the distinction between making a decision to forgive and the emotional process helpful for understanding the task of forgiveness?

8. Do you agree with Jeffrie G. Murphy when he says that "vindictiveness" can sometimes be a good and healthy response to being wronged?

9. Can forgiveness be extended too quickly? When is the appropriate time for a victim to forgive his or her offender?

10. Do you know of religious leaders who have pressured victims to forgive too quickly? How can religious communities promote the

practice of forgiveness without putting undue pressure on victims to "get over" their hurt?

Chapter Eleven: What About Shunning?

1. What is the purpose of Members Meetings in the life of the Amish church? Are you aware of other religious communities that pursue the same purpose in a different way?

2. What rationale, biblical or otherwise, do the Amish have for disciplining wayward church members? Do you find their rationale convincing?

3. Although the Amish do not equate the *Ordnung* with divine law, they nonetheless discipline church members who do not abide by it. What is their rationale for enforcing rules that are not, even in their view, divinely given? Is that a justifiable rationale?

4. What, according to the Amish, is the goal of shunning?

5. Some Amish people use the analogy of disciplining (or spanking) children to explain shunning, arguing that is possible to both discipline and love someone. Is this a good analogy?

6. The authors contend that there is no inherent contradiction between Amish forgiveness and their practice of shunning, as long as forgiveness is correctly understood. Do you agree?

7. Should religious communities discipline members who don't abide by their rules? If so, how can this be done in a way that is both loving and effective?

8. Do you agree with the Amish that pardoning someone of wrong-doing is not always in that person's best interest?

9. This chapter outlines the process of excommunication and the practice of shunning. How does this description square with popular perceptions of Amish shunning?

10. "Some people think that shunning is barbaric," said one Amish person who was interviewed for this book. Would you call shunning barbaric? If not, what adjectives would you use to describe it?

Chapter Twelve: Grief, Providence, and Justice

1. Did anything in the descriptions of Amish grief surprise you?

2. All communities practice particular grieving rituals. What is unique about the grieving rituals practiced by the Amish? How do their rituals compare with what you've witnessed in your own community?

3. Was there anything about the memorial poem quoted in this chapter that caught your attention?

4. This chapter provides a definition and description of "God's providence." Have you ever thought about God's providence? If so, how would you describe it?

5. The authors identify three general answers posed by Christians to the problem of evil. Which of these three answers, if any, do you find most attractive? Why?

6. One Amish person asserted that the school shooting was a part of "God's plan" but also said that God didn't "will it" to happen? Are those two assertions contradictory?

7. What evidence did Amish people offer to claim that "good" had come from the school shooting? Is it appropriate for people to look for good in something so horrific?

8. "We should not put a question mark where God puts a period." What do Amish ministers mean by that? Do you agree with them?

9. What do you think about the Amish reluctance to speculate on their eternal destiny (and on that of Charles Roberts)?

10. What do the authors mean by the Amish "two-kingdom ethic"? Do you think it's appropriate for people to accept the state's authority to use force (as when restraining criminals) yet refuse to participate in those coercive practices themselves?

Chapter Thirteen: Amish Grace and the Rest of Us

1. What do you think of the book's title? Did forgiveness transcend tragedy in this instance? Did forgiveness redeem tragedy?

2. The authors write that for the Amish, the willingness to forgive others "is absolutely essential to the Christian faith." Would that be true for most North American Christians?

3. Chapter Six characterized forgiveness as a "habit." Is it possible to imitate a habit?

4. The authors contend that many commentators writing in the aftermath of the shooting "missed the countercultural dimension of Amish forgiveness." What do the authors mean by that?

5. Why would an Amish community forbid one of its members to give public lectures on Amish forgiveness?

6. What do you think about the tendency of op-ed writers to apply the lesson of Amish forgiveness to contemporary world problems? Do you agree with the authors' reservations about doing that?

7. The authors write that forgiveness is a "divine act that is broadly available to the human community." Is it?

8. The authors suggest that vengeance is often glamorized in American society. They also suggest that Americans are obsessed with "getting their due." Do you agree with their assessment? Or are you more inclined to say that Americans have a healthy and realistic sense of justice?

9. Have you had experiences of forgiveness in your life—either extending it to someone or receiving it from someone? Was there anything in this book that deepened your understanding of that experience?

10. What are some ways that religious communities can help their participants become more forgiving people? Do the Amish provide any clues in this regard?

The Fetzer Institute

Change everything.
Love and forgive.

FETZER INSTITUTE
www.fetzer.org

The Fetzer Institute's mission, to foster awareness of the power of love and forgiveness in the emerging global community, rests on the conviction that efforts to address the critical issues facing the world must go beyond political, social, and economic strategies to their psychological and spiritual roots. In a world dominated by fear and violence, the Institute works with global leaders, other organizations, and individuals to bring the power of love and forgiveness to the center of individual, community, and organizational life.

The Institute has provided research funds for *Amish Grace* as part of its Campaign for Love & Forgiveness.

The interpretations and conclusions contained in this publication represent the views of the authors and not necessarily those of the John E. Fetzer Institute, its trustees, or officers.